P9-EJU-390

READY OR NOT!

150+ MAKE-AHEAD, MAKE-OVER, AND MAKE-NOW RECIPES BY

nom nom paleo

MICHELLE TAM + HENRY FONG

Andrews McMeel
PUBLISHING®

FOR OUR PARENTS, **GENE + REBECCA TAM** AND **KENNY + WENDY FONG**.

THANK YOU FOR EVERYTHING. ESPECIALLY FOR FEEDING US.

CONTENTS

WELCOME!

HELLO!

Hey! Remember me? The lifelong food nerd who cleaned up her diet but stayed gleefully obsessed with all the pleasures of gastronomy? The nightshift-working mom who started sharing her recipes and blogging about Paleo cooking and lifestyle? The one who wrote a cookbook, and somehow convinced her publisher to let her write another one?

WELL, I'M BAAA-ACK!

My posse's here, too: my husband and co-author, Henry, whom you might not recognize with his new, scraggly, midlife-crisis beard…

"SCRAGGLY"?!? I THINK YOU MEAN "DISTINGUISHED"!

…and our two boys, Owen (a.k.a. Big-O), and Ollie (a.k.a. Lil-O), who are growing like weeds.

OR LIKE DAD'S BEARD HAIRS!

There! Now that we're reacquainted, let's cut right to the chase. This time around, I'm going to skip the biographical backstory, so if you want the full scoop on how Paleo transmogrified me from an exhausted, belly-aching, and muffin-topped crank into a happy, healthy, and energized mom, you'll have to buy, borrow, or steal a copy of my first book, *Nom Nom Paleo: Food for Humans*. (On second thought, please don't steal it. Stealing is bad.)

I'll go over the ancestral approach to eating and how to implement it for a modern lifestyle, but this book is not an all-encompassing guide to Paleo, nor is it a comprehensive treatise on nutritional science. And I'm certainly not going to lecture you about sticking to a strict set of eating rules, because I'm no "Paleo perfectionist" myself. Like you, I live in the real world.

Instead, this book is focused on one basic life skill that can make a huge impact on your health: *cooking your own food—whether you're ready to cook or not.*

Getting healthy, tasty, made-from-scratch meals on the dinner table can sometimes seem impossible, which explains why so many of us opt for unhealthy convenience foods. But with this handy cookbook, you'll always come home to plenty of deliciously nourishing options—from make-ahead, reheat-and-eat dishes to super-fast pantry creations.

NO MATTER IF YOU'RE A FASTIDIOUS PLANNER, A LAST-MINUTE IMPROVISER, OR SOMETHING IN-BETWEEN, THIS BOOK WILL MAKE COOKING A BREEZE!

Face it: Cooking is an essential, non-negotiable part of your day—like brushing your teeth. But unlike dental hygiene, meal prep doesn't have to feel like a daily chore. In fact, this book is designed to make cooking so easy, enjoyable, and fulfilling that it becomes a habit you'll never want to break.

Okay—enough chitchat. Let's get in the kitchen!

OLLIE WANTS EVERYONE TO KNOW THAT HE SNAPPED THIS PHOTO.

ONE OF THE BEST WAYS TO BOOST YOUR HEALTH IS TO ACTUALLY COOK YOUR OWN FOOD!

HENRY: Wait—*cooking*? Aren't sleep and exercise the true keys to better health? Stress reduction, too? And happiness and mindfulness? Community?

MICHELLE: Sure—all of those things are important, but if your diet consists mainly of processed garbage and cheap convenience foods, all the sleep, exercise, and meditation in the world won't get you anywhere. If anything, eating crap is going to wreck your sleep, hurt your athletic performance, and keep your body inflamed and stressed out.

HENRY: It's not easy to give up the convenience of packaged foods or quick take-out meals, though.

MICHELLE: But here's the crazy thing: The average American spends over 8 hours each day consuming media from TVs, computers, and handheld devices— but fewer than 30 minutes a day on food prep. What does that say about our priorities?

HENRY: It says we'd rather watch cooking shows on TV than actually cook. Cooking can be difficult, time-consuming, and boring—and more often than not, the results just aren't as tasty as the chemically-engineered junk concocted by flavor scientists.

MICHELLE: I get it. There are times when I *dread* cooking—especially when I'm short on time, energy, or both. But when it's done right, cooking is fun, easy, and one of the most pleasurable things in life. Plus, it yields results that are way more fresh and tasty than anything that comes out of an industrial kitchen. There's nothing more satisfying than literally stuffing your mouth with the fruits of your own labor.

HENRY: And don't forget that cooking is responsible for our very existence! It enabled human evolution,

making new food sources available to our ancestors. Over the millennia, humans came up with techniques like fermentation that not only preserved food but also made it more nutritious and delicious. Cooking became a ritual imbued with rich traditions. But it's not just backwards-looking, either; it's also an outlet for creativity and innovation. Cooking is an art form.

OWEN: Plus, people who know how to cook will survive longer. Survival of the fittest!

MICHELLE: Knowing how to prep meals from scratch doesn't just make you a more rounded individual or hearty survivalist—it makes you more mindful of the ingredients you're putting in your body. By cooking at home, I know exactly what goes into my food. I never have to guess whether my dishes were cooked with ingredients that don't sit well with me.

HENRY: And you're able to control all the flavors of your dishes. You can substitute ingredients to suit your tastes, and be a much more versatile home cook. You can go with the flow and hit a culinary home run even when life throws knuckleballs at you.

MICHELLE: This cookbook is designed to unlock all of that culinary potential. In these pages, I'll share with you my favorite make-ahead recipes, leftover makeovers, and quick and easy meals. And once you know what you're doing, your time in the kitchen won't just be fun—it'll be meditative, too. Cooking's a great way to unwind after a long day—and still produce something that's nomtastically delicious.

HENRY: Okay, we should stop. I think we're starting to sound like a cheesy infomercial.

OLLIE: And FYI, mom: Cheese is not Paleo.

YOU MAY BE WONDERING: **WHAT IS PALEO,** ANYWAY?

IT SOMETIMES DEPENDS ON WHO YOU ASK, BUT THIS IS HOW I THINK ABOUT IT!

---

① **Paleo is an ancestral approach that prioritizes eating real, whole, nutrient-dense foods.**

At its core, Paleo is about trying to eat real, naturally occurring ingredients that are healthful rather than harmful. Biologically, our bodies respond best to real, whole, nutrient-dense foods like plants, meat, and seafood—all of them packed with the nutrients our bodies evolved to thrive on. It was only after industrialized food production and lab-engineered edibles took over our diets that the "diseases of civilization" exploded. Today, wheat, soy, sugar, and highly processed foods continue to drive up rates of autoimmune disorders, cardiovascular disease, type-2 diabetes, and obesity. But by getting back to eating real food, we can stay healthier and happier.

Paleo also means not having to stress out about counting calories, balancing macronutrients, or starving ourselves to get healthy. Although Paleo isn't specifically intended to be a low-carb or weight-loss diet, by filling our plates with deliciously nourishing foods like vegetables, meat, and healthy fats, we can eat until we're satiated and still improve our body composition and overall health.

---

② **The caveman's just a mascot.**

I know that a lot of people still call it the "caveman diet," but Paleo isn't about slavishly and mindlessly replicating the actual diets of Paleolithic humans. If it was, this cookbook would be packed with recipes featuring ingredients like bugs and brains. (Spoiler alert: it's not.) The caveman isn't our role model—it's just a fun shorthand we use to refer to an ancestral approach to eating. It's funny—whenever someone tells me I can't possibly be Paleo because "cavemen never made ranch dressing" or "cavemen didn't use pressure cookers," I'm tempted to point out that cavemen didn't write food blogs, either.

YOU SURE ABOUT THAT?

---

③ **Paleo is about eating as broadly as possible, not as restrictively as possible.**

When the Paleo approach first arrived on the scene, it made sense to define exactly what it was all about. Broad rules were established (*no dairy! no rice! no beans!*), and people stuck to them. It wasn't a surprise that the rules worked. After all, who can argue with cutting out inflammatory foods and replacing them with wholesome ingredients like sustainably raised meat, wild seafood, pesticide-free vegetables and fruit, and healthy fats? By eliminating potentially harmful foods from our diets, these rules helped change our behaviors and boost our health.

But over the years, it became clear that a one-size-fits-all approach may not always be best. We're not all the same; every one of us is a unique snowflake, so we each need to figure out how different foods affect our individual health. For example, even if raw, full-fat dairy doesn't play nicely with my gut, it may be perfectly fine for you—and if you're told you can never have your precious dairy again, you're less likely to stick with Paleo. To be sustainable over the long term, Paleo needs to be about eating as much variety as possible, and not about deprivation.

Here's what I recommend: Treat Paleo as a starting point. Get yourself back to a clean slate by doing a dietary reset like the Whole30: Eliminate all grains, legumes, dairy, sugar, and chemically processed vegetable and seed oils from your diet for a month. Once a baseline of health is established, slowly reintroduce some of these foods (like dairy, white rice, and dark chocolate—not hyper-processed junk foods!) one at a time to see where you sit on the spectrum of food tolerance. We all share the goal of finding a lifelong template for optimal nutrition and health, but you just might find that your template allows for a wider range of foods than mine.

---

④ Strive for progress, not "Paleo perfection." Just make mindful food choices.

As I already mentioned, the Paleo template simply gives us a starting point from which to decide how to feed ourselves in the modern world. I make my own choices by weighing the health consequences of the foods I eat—and I also consider the gustatory pleasure of the experiences, too.

Over the past few years, my attitude toward food has evolved. When I first adopted a Paleo lifestyle, I strictly followed the rigid dictates of the Paleo diet because this new way of eating made me feel so much better. I didn't even think to question *why* it worked. But with time, I've learned that it's more important to stay curious about the science behind the approach, and to be fully conscious of my food choices. I learned that I don't need to strive for "Paleo perfection" as long as I'm mindful of what I'm choosing to put into my mouth, and why.

⑤ Paleo is a long-term lifestyle change, and to be sustainable, it needs to be simple, quick, and crazy-delicious.

Going Paleo for just a few days or weeks isn't going to do you much good. The Paleo approach isn't meant to be a quick-fix crash diet that burns off the pounds just in time for your wedding, high school reunion, or beach vacation—only to be put aside once you slip back into baggy sweatpants and resume your customary diet of pizza and beer. Short-term weight-loss diets aren't designed to be sustainable.

But Paleo is different. It's a lifestyle change that produces long-term health benefits—as long as you stick to it. That means Paleo needs to be both doable and delicious to be sustainable over a lifetime.

I've said it before: Cooking becomes overwhelming whenever we get too wrapped up in frustratingly complicated and time-consuming recipes that may not work. As a practical matter, ancestral eating has to be something that we can sustain on a day-to-day basis. At the same time, Paleo dishes have to be able to go head-to-head against lab-concocted convenience foods that are specifically engineered by flavor scientists to be addictively tasty. That's why I've devoted myself to creating healthy recipes that are both easy to make and insanely good.

The recipes in this cookbook were designed with these principles in mind: healthfulness, mindfulness, practicality, and deliciousness—and zero patience for dogma or deprivation.

REGULARLY FUELING MYSELF WITH THE HEALTHIEST POSSIBLE FOOD MAKES ME FEEL AWESOME, BUT SO DOES SHARING A SWEET BIRTHDAY TREAT WITH MY FAMILY. IT'S WORTH IT!

PRIORITIZE WHOLE, UNPROCESSED, NUTRIENT-RICH, NOURISHING FOODS.

EAT VEGETABLES, GRASS-FED AND PASTURED MEAT AND EGGS, WILD-CAUGHT SEAFOOD, HEALTHY FATS, FERMENTED FOODS, FRUIT, NUTS, SEEDS, AND SPICES.

AVOID FOODS THAT ARE LIKELY TO BE MORE HARMFUL THAN HEALTHFUL.

ESPECIALLY WHEN REGULARLY AND HEAVILY CONSUMED, FOODS LIKE GRAINS, DAIRY, SOY, SUGAR, AND PROCESSED SEED AND VEGETABLE OILS CAN TRIGGER INFLAMMATION, CAUSE DIGESTIVE PROBLEMS, OR DERAIL OUR NATURAL METABOLIC PROCESSES.

BUT LET'S NOT FOCUS ON WHAT WE SHOULDN'T EAT. LET'S FOCUS ON ALL THE AWESOME STUFF WE CAN EAT!

14

WANNA TURN YOUR PLATE PALEO? HERE'S HOW!

FRUIT!

NUTS & SEEDS!

1. Start with a hand-size portion of high-quality animal protein. The most sustainable, nutrient-rich, and flavorful meat comes from healthy beasts that chow on whatever nature intended them to eat, so prioritize grass-fed (and grass-finished) beef, bison, lamb and goat, pastured pork and poultry, and wild game. These animals offer meat that's full of anti-inflammatory omega-3 fatty acids, antioxidants, and other nutrients. Eggs and wild-caught seafood are awesome sources of protein, too.

2. Fill the rest of your plate with plants. Buy or grow in-season, pesticide-free produce, and supplement your haul with frozen organic veggies.

3. Next, replace the grains that normally dominate your plate with even *more* vegetables. Pasta and bread are nutrient-poor compared to veggies—and many grains contain proteins like gluten that can cause gut issues and inflammation. Even if you don't suffer from celiac disease, stuffing yourself with grains in place of vegetables, meat, or fish isn't doing your health any favors.

4. Choose healthy saturated fats that remain stable when exposed to heat, like ghee, coconut oil, and high-quality rendered animal fats. Olive oil and avo-cado oil are also great. Steer clear of vegetable and seed oils, which—believe it or not—are processed with chemical solvents like hexane. These oils are also high in omega-6 polyunsaturated fatty acids and highly susceptible to oxidation and rancidity.

5. One of the best things you can do for gut health is to eat fermented foods, so make sure you regularly plop some kimchi or sauerkraut on your plate, too.

6. Enjoy fruit, nuts, and seeds, but don't go over-board. Fruit is fine, but vegetables are generally more nutrient-rich and lower in sugar. And while nuts and seeds can add wonderful texture and flavor to your dishes, don't go nuts with nuts.

7. Try your best to keep ultra-processed foods off your plate, as they usually contain terrible-for-you additives like hydrogenated oils (a.k.a. trans fats), artificial dyes, chemical preservatives, high-fructose corn syrup, and/or soy. Most commercially available soy is genetically modified, contains isoflavones that can disrupt normal endocrine function, and is all-around awful for you. Stick to real food instead.

WHILE WE'RE AT IT, SHOULD WE ANSWER THESE READERS' QUESTIONS? THEY'RE STARTING TO PILE UP.

WELL, LET'S SEE HOW MANY WE CAN TACKLE IN THE NEXT TWO PAGES BEFORE WE RUN OUT OF SPACE. THEN, IT'S TIME TO DIVE INTO THE RECIPES!

CAN'T WE DO THIS AFTER I BEAT THIS LEVEL?

Q: Do you ever get bored of Paleo?

MICHELLE: I actually don't. To me, Paleo is about eating real, natural, wholesome foods, which I find to be incredibly satisfying and delicious. A lot of people assume Paleo means deprivation—but it doesn't. We don't subsist on boiled meat and limp vegetables. There's a huge world of possibilities out there, and we haven't even scratched the surface of all the wonderful and diverse Paleo-friendly ingredients and flavor combinations in existence.

Q: Do you eat rice and white potatoes? Aren't they off-limits on the Paleo diet?

MICHELLE: When Paleo first spiked in popularity, rice and potatoes were strictly considered off-limits, and it's true that these starchy foods may not be the best option for everyone at all times. For people who don't do well with excess carbohydrate intake, it may be worth cutting them out. However, an increasing number of Paleo eaters have found that as long as they're active and healthy, these foods are unlikely to cause problems. I've always said that Paleo shouldn't be about eating as restrictively as possible; instead, we should try to eat as broadly and sustainably as possible while being thoughtful about how certain foods make us feel. It's more important to be mindful of our food choices than it is to blindly follow rules.

HENRY: Besides, research now suggests that once white rice and potatoes are cooked and cooled, they form resistant starch that passes through our guts and feeds the beneficial bacteria in our microbiomes. Once we learned about this, we gradually started re-incorporating these foods back into our diets.

MICHELLE: And we still feel awesome! Don't avoid rice and potatoes just because once upon a time someone decreed that these ingredients are the devil. Paleo is personal, so make your own choices based on how different foods actually affect you.

HENRY: That being said, for those who remain rice-averse, we didn't include any rice-based recipes in this cookbook. But if you want, you can still serve white rice to accompany any of the dishes found in these pages. We certainly do.

MICHELLE: For you potato lovers out there, we did include two recipes with potatoes or potato starch in the ingredients: Hobo Stew (page 250) and Salt + Pepper Fried Pork Chops (page 124). I included these recipes because I didn't want to shy away from showing how we eat in real life. In any event, potatoes are now considered by most modern Paleo eaters to be fine. They're even Whole30-friendly!

Q: Do you ever "cheat" while eating Paleo?

MICHELLE: No, because I don't think of Paleo as a rigid set of rules. Instead, I consider Paleo to be a roadmap I'm using to get to my desired destination of optimal wellness. Paleo is like a compass or a GPS system that tells me which direction I need to go, but it doesn't stop me from taking an occasional detour off the road when there's something worthwhile to check out. I'm on a lifelong health journey—and what's the point of a long road trip if you can't see the sights or take a detour when it's worth it?

HENRY: But know your limits. For example, Michelle, you can't eat gluten without a severe reaction. So your dietary "detours" aren't off-the-rails pizza-fests or pasta parties. You'll only take a detour if you know it's worth steering away from the main road for a bit.

MICHELLE: Right. I'm mindful of what will wreck me, so I try my best to take a thoughtful, balanced approach. Just like in real life, if you're driving across America, a side trip to see the Grand Canyon is a spectacular experience—even if it takes you away from your intended route for a bit. But you're not going to purposefully crash through the guardrails that keep you from plunging down into the bottom of the canyon, right? At least, I hope not.

Q: Isn't eating all that red meat unhealthy?

MICHELLE: Context matters. Contrary to what you may have heard, red meat isn't necessarily bad for you. As my friend Diana Rodgers puts it, "meat itself isn't evil, it's the method by which we farm it (feed lots and CAFOs—Confined Animal Feeding Operations) and how we prepare it (breaded and deep fried), and what we eat alongside it (fries and a large soda)." Quality matters, too. I know that it can be challenging sometimes to find high-quality meat, but that's why I tend to choose cheaper cuts of meat that are still sustainably raised and sourced, like chuck roast, brisket, pork shoulder, oxtail, and offal.

HENRY: We should also point out that it's a myth that Paleo people eat nothing but red meat. In fact, if you look at our dinner plates (and the recipes in this book), we're obviously crazy about vegetables. Sustainable, well-raised meat happens to be an awesomely nutrient-dense source of protein and fat, so we eat it in reasonable portion sizes, but it's not like we gorge on plates of bacon every day.

OWEN: Plates of bacon sound pretty good, though!

Q: Do you use Paleo sweeteners like stevia or lower-calorie sugar alcohols?

MICHELLE: I know a lot of people have had success with those ingredients, and there are some Paleo-friendly products in stores that are sweetened with them. But I don't normally cook with any sweeteners other than some fruit, and occasionally a bit of honey or maple syrup. I don't often treat myself to dessert, but if I'm going to indulge in something sweet, I don't think it makes much of a difference which sweetener I use, as long as it's not an artificial one like aspartame. To me, sugar is sugar is sugar.

Q: Why is it so important to eat fermented foods like kimchi, sauerkraut, and kombucha?

MICHELLE: We love fermented foods, but especially sauerkraut and the Spicy Kimchi on page 62. It's easy to add to breakfast, lunch, or dinner—I just serve a little bit of kimchi or sauerkraut on the side. People have been fermenting stuff for generations not just because it preserves food; it also boosts umami, increases the bioavailability of nutrients, and helps repopulate the good bacteria in human guts.

OLLIE: Bacteria? Human guts? Gross. And awesome!

Q: How do you handle feeding picky eaters?

MICHELLE: Ollie, you're the resident picky eater in this family. How do we get you to try new things?

WELL, YOU TELL ME I HAVE NO CHOICE.

OWEN: Yeah—mom's a real dictator. Ha, ha!

Q: How do you stay motivated to cook and eat healthy all the time?

MICHELLE: I like feeling energized and healthy, so I don't feel like it's worth eating things that tire me out or make me feel like crap. I'm in my 40s now, and I want to be able to keep up with my kids and be the best version of myself. Thankfully, I've found Paleo to be a sustainable, healthy approach that offers a whole universe of amazing ingredients and complex flavors. As long as Paleo continues to be delicious and fun, it's easy for me to stay committed to this way of eating. After making your way through this book, I hope you'll agree with me!

THAT'S WHY WE'VE ORGANIZED THIS BOOK INTO COLOR-CODED CHAPTERS THAT YOU CAN TURN TO NO MATTER WHAT SCENARIO YOU'RE FACING!

READY OR NOT!
150+ nom nom paleo
MICHELLE TAM + HENRY FONG

FIRST, IN THE "GET READY" SECTION, I'LL WALK YOU THROUGH STOCKING UP YOUR KITCHEN FOR SUCCESS, AND SHARE WITH YOU A BUNCH OF BASIC BUILDING BLOCKS TO BUY OR MAKE AHEAD OF TIME. THIS IS THE PURPLE SECTION OF THE BOOK!

WHEN YOU'RE READY TO WHIP UP SOMETHING SPECIAL IN THE KITCHEN, FLIP TO THE GREEN SECTION. I TURN TO THESE "READY" RECIPES WHEN I FEEL LIKE DOING SOME MAKE-AHEAD COOKING. THAT WAY, I CAN GET A HEAD START ON THE WEEK!

THE ORANGE SECTION IS FOR WHEN YOU'RE ONLY "KINDA READY." TURN HERE WHEN YOU WANT TO QUICKLY TRANSFORM PRE-MADE COMPONENTS INTO SOMETHING NEW AND TASTY, OR WHEN YOU WANT TO GIVE YOUR LEFTOVERS A MAKEOVER!

AND WHEN YOU'RE "NOT READY" AT ALL, HEAD TO THE RED SECTION, WHICH IS JAM-PACKED WITH SIMPLE, SPEEDY RECIPES THAT CAN BE MADE IN 45 MINUTES OR LESS. SOME OF THEM TAKE AS LITTLE AS 15 MINUTES FROM START TO FINISH!

THE BLUE SECTION AT THE END CONTAINS 4 WEEKS OF DINNER PLANS AND A BUNCH OF "NO RECIPE" RECIPES!

AND LAST BUT NOT LEAST, YOU'LL FIND NOT JUST A REGULAR INDEX IN THE BACK OF THE BOOK, BUT ALSO A RECIPE INDEX WITH SPECIAL DIETS AND ALLERGY INFORMATION!

MOM! I KNEW YOU'D FORGET DESSERTS!

GET SET!

THE STUFF YOU NEED TO COOK ANYTIME

WHAT DO I NEED TO DO TO
GET SET?

The hardest part of cooking is getting started.

I hate getting started, too. Some folks assume that I'm head-over-heels in love with cooking, but to be totally honest, my favorite meal is whatever someone else is nice enough to cook for me. After all, when I'm sprawled on the couch with my nose in a gossip magazine, it takes a lot for me to get off my butt and into the kitchen. Inertia is a powerful force.

But as I said earlier, cooking is non-negotiable, which means we're not going to make excuses for why we can't cook. Your pantry is bare? No problem—we'll go shopping! Don't know the difference between a skillet and a saucepan? We'll figure it out! Over the years, I've heard from many Nomsters—especially those who are brand new to Paleo—who want to dive right in, but need some help getting started. In this section, I'm going to show you how to stock your kitchen with Paleo essentials so you can make nomtastically butt-kicking meals at any time.

So here's the game plan:

First, we'll go over all the kitchen tools you'll need for everyday cooking—from basics like sharp knives and wire racks to more specialized equipment like rasp graters and spiralizers…

> …AND PRESSURE COOKERS!

> PLUS A CAT TO KEEP YOU COMPANY!

Then, we'll get to work stocking your kitchen with all the stuff that'll end up in your belly. We'll review the ingredients that will not only make you healthier and happier, but also make your food taste amazing.

> LIKE HEAVENLY, GLORIOUS, UMAMI-RICH FISH SAUCE!

> "PUNGENT" IS THE WORD I'D USE!

Next, we'll tackle a bunch of easy prep-ahead sauces, dressings, and other essential building blocks that you can whip up and stash in your kitchen. These foundational components will come in handy later, when you're scrambling to cobble together a meal from whatever you can scavenge from your fridge.

> FOR INSTANCE, IF WE COMBINE ROAST-AHEAD CHICKEN BREASTS (PAGE 84) WITH SRIRACHA RANCH DRESSING (PAGE 57) AND SOME SALAD GREENS, WE'LL HAVE A SIMPLE AND YUMMY LUNCH READY IN NO TIME FLAT!

Later, we'll brainstorm some fun and creative ways to mix-and-match these building blocks to get the most out of your prep work.

By the time we're done with this section, you'll have all the fundamentals you need to whip up meals at the drop of a hat. Your shelves will be filled with pantry essentials and versatile kitchen tools. With an arsenal of prepared flavor boosters on hand, you'll have a head start on a number of the recipes you'll encounter later in this book. And your noggin will be bursting with enough Paleo expertise to make you an obnoxious know-it-all (if you choose to be, and for your own sake, I hope you won't).

Okay, gang. Ready to get set?

Outfitting your kitchen with cooking implements for the very first time? Or just sick and tired of your cruddy old culinary tools, like that sad-looking plastic spatula with the melted front edge? Either way, it's time to level up your kitchen game. After all, having the right tools can mean the difference between a perfectly cooked steak dinner and a total waste of a pricey cut of grass-fed meat.

In the next few pages, I'm going to share with you my favorite culinary essentials. And don't you worry your pretty little head—I won't recommend anything crazy-expensive or any one-trick ponies that'll clutter your countertop unnecessarily.

CHEF'S KNIFE

With a well-balanced chef's knife in the palm of your hand, you can slice and dice with the best of them. It's not just a matter of aesthetics; a good blade can make a huge impact on your cooking.

Just make sure to keep your chef's knife razor-sharp, because a dull blade is much more dangerous than a newly sharpened one. With a dull knife, you'll end up exerting more force as you chop, increasing the chances that your blade will slip off the food and cut you. You can get your knives sharpened at your local butcher shop or at most farmer's markets—or just do it yourself with an electric knife sharpener.

PARING KNIFE

I know what you're thinking: If I already have a chef's knife, why do I need a baby blade, too? Answer: A chef's knife is too big and clunky when a recipe calls for fine, detailed knifework. Sometimes, you just need to pick out the seeds in an apple or jab a few small slits in a slab of pork shoulder. There's no need to blow your budget on an expensive paring knife, though—even a cheap one can help make quick work of small tasks on the cutting board.

CUTTING BOARD

Speaking of cutting boards, you'll need one. People often ask whether wooden or plastic cutting boards are best, and my response is always the same: It depends on your personal preference and budget. There's no real difference sanitation-wise; research shows that both types can be cleaned easily and thoroughly. Personally, I've got both wooden and plastic boards in my kitchen, though I tend to lean more on my plastic ones for day-to-day tasks. If your cutting boards don't have slip-resistant edges or feet, lay a damp towel underneath to keep them from moving while you chop.

SAFETY FIRST, PEOPLE!

PEELERS

I recommend stashing at least two vegetable peelers in your kitchen drawer so you'll always have one on hand to quickly remove the skins and peels of fruits and vegetables. (Okay, you can get away with just a single peeler if you're good about washing your cooking utensils as you go.) You can also jazz up your salads by peeling your carrots, cucumbers, and zucchini into thin noodles or ribbons.

TIME FOR A SOAK!

My favorite new kitchen shortcut? It may be old news to you, but I've been making it a habit to keep a large stainless steel bowl filled with warm, soapy water in the sink so I can chuck dirty utensils and dishes into it as I cook. *Presto!* Washing dishes just got a lot easier!

KITCHEN SHEARS

A dedicated pair of scissors for cooking duties might seem like an unnecessary extravagance, but it's not. Kitchen shears are a must in my kitchen. Knives can deliver more precise cuts, but shears offer speed and power. I use shears for everything from snipping fresh herbs to removing the backbone from a chicken. Buy a pair of well-balanced, high-carbon stainless steel shears with micro-serrations on the blades to help firmly grip the slippery foods (like raw chicken) you'll be cutting. And for easy cleaning, make sure the blades can be fully separated.

RASP GRATER

Microplane makes rasp graters with tiny, sharp teeth that slice food into feathery-light ribbons, which in turn adds subtle flavors and essences to your dishes without any annoying fiber or grittiness. I'll reach for my rasp grater to finely zest citrus without digging into the bitter white pith, shave frozen ginger to create flavorful snow that melts into hot dishes, and tame raw garlic so that none of my dinner guests are surprised by a big chunk of unpleasant spiciness.

SILICONE SPATULAS

Traditionalists swear by their wooden spoons, but while wood is a great material for cooking tools, I've come to prefer utensils that won't stain or scorch over time. That's why I switched to flat-edged, silicone spatulas a few years ago. For a while, I got the ones with the silicone heads and wooden handles, but the handles eventually got warped and mildewy. Now, the spatulas I keep in my kitchen are constructed of a single piece of silicone with no holes or seams, which makes cleaning a breeze.

SILICONE SPATULAS MAKE GREAT BACK-SCRATCHERS, TOO!

TONGS

Many restaurant chefs scoff at the idea of cooking with tongs, but I'm just a home cook who can't live without a good pair of dishwasher-safe locking tongs with wide-scalloped pincers. I use tongs to nimbly turn ingredients roasting in the oven, transfer hot foods from the stovetop, or grab stuff straight off the grill. I also like to pretend they're my robot hands.

MEASURING TOOLS

If you're a rookie in the kitchen, follow my recipes precisely, and you'll get a no-fail dish on your first try. Then, as you gain more confidence and experience, you can forgo the measuring tools and add a dash, splash, or pinch as you wish. But for now, get a kitchen scale, a ruler, measuring cups, and measuring spoons. When buying liquid measuring cups, avoid the cheap plastic ones. Go with glass, which does a better job of withstanding heat. And when selecting measuring spoons, choose the narrow, flat-bottomed ones; not only will they actually fit inside the mouths of your spice containers, but you can rest them on your kitchen counter without fear of spilling.

HEAT-RESISTANT OVEN MITTS

Whenever you handle hot cookware, slip on a pair of heat-resistant oven mitts so you don't burn yourself. Yes, a kitchen towel can work in a pinch, but I'm all for maximum hand protection. Nothing kills a good cook-up faster than a painful, debilitating burn.

GET SUPER-HEAT-RESISTANT KEVLAR OR NOMEX GLOVES WITH FIVE FINGERS FOR MAXIMUM DEXTERITY!

INSTANT-READ THERMOMETER

Yes, with experience, you'll figure out how to tell when your meat is cooked to your liking. But let's be frank: The only way to guarantee that your protein is perfectly cooked is to make sure it reaches the right temperature. If you're just starting out in the kitchen and cooking up high-quality meat, do yourself a favor: Invest in a reliable instant-read thermometer. After all, you'll never want to cook meat again if your expensive steak comes out gray and powdery.

RIMMED BAKING SHEETS

Most cooks know them as cookie sheets, but that doesn't mean they have to only be used to bake cookies. I use rimmed baking sheets to roast meats and vegetables. I recommend getting a few sheets that are no smaller than 13 by 18 inches—otherwise known as half-sheets. You can find them in your local kitchen supply store or online.

YOU MIGHT BE TEMPTED TO GET A FULL BAKING SHEET, BUT WATCH OUT: THEY'RE TOO BIG FOR MOST HOME OVENS.

OVEN-SAFE WIRE RACKS

I use wire racks to keep my roasted meats from sitting in a puddle of grease in the oven, and to prevent crunchy stuff from going limp and soggy. Wire racks also come in handy for cooling, resting, and draining food. Dishwasher-safe stainless steel racks are my favorite because they're practically indestructible—unlike the chrome-lined ones that flake off with use.

HEAVY DUTY SKILLETS

In my kitchen, I make heavy use of a pre-seasoned 12-inch cast-iron skillet, as well as an 8-inch version. They're fantastically versatile, but don't presume that the factory-applied "pre-seasoning" on the cast-iron surface is sufficient. You'll still need to season the skillets until a non-stick coating naturally develops with repeated use.

To maintain your cast-iron skillets, clean them after each use; then wipe them out and put them on a hot burner to dry before rubbing a bit of melted fat onto all surfaces. Cast-iron skillets are cheap and reliable, but if you have money burning a hole in your pocket, you can invest in stainless steel tri-ply skillets (made with stainless steel bonded to an aluminum core). In general, I don't recommend skillets with non-stick surfaces because they don't tend to stand up well to high heat. Besides, a non-stick surface prevents the tasty fond (the delicious brown bits that develop when you cook) from forming on the bottom of the pan and adding to the complexity of your dishes.

CAST-IRON SKILLETS WILL ALSO MAKE EXCELLENT WEAPONS DURING THE COMING ZOMBIE APOCALYPSE!

HEAVY DUTY STOCKPOT

Comforting stews and soups can be simmering on your stovetop in the wintertime—but only if you've got a big stockpot.

EVEN IF YOU'RE ONLY COOKING FOR A SMALL CREW, A BIG POT ENABLES YOU TO MAKE ENOUGH TO FREEZE FOR LATER!

HEAVY DUTY SAUCEPAN

A lidded, high-sided pan is perfect for making sauces and reheating small portions of leftovers. Get a long-handled stainless steel saucepan with an aluminum core. Unless you're feeding an army, a small (2-quart) saucepan will work fine for most families.

BLENDER + FOOD PROCESSOR

With an immersion blender (a.k.a. hand blender), whipping up sauces, condiments, and puréed soups is a cinch. It's relatively inexpensive, too.

Got a bit more money to spend? Invest in a high-powered countertop blender. It will yield faster and more consistent results. Besides, if you're frequently blitzing a lot of sauces, soups, and smoothies, you certainly won't regret the purchase.

Similarly, if you always find yourself buried under an avalanche of ingredients to cut into small pieces, a food processor may be well worth the price, too.

SLOW + PRESSURE COOKER

The slow cooker is a countertop appliance that cooks food at a low, steady temperature for hours. There's no need to babysit the slow cooker—I just set it and forget about it. Hours later, my kitchen will be filled with the intoxicating aroma of a delicious, ready-made meal. No fuss, no muss!

But these days, even when I have enough time to use a slow cooker, I'll whip out my electric pressure cooker to speed up my meal prep. Once it's done cooking, this smart little appliance de-pressurizes and keeps our food warm until we're ready to eat.

Pressure cooking is a game-changer—especially for busy home cooks like me. When I'm short on time but hankering for dishes that normally take forever to cook (like bone broth, tough cuts of meat, or winter braises and stews), I turn to my pressure cooker.

DON'T WORRY: ALL THE PRESSURE COOKER RECIPES IN THIS BOOK ARE ACCOMPANIED BY NON-PRESSURE COOKER VARIATIONS, TOO!

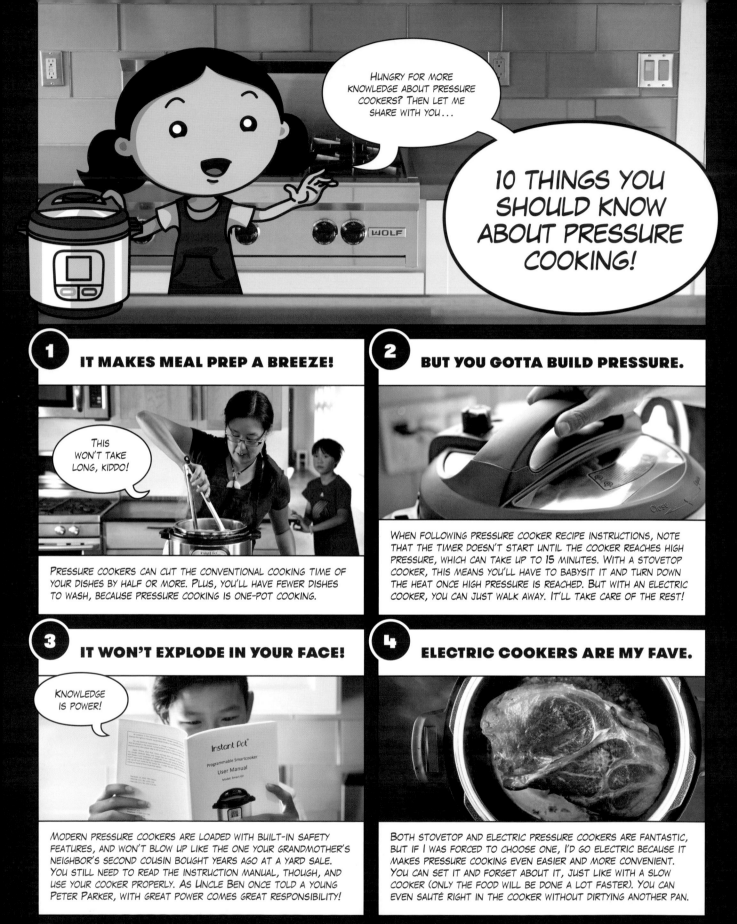

HUNGRY FOR MORE KNOWLEDGE ABOUT PRESSURE COOKERS? THEN LET ME SHARE WITH YOU...

10 THINGS YOU SHOULD KNOW ABOUT PRESSURE COOKING!

1 IT MAKES MEAL PREP A BREEZE!

THIS WON'T TAKE LONG, KIDDO!

PRESSURE COOKERS CAN CUT THE CONVENTIONAL COOKING TIME OF YOUR DISHES BY HALF OR MORE. PLUS, YOU'LL HAVE FEWER DISHES TO WASH, BECAUSE PRESSURE COOKING IS ONE-POT COOKING.

2 BUT YOU GOTTA BUILD PRESSURE.

WHEN FOLLOWING PRESSURE COOKER RECIPE INSTRUCTIONS, NOTE THAT THE TIMER DOESN'T START UNTIL THE COOKER REACHES HIGH PRESSURE, WHICH CAN TAKE UP TO 15 MINUTES. WITH A STOVETOP COOKER, THIS MEANS YOU'LL HAVE TO BABYSIT IT AND TURN DOWN THE HEAT ONCE HIGH PRESSURE IS REACHED. BUT WITH AN ELECTRIC COOKER, YOU CAN JUST WALK AWAY. IT'LL TAKE CARE OF THE REST!

3 IT WON'T EXPLODE IN YOUR FACE!

KNOWLEDGE IS POWER!

MODERN PRESSURE COOKERS ARE LOADED WITH BUILT-IN SAFETY FEATURES, AND WON'T BLOW UP LIKE THE ONE YOUR GRANDMOTHER'S NEIGHBOR'S SECOND COUSIN BOUGHT YEARS AGO AT A YARD SALE. YOU STILL NEED TO READ THE INSTRUCTION MANUAL, THOUGH, AND USE YOUR COOKER PROPERLY. AS UNCLE BEN ONCE TOLD A YOUNG PETER PARKER, WITH GREAT POWER COMES GREAT RESPONSIBILITY!

4 ELECTRIC COOKERS ARE MY FAVE.

BOTH STOVETOP AND ELECTRIC PRESSURE COOKERS ARE FANTASTIC, BUT IF I WAS FORCED TO CHOOSE ONE, I'D GO ELECTRIC BECAUSE IT MAKES PRESSURE COOKING EVEN EASIER AND MORE CONVENIENT. YOU CAN SET IT AND FORGET ABOUT IT, JUST LIKE WITH A SLOW COOKER (ONLY THE FOOD WILL BE DONE A LOT FASTER). YOU CAN EVEN SAUTÉ RIGHT IN THE COOKER WITHOUT DIRTYING ANOTHER PAN.

5. PRESSURE AFFECTS TIMING A BIT.

STOVETOP PRESSURE COOKERS COOK AT A SLIGHTLY HIGHER PRESSURE (15 PSI) THAN ELECTRIC COOKERS (10 TO 12 PSI), SO IT ACTUALLY TAKES A BIT LESS TIME FOR STOVETOP COOKERS TO DO THEIR THING. FOR THE PRESSURE COOKER RECIPES IN THIS BOOK, I'LL POINT OUT ANY RELEVANT DIFFERENCES IN COOKING TIME.

6. NOT EVERYTHING SHOULD BE P.C.!

AND BY "P.C.," I MEAN PRESSURE-COOKED. IF I WERE YOU, I'D AVOID COOKING ANYTHING IN A PRESSURE COOKER THAT CAN BE QUICKLY PREPARED USING A CONVENTIONAL METHOD LIKE SAUTÉING OR STIR-FRYING. OTHERWISE, YOU'LL RISK OVERCOOKING YOUR FOOD IN THE PRESSURE COOKER, AND IN THE END, YOU WON'T SAVE MUCH TIME.

7. PRESSURIZE THOSE CHEAP CUTS!

THE BEST DISHES TO PRESSURE-COOK ARE STEWS AND BRAISES THAT CALL FOR CHEAPER, COLLAGEN-RICH CUTS LIKE PORK BUTT, CHUCK ROAST, AND LAMB SHANKS. THEY'LL END UP TENDER AND DELICIOUS. IF THE MEAT'S STILL TOUGH, JUST PRESSURE-COOK IT FOR ANOTHER 5 TO 10 MINUTES. THESE CUTS WON'T GET TOUGHER AS THEY COOK.

8. IT'S TRUE, GUYS: SIZE MATTERS.

IDEALLY, YOUR INGREDIENTS SHOULD BE CUT TO ROUGHLY THE SAME SIZE. THAT WAY, THEY'LL COOK IN THE SAME AMOUNT OF TIME.

9. DO YOU NEED EXTRA LIQUID?

MOST INSTRUCTION MANUALS CALL FOR ADDING AT LEAST 1 CUP OF EXTRA LIQUID TO THE PRESSURE COOKER, BUT IT MAY NOT ALWAYS BE NECESSARY. MANY INGREDIENTS WILL RELEASE THAT AMOUNT OF MOISTURE (OR MORE) WHEN COOKED UNDER HIGH PRESSURE. THAT'S WHY SOME OF MY RECIPES DON'T CALL FOR AN EXTRA CUP OF LIQUID.

10. BLOW OFF STEAM THE RIGHT WAY!

PUT YOUR ELECTRIC COOKER UNDER YOUR STOVETOP HOOD SO THAT WHEN YOU RELEASE THE PRESSURE, THE ESCAPING STEAM WON'T RUIN YOUR CABINETS. JUST DON'T TURN ON THE STOVE, YA DUMS!

PLANTS!

After all this time, people still assume that Paleo is a total meat-fest, but it's not. It's become a tired cliché in Paleo circles, but I eat more vegetables than I did back when I was a vegetarian. (My flirtation with vegetarianism in college didn't last long; I soon got sick of microwaveable mac 'n' cheese and sad-looking bean burritos.) These days, our dinner plates are always overflowing with vegetables.

IT'S LIKE A GARDEN EXPLODED ON OUR PLATES!

Most plants are rich in micronutrients like potassium, magnesium, folate, and vitamins A, C and E. In addition, many vegetables are also packed with prebiotics—a special form of dietary fiber that helps feed the beneficial gut bacteria in our bodies. And best of all, plants are incredibly delicious.

When shopping, prioritize in-season, pesticide-free produce, and grab a variety of fruits and vegetables. Eat all the colors of the rainbow so you can get the broadest range of micronutrients.

FRUIT IS GOOD, TOO, BUT IT'S NOT QUITE AS NUTRIENT-RICH. SO EAT FRUIT ALONG WITH YOUR VEGGIES, NOT INSTEAD OF THEM!

Garden-fresh produce is always the best choice, but I also stock up on "emergency greens": frozen organic vegetables, pre-washed organic salad greens, and packaged baby kale and spinach. Yes, convenience costs extra, but knowing I have prepped vegetables on hand means I have no excuse not to eat them.

The bottom line: Listen to your mother, and eat your vegetables. They're good for you.

GET MORE VEGETABLES ON YOUR PLATE!

- Make a deal with yourself to add vegetables to every single meal. It can be as easy as slicing a cucumber to eat with breakfast or roasting some broccoli to serve with a meaty sauce at lunchtime.

- When you get home from the store, take a few minutes to wash, dry, and store your leafy greens. Most greens will stay fresh in a sealed, paper towel–lined container for up to 1 week.

- Stock up on vegetables that can be eaten raw, like carrots, cucumbers, celery, bell peppers, and jicama. Pair them with your favorite nut butter, salsa, or dressing, and they'll quickly become your go-to snack.

- Don't let your produce go to waste. Instead of throwing out your wilted veggies, roast them with your favorite cooking fat, or use them to make a giant pot of vegetable soup—a.k.a. "Garbage Soup" (page 328)!

ANIMALS!

The best protein comes from healthy animals that consume whatever nature intended. So whenever possible, fill your freezer or fridge with grass-fed and grass-finished meats, wild game, pastured poultry and eggs, and wild-caught seafood.

Yes, high-quality animal protein doesn't come cheap, but who says you have to eat steak every night? I keep costs down by buying whole chickens, eggs, ground meat, and less pricey braising cuts like chuck roast and pork shoulder—and I always stock up when there's a sale. If you've got room in your freezer (a standalone chest freezer is a great investment, by the way), you can save even more money by purchasing a whole, half, or quarter animal from a local farmer or rancher. Learn to be a nose-to-tail eater!

Sourcing healthy, ethically raised animal protein can be a pain, but just do the best you can. Don't be paralyzed by the fear of being less than perfect.

As an insurance policy, I always keep pre-cooked "emergency protein" on hand so I can whip up quick meals whenever I'm too busy, tired, or lazy to make more complicated recipes. My favorite emergency proteins include hard-cooked eggs, canned seafood (like wild salmon, sardines, and tuna), sausages, and organic deli meat.

And when I've got absolutely *nothing* in the house, I'll swing by my neighborhood grocery store and buy a salt-and-pepper-seasoned rotisserie chicken to serve with a giant green salad. Did those birds freely roam around, chowing only on what nature intended? Probably not—but sometimes, you just have to get dinner on the table. And didn't I just finish telling you to stop worrying about being perfect all the time?

MAKE EXTRA!

It's usually faster and easier to throw together a vegetable side dish than to cook up a meaty entrée, so don't be shy about batch-cooking your proteins. After all, leftover meat can always be repurposed in different ways to keep your meals exciting.

HEALTHY FATS!

I know what you're thinking: "Healthy fat? Isn't that an oxymoron?" Not at all!

For decades, we were told to banish dietary fat from our diets (want a glass of watery skim milk with your dessicated fat-free cookies, anyone?). And of course, some fats are, in fact, terrible for our bodies. We all know about partially hydrogenated oils containing trans fats, but margarine isn't the only fat to avoid. Even vegetable and seed oils—which are usually marketed as "heart-healthy"—are highly processed with chemical solvents and packed with omega-6 polyunsaturated fatty acids. They're so unstable that even when kept at room temperature, they oxidize and turn rancid to some degree. Heat accelerates this oxidation, and promotes the formation of free radicals that assault the healthy cells in your body.

I DON'T KNOW WHAT ALL THAT SCIENTIFIC MUMBO-JUMBO MEANS, BUT I DON'T THINK FOOD SHOULD BE RANCID AND ASSAULT ME.

But the solution isn't to shun dietary fats altogether. Fat is a terrific source of energy, and it helps humans absorb many vitamins and minerals. It builds our cell membranes and the sheaths surrounding our nerves. Fat isn't the enemy. You just need to make sure the fats you consume are the *right* fats. And in fact, there are plenty of good, healthy fats that offer incredible health benefits—and taste great, too.

I promised you I wouldn't geek out on food science in this book, so I won't bore you with a lecture on the chemical properties of fat. But here's the deal: promise me you'll replace the bottles of highly processed, omega-6 dominant vegetable oils on your shelves with healthy cooking fats like ghee, coconut oil, rendered animal fats (like lard, tallow, bacon drippings, schmaltz, and duck fat), avocado oil, macadamia nut oil, or extra-virgin olive oil. Deal?

MAKE YOUR OWN GHEE!

As you'll soon see, one of my go-to healthy cooking fats is ghee, a traditional Indian preparation of clarified butter. You can buy ghee at the store or online, but it's easy to make your own ghee at home, too.

Here's how to do it:

1. Melt a cup of unsalted butter in a saucepan over low heat. As it melts, the clear fat will separate from the milk solids. The surface of the butter will initially bubble, and then settle into a foam.

2. Once the milk solids turn a deep golden brown, clump together, and begin to drift to the bottom of the saucepan (about 8 to 10 minutes after the butter initially started bubbling), remove the pan from the heat, and strain the butter through a triple layer of cheesecloth.

3. Discard the milk solids, and store the ghee in a sealed container. With the milk solids removed, the ghee should be shelf-stable for months.

Folks with dairy sensitivities generally do fine with ghee because the problematic milk proteins have been removed during the clarification process, leaving behind just pure butter oil. Of course, if you have an extreme sensitivity to dairy, you should exercise caution, as ghee may still contain trace amounts of lactose and casein. In that case, you may want to use coconut oil, avocado oil, and/or olive oil instead.

FERMENTED STUFF!

Okay—I lied. Forgive me, but I'm going to indulge in a teeny-tiny bit of science-geekery here. But who wouldn't nerd out over a subject as fascinating (and wonderfully delicious) as fermentation?

Human bodies are complicated ecosystems. Each of us house somewhere between 10 to 100 trillion microbes representing thousands of species just in our gastrointestinal tract—and they're not there just to hang out. According to Dr. Justin Sonnenburg, a Stanford professor and pioneer in immunology and microbiology, our gut microbiota "is a control center for multiple aspects of our biology, including our immune status, metabolism, and neurobiology." In other words, I'm not just me, and you're not just you; we're actually "composite organisms consisting of microbial and human parts."

WE'RE IN A SYMBIOTIC RELATIONSHIP WITH OUR MICROSCOPIC GUT-BUDDIES!

Recent studies suggest that a diverse microbiota may be critical to our overall health, so I want to make sure my own gastrointestinal tract is well-populated with beneficial bacteria. How? By eating fermented foods, as well as feeding my gut good bacteria by consuming lots of fiber-rich vegetables and fruit.

Our ancestors fermented their foods for a different reason, of course. For thousands of years, humans have used fermentation to preserve food, and to transform and deepen flavors. We now have good reason to believe that fermentation also increases nutrient bioavailability, and introduces our guts to good bacteria. By enjoying fermented foods, we can restore balance to our immune systems.

Look, I'm not saying that eating fermented foods will cure you of all sickness and disease. But I *am* telling you that consuming fermented foods will expose your gastrointestinal system to diverse microbes, and that's a good thing.

SO...WHEN WE EAT FERMENTED FOODS, WE'RE EATING BACTERIA, AND THEN WE EAT VEGETABLES TO FEED THE BACTERIA IN OUR GUTS?

COOL!

There are lots of different fermented foods you can incorporate into your diet. Kimchi and sauerkraut are favorites of mine, as are lacto-fermented pickles. Henry loves kombucha, and both dairy-free yogurt and kefir can regularly be found in our fridge.

I've discovered that the best way to consume a variety of fermented foods is by having a little bit every day. That's really all you need; fermented foods are pretty potent both flavor-wise and health-wise, so a little goes a long way. To some, fermented foods are an acquired taste, so if you're new to them, start with baby steps. Have a bite of sauerkraut with grilled sausages, or throw some lacto-fermented pickles on your lettuce-wrapped burger patty.

THAT'S HOW WE GET OUR KIDS TO EAT FERMENTED FOODS: AS CONDIMENTS!

FLAVOR BOOSTERS!

Raise your hand if you love bland food!

Yeah, I didn't think so. No one wants to eat *blah*-tasting food. That's why it's imperative to have flavor boosters on hand to magically transform meat and veggies from boring to nomtastic. As you'll see, I prioritize ingredients that naturally boost umami—a.k.a. the fifth taste. By the time you finish this book, you'll be sick of reading about umami, but I'm never going to stop extolling its virtues. After all, it's the ultimate shortcut to deliciousness.

WANT TO LEARN MORE ABOUT UMAMI? TURN TO PAGE 284!

IN THE MEANTIME, LET'S TALK ABOUT MY GO-TO FLAVOR BOOSTERS!

SALT

Human bodies need enough salt to regulate fluids in the body. But it's not just essential for life—it's also a key flavoring agent. I use kosher salt in most of my savory dishes; I like its coarseness, which makes it easy to pinch and sprinkle. This may also explain why it's the standard salt used by most restaurant chefs.

This is important, you guys: Not all salts are the same. This book's salt measurements were made using Diamond Crystal kosher salt, which is lighter and less salty by volume than Morton's kosher salt, fine sea salt, or regular table salt. If you use those other salts, use roughly half the amount called for in my recipes. But as always, you should salt to taste while you're cooking, because saltiness is a personal preference.

DRIED SPICES + SEASONINGS

Spices go a long way toward perking up our palates. Seek out your local spice purveyor and follow your nose. Stock up on curry powder, cumin, cinnamon—whatever floats your boat. One of my new favorites is *gochugaru*, a coarsely ground blend of Korean red pepper flakes. My spice cabinet always contains plenty of black pepper, dried thyme, bay leaves, and granulated onion and garlic. I also keep several spice blends that I sprinkle on emergency stir-fries (see page 329) and impromptu ground beef dinners.

DRIED HERBS AND SPICES DON'T LAST FOREVER, SO PURGE YOUR PANTRY EVERY 6 MONTHS OR SO TO KEEP THINGS SPICY!

FRESH HERBS

Fresh herbs add wonderful brightness and flavor to your meals, so make sure you have plenty on hand. I especially love basil, mint, cilantro, Italian parsley, chives, thyme, and rosemary.

At the market, pick herbs with a clean, fresh aroma and vibrantly colored leaves. Better yet, grow your own herb garden. Leafy herbs like parsley and cilantro can be kept perky for at least a week if you trim the stems and place the cut ends in a jar or glass filled halfway with water. Cover loosely with a plastic bag before refrigerating the jar—and be careful not to knock it over while rummaging for a snack.

OR, YOU CAN WRAP YOUR HERBS IN PAPER TOWELS AND REFRIGERATE THEM IN AN AIRTIGHT CONTAINER.

THEY WON'T LAST QUITE AS LONG AS HERBS STORED LIKE FRESH FLOWERS, THOUGH!

AROMATICS

Asian cuisine is my comfort food, so you'll always find ginger, scallions, and garlic—the holy trinity of Chinese cooking—in my house. But frankly, all sorts of international flavors are built on the same basic building blocks that you can find in every grocery store, like fresh celery, carrots, shallots, onions, and leeks. I keep all of these aromatic vegetables in my kitchen, so that I can bust out just about any dish, no matter how diverse in origin.

When in doubt about what to make, just start cooking sliced or diced onions with your fat of choice in a skillet over medium-low heat. By the time you figure out what's for dinner, the onions will be softened, sweet, and ready to be incorporated into your dish. Better yet, slowly cook a giant batch of caramelized onions in advance, and freeze them in ice cube trays. Later, when you need a punch of instant flavor, you can add it—one onion-y cube at a time.

DRIED MUSHROOMS

Add an extra blast of umami to all your stews and braises by simply tossing in a few reconstituted dried mushrooms. These little guys are a game-changing flavor booster: Not only are dried 'shrooms scientifically proven to contain exponentially more umami power than their fresh counterparts, but they'll keep for months and never get slimy.

Whenever I see organic dried mushrooms on sale, I go into full-on buy-and-hoard mode, and you should, too. My two favorite varieties of dried mushrooms are shiitakes (perfect for Asian dishes!) and porcinis (delicious in Italian dishes!).

IF YOU'RE USING DRIED MUSHROOMS IN A PRESSURE COOKER RECIPE OR IN A LONG-COOKING BRAISE, YOU DON'T NEED TO RECONSTITUTE THEM IN WATER. JUST RINSE THEM AND TOSS 'EM IN!

TOMATO PASTE

Just one spoonful will add incredible depth and concentrated umami to your stews and braises. I like to buy the paste sold in toothpaste-like tubes so that I can squeeze out exactly the amount I want.

SO THIS ISN'T TOMATO-FLAVORED TOOTHPASTE?

BACON

When I first started eating Paleo, I went overboard with bacon. (Don't judge. You know you did it, too.) These days, I use bacon more as a flavoring agent than as the main dish. I don't need to tell you how much smoky goodness bacon imparts to dishes. Try to buy bacon made with pastured pork and no crazy additives, and if you're on a strict Paleo challenge, avoid bacon with added sugar.

By the way, I recommend freezing uncooked bacon in 3-slice portions, which will make it easier to slice when a recipe calls for it. Otherwise, slicing bacon can be a slippery exercise in frustration. Besides, I'd really like to keep all my fingers if at all possible.

BONE BROTH + STOCK

The terms "bone broth" and "stock" are often used interchangeably because, well, they're pretty much the same thing. Technically, "stock" is made from bones and cartilage, whereas "broth" is made with both bones and meat. My bone broth recipe (which you can find on page 76) incorporates both meat and bones to deliver a full, rich mouthfeel and deep flavor, while also yielding the health benefits of the gelatin produced by long-simmering bones.

I like to drink bone broth straight (it's delicious!), but I also use it as the foundation for my soups and as a critical flavoring agent in many of my dishes. In a pinch, you can substitute store-bought stock for bone broth in my recipes, but remember: The final result will only be as delicious as the base, so don't just use hot ham water. (Hot ham water is gross.)

COCONUT AMINOS

This dark, salty, aged coconut tree sap tastes a lot like soy sauce, but without gluten or soy. I like to mix coconut aminos with fish sauce to make it an even more umami-rich substitute for soy sauce.

VINEGARS + CITRUS

Acids are a key component in good cooking, and one of the most valuable flavor enhancers in your pantry. A splash of vinegar or a squeeze of fresh lemon or lime juice can add much-needed tartness and brightness to your finished dishes. To stay Paleo, just make sure that the vinegars you're using don't contain gluten (like malt vinegar) or weird additives.

SAUCES + DRESSINGS

It's always best to make your own sauces and dressings from scratch, but to stay sane, I keep a few bottles of store-bought marinara sauce, Thai curry paste, and spicy salsa in my kitchen. All feature Paleo-friendly ingredients, and make it even easier to quickly throw together a fast and tasty meal.

COCONUT MILK

Coconut milk is a Paleo staple, and it's wonderful in dishes as wildly different as Thai curries and dairy-free chocolate cake. But be careful when shopping for coconut milk, as many brands contain chemical additives. Go for the shelf-stable, full-fat, sulfite-free variety in BPA-free cans. One more thing: Don't confuse sweetened "cream of coconut" for coconut milk. Trust me: It's not the same thing.

TEXTURE BOOSTERS

Arrowroot powder, tapioca flour, and potato starch are useful for thickening sauces and gravies, and for making batters for coating fried foods.

WHAT IS ALL THIS STUFF?

Not familiar with these texture boosters? Pure arrowroot powder is a gluten-free starch made from the pulp of arrowroot tubers. Tapioca flour is similar, but it's derived from the cassava root. Potato starch is the starch extracted from, well, potatoes. (As I said on page 16, potatoes are not the enemy, so chill out, 'tater haters.) I use all of these ingredients in place of non-Paleo-friendly white flour and cornstarch to thicken and coat foods. A light dusting of these starches on the outside of your favorite protein yields a thin, crunchy coating on deep-fried eats.

By the way, arrowroot powder and tapioca flour can lose their thickening power at high temperatures, so remove your food from the heat as soon as it's ready.

"FLOURS" + SWEETENERS

For celebratory occasions that call for a yummy grain-free treat, I turn to alternative flours like almond, cassava, and coconut flour, and reach for natural sweeteners like raw organic honey, coconut sugar, maple syrup, dates, applesauce, or fruit juice.

WEIRD ... MOM FORGOT TO MENTION FISH SAUCE.

JUST WAIT 'TIL YOU TURN THE PAGE!

FISH SAUCE

MICHELLE: It's true—I'm always touting the virtues of fish sauce, but for good reason: It's truly magical. I know some people are turned off by the thought—or smell—of fish sauce, but if only they knew its transformative power, they'd be a convert like me.

HENRY: Fish sauce is made with salted, fermented anchovies, which may explain why so many folks steer clear of it. Most Americans think of anchovies as a briny, pungent pizza topping they'd rather avoid.

MICHELLE: But if people can manage to put aside any preconceived notions, they'll realize how much anchovies add to their favorite dishes. For example, the world's best Caesar salad dressings incorporate chopped-up anchovies, and folks love Worcestershire sauce, which is made with vinegar, tamarind, and anchovies. Restaurant chefs know that anchovies are a wonderful source of umami, adding a deep, satisfying dimension to just about any savory dish. Unless you dine out only at vegetarian places, you've probably consumed—and enjoyed—anchovies in all sorts of soups, sauces, stews, and sides.

HENRY: I read somewhere once that everyone loves anchovies—they just don't know it yet.

MICHELLE: Same goes for anchovy-rich fish sauce, which is a key flavoring agent in the cuisines of southern China, Thailand, Vietnam, and Indonesia. It's a big part of why Southeast Asian cooking has such a distinct flavor profile, and why I incorporate fish sauce in so many of my Asian-inspired dishes.

HENRY: But fish sauce isn't just for Asian recipes. Its funky brininess enhances Italian dishes, African dishes—even burgers. During the Roman Empire, many dishes featured a fish sauce called *garum* that was made by fermenting fish and salt. The modern version of this ancient Roman sauce is called *colatura di alici*, and it's increasingly popping up on the menus of trend-setting Italian restaurants these days.

MICHELLE: When I decided to make it my mission in life to make restaurant-quality dishes using real, whole ingredients, a Paleo-friendly fish sauce was at the top of my shopping list. But whenever I'd venture into Asian grocery stores to look for fish sauces made with just anchovies and salt, I'd come away disappointed. Every brand on the shelves contained sugar, preservatives, and other chemical additives. To make matters worse, many of them were "stretched" or thinned out with water or other liquids. Ugh.

HENRY: Would you have stuck with Paleo if you didn't manage to find a Paleo-friendly fish sauce?

MICHELLE: Thankfully, it never came to that. In early 2011, my sister told me about Red Boat Fish Sauce, a family-made artisanal product from the Vietnamese island of Phú Quốc that was just hitting the market. It contains just two ingredients: freshly caught black anchovies and salt. One taste, and I was hooked.

HENRY: We've since learned of a few other Paleo-friendly, two-ingredient fish sauce brands on the market, too, like Son Fish Sauce and 3 Miền.

MICHELLE: Remember: Fish sauce is powerful stuff. Just a few drops of this amber-colored magic will greatly amplify the umami flavor of savory food—without making it fishy-tasting. Now go get some!

NOT TOO LONG AGO, WE TOOK A TRIP TO VIETNAM AND VISITED PHÚ QUỐC ISLAND.

SWEATY

PHÚ QUỐC SITS IN THE GULF OF THAILAND, WHERE THE WATERS ARE TEEMING WITH FISH AND THE BUSTLING WET MARKETS ARE PACKED WITH FRESH SEAFOOD.

THE ISLAND IS FAMOUS FOR THREE THINGS: PEPPER TREES, STUNNING BEACHES...

...AND FISH SAUCE. FOR OVER 200 YEARS, THE ANCHOVIES CAUGHT IN THE WATERS OFF THE ISLAND HAVE BEEN USED TO MAKE SOME OF THE WORLD'S BEST FISH SAUCE.

SOON AFTER OUR ARRIVAL, RED BOAT'S FOUNDER, CUONG PHAM, TOOK US TO SEE A FRESH HAUL OF ANCHOVIES GET SALTED RIGHT ON THE DECK OF THE FISHING BOAT.

WE WERE MILES FROM LAND, BUT CUONG EXPLAINED THAT IT'S ESSENTIAL THAT THE SALTING PROCESS BEGIN IMMEDIATELY.

THE SALTED ANCHOVIES WERE PACKED INTO SACKS, AND THEN TRANSFERRED TO CUONG'S LITTLE RED BOAT SO WE COULD FERRY THEM BACK TO PHÚ QUỐC ISLAND.

ONCE THEY ARRIVED AT RED BOAT'S BARREL HOUSE, THE ANCHOVIES WERE UNLOADED AND CAREFULLY SORTED...

...BEFORE BEING PLACED INTO GIGANTIC WOODEN BARRELS AND COVERED WITH EVEN MORE SALT TO SLOWLY FERMENT AND DEVELOP INTO THE RICH AND DEEPLY FLAVORFUL CONDIMENT THAT WE ALL LOVE.

THE RESULT: AN UMAMI-RICH FISH SAUCE CRAVED BY CHEFS AND FOODIES ALIKE.

YES, THE AROMA IS POWERFUL, BUT NO ONE'S EXPECTED TO CLIMB INTO A BARREL AND TAKE A SWIM. THIS STUFF IS SUPER-CONCENTRATED, SO JUST A LITTLE BIT WILL MAKE YOUR FOOD POP WITH FLAVOR.

PALEO-FRIENDLY FISH SAUCE IS ONE OF THE KEYS TO AWESOME COOKING, SO MAKE SURE YOU ALWAYS HAVE SOME ON HAND.

So...are you itchin' to get in the kitchen?

Good, 'cause we've got over 150 recipes to scratch that itch!

MICHELLE: But before we jump into the meat of this book, let me explain what you're about to see. For folks who are accustomed to standard cookbook formatting, our recipes are going to look a little... unorthodox. That is, unless you read comic books.

HENRY: True! Our recipes are formatted like pages out of a comic book. Nom Nom Paleo has always featured recipes with photos of each step, so what better way to present our dishes than by sharing the action-packed sequences that magically turn raw ingredients into ready-to-eat meals?

MICHELLE: It's easy to navigate the recipe steps: Just follow the numbered instruction boxes on each photo. They look like this:

9 NEXT, TRANSFER THE COOKED VEGETABLES TO A PLATTER. SPREAD IT OUT IN A SINGLE LAYER AND COOL TO ROOM TEMPERATURE.

HENRY: Below the title of each recipe, you'll also find information about serving size suggestions. We based serving sizes on how we actually feed our family: a palm-size portion of protein and a whole lot of vegetables per person. But if you happen to be

eating for athletic performance or feeding ravenous teenagers, feel free to make extra.

MICHELLE: Below the serving size information is the anticipated total cooking time for each recipe. This may include time you're not actually having to do anything except wait around; in these cases, we've also noted the hands-on time. Here's an example:

> ### MAKES 4 SERVINGS
> ### ⏱ 1 HOUR
> ### (30 MINUTES HANDS-ON)

HENRY: In this book, we've also included a bunch of recipe variants—different versions of dishes that you can create with just a few changes to the instructions or ingredients. These variations are marked with a circular symbol with two rotating arrows like this:

> ### SWITCH IT UP:
> ## UMAMI BOK CHOY

MICHELLE: Of course, each recipe will also feature a headnote, detailed information about prepping ingredients, and any special notes or tips to keep in mind. Most will also include storage instructions.

HENRY: We'll also butt in every now and then to talk about topics that might be of interest, like what to eat for breakfast. Anything else to cover before we dive into the recipes, Michelle?

MICHELLE: Nope. Let's get the show on the road!

SMOKY LIME PEPITAS

MAKES 1 CUP
⏱ 20 MINUTES
(5 MINUTES HANDS-ON)

Let's start with something simple.

When it comes to toasting nuts and seeds, there's really not much work involved, but when it's done correctly, the results can be out-of-this-world. Take these Smoky Lime Pepitas, for example. Pumpkin seeds aren't anything special, but once roasted, they take on a rich, dark, meaty texture. Nicely balanced between the spice and tang of chile and lime, these seeds are perfect for snacking. Set them out in small bowls for your guests while they mingle before dinner, or just sprinkle them on a casually thrown-together salad for lunch like the Mexican Watermelon + Cucumber Salad on page 189.

INGREDIENTS:

1   **cup raw pepitas**

1   **teaspoon olive oil or avocado oil**

¾   **teaspoon salt**

½   **teaspoon smoked paprika or ancho chili powder**

¼   **teaspoon cayenne pepper**

     Juice from 1 medium lime

GUESS WHAT? THIS RECIPE WORKS WITH NUTS LIKE ALMONDS AND CASHEWS, TOO!

INSTRUCTIONS:

1 PREHEAT THE OVEN TO 325ºF WITH THE RACK PLACED IN THE MIDDLE POSITION.

2 IN A MEDIUM BOWL, COMBINE THE PEPITAS, OLIVE OIL, SALT, PAPRIKA, AND CAYENNE.

3 ADD THE LIME JUICE AND MIX WELL.

4 SPREAD THE SEASONED PEPITAS IN A SINGLE LAYER ON A PARCHMENT-LINED RIMMED BAKING SHEET.

5 TOAST THE SEEDS FOR 12 TO 15 MINUTES IN THE OVEN, STIRRING AT THE HALFWAY POINT, UNTIL FRAGRANT AND CRUNCHY.

6 COOL TO ROOM TEMPERATURE. YOU CAN KEEP THE SMOKY LIME PEPITAS IN A SEALED CONTAINER FOR UP TO 1 WEEK.

TRY SPRINKLING THEM ON TOP OF ROASTED ONION SOUP (PAGE 96)!

THAI CITRUS DRESSING

MAKES 1 CUP
⏱ **5 MINUTES**

INGREDIENTS:

- 3   **tablespoons extra-virgin olive oil**
- 3   **tablespoons fresh lime juice**
- 3   **tablespoons fresh orange juice**
- 3   **tablespoons fish sauce**
- 3   **tablespoons coconut aminos**
- 2   **teaspoons honey (optional)**
- 1   **small garlic clove, minced**
- ½   **teaspoon crushed red pepper flakes**

INSTRUCTIONS:

① TOSS ALL THE INGREDIENTS INTO A JAR, SMALL BOWL, OR MEDIUM MEASURING CUP.

② WHISK WELL (OR IF MAKING THIS DRESSING IN A JAR, JUST SEAL AND SHAKE). TASTE THE MIXTURE AND ADJUST FOR SEASONING.

Thai salads are my latest obsession, which is why I like to keep a jar of this easy Asian dressing in my refrigerator at all times. All five tastes are perfectly balanced in this dressing: sweet, savory, spicy, tangy, and umami. Best of all, Thai Citrus Dressing can be used on dishes other than salads. Drizzle it on roasted vegetables or grilled steaks, and you'll see what I mean.

③ THIS DRESSING CAN BE KEPT IN THE FRIDGE FOR UP TO 1 WEEK. JUST REMEMBER TO SHAKE OR STIR WELL BEFORE USING.

WHEN YOU HAVE PRE-MADE DRESSINGS AND TOPPINGS ON HAND, BUTT-KICKING SALADS ARE A BREEZE TO MAKE. HERE'S A SIMPLE SALAD TOSSED WITH *THAI CITRUS DRESSING* AND TOPPED WITH *SMOKY LIME PEPITAS*!

YOU CAN ALSO USE THIS DRESSING IN PLACE OF THE MARINADE FOR *PAPER-WRAPPED CHICKEN* (PAGE 204), AS AN ALTERNATIVE DRESSING FOR *CHILLED ASIAN ZOODLE SALAD WITH CHICKEN + AVOCADO* (PAGE 183), OR AS AN ACCOMPANIMENT FOR *NO LÁ LỐT MEATBALLS* (PAGE 296).

GREEN BEAST DRESSING

MAKES 2 CUPS
⏱ **15 MINUTES**

Traditionally made with sour cream, mayonnaise, chives, chervil, and anchovy, Green Goddess Dressing was named after a 1921 stage play called—you guessed it—*The Green Goddess*. But when I devised my own version of this verdant sauce, my two boys declared that it needed a "tougher-sounding" name, and dubbed it "Green Beast Dressing."

I was taken aback at first—who says goddesses aren't tough? But after mulling it over, I agreed to go with the boys' name of choice—under one condition: This "Green Beast" refers to a girl. A really tough girl. One whose namesake dressing will knock you out with a single punch to the mouth.

INGREDIENTS:

- ½ medium avocado, pitted and peeled
- ½ cup Italian parsley, chopped
- ½ cup fresh basil
- ¼ cup chopped chives
- 1 garlic clove, minced
- ¾ cup extra-virgin olive oil
- ½ cup water, plus more as needed
- ¼ cup fresh lemon juice, plus more to taste
- 2 tablespoons tahini
- 1 teaspoon kosher salt
- ¼ teaspoon freshly ground black pepper

INSTRUCTIONS:

1 TOSS ALL THE INGREDIENTS INTO A HIGH-SPEED BLENDER.

2 PURÉE UNTIL SMOOTH.

3 TASTE THE DRESSING AND ADJUST THE SEASONING AS NEEDED. IF THE DRESSING'S TOO THICK FOR YOUR LIKING, YOU CAN THIN IT OUT WITH A LITTLE MORE WATER.

4 IN A SEALED CONTAINER, THIS DRESSING CAN BE REFRIGERATED FOR UP TO 1 WEEK. JUST STIR VIGOROUSLY BEFORE USING.

5 TOP YOUR SALADS, SOUPS, MEATS, AND VEGETABLES WITH THIS VIBRANT, VERSATILE DRESSING.

FOR EXAMPLE, I DRIZZLED GREEN BEAST DRESSING ON THIS SIDE SALAD OF LETTUCE, CARROT, CUCUMBER, RADISH, BELL PEPPER, AND MACADAMIA NUTS. EASY DOES IT!

CREAMY ONION DRESSING

MAKES 3 CUPS
⏱ 2 HOURS
(15 MINUTES HANDS-ON)

Yes, I know you can make a simple vinaigrette in less than 5 minutes. After all, vinegar plus oil plus a bit of mustard and some salt and pepper make for a nice, basic dressing in a pinch. But if you have a sack of onions and some time to kill, you owe it to yourself to make this dressing. Even if you're already a salad-making Yoda, roasted onion and garlic will elevate your salad game to the next level.

INGREDIENTS:

- **6** unpeeled garlic cloves
- **3** medium unpeeled yellow onions (about 1½ pounds)
- **1¼ cup** extra-virgin olive oil or avocado oil, divided
- **¼ cup** fresh lemon juice
- **¼ cup** apple cider vinegar
- **1** tablespoon kosher salt
- Freshly ground black pepper

INSTRUCTIONS:

1 PREHEAT THE OVEN TO 425°F WITH THE RACK IN THE MIDDLE. PLACE THE GARLIC AND ONIONS IN A BAKING DISH, AND DRIZZLE ¼ CUP OF THE OLIVE OIL ON TOP.

2 ROAST IN THE OVEN FOR 1 HOUR OR UNTIL TENDER AND CHARRED.

3 COOL TO ROOM TEMPERATURE.

4 PEEL THE ONIONS AND GARLIC. TRIM THE ROOT ENDS OFF THE ONIONS, AND ROUGHLY CHOP 'EM INTO UNIFORM PIECES.

5 PURÉE THE ONIONS, GARLIC, LEMON JUICE, AND VINEGAR IN A BLENDER 'TIL SMOOTH.

6 WITH THE BLENDER ON, SLOWLY ADD 1 CUP OF OLIVE OIL UNTIL WELL INCORPORATED.

7 ADD THE SALT. SEASON WITH PEPPER AND MORE SALT IF NEEDED. THIS DRESSING CAN BE KEPT IN THE FRIDGE FOR UP TO 1 WEEK, OR FROZEN FOR UP TO 6 MONTHS.

PALEO MAYO

MAKES 1 CUP
⏱ **5 MINUTES**

Do it! Make your own mayonnaise!

INGREDIENTS:

1   large egg yolk

1   tablespoon fresh lemon juice

1   tablespoon water

1   teaspoon Dijon-style mustard

1   cup avocado oil or macadamia nut oil

Kosher salt

INSTRUCTIONS:

1 There are different ways to whip up your own mayo, but this immersion blender method by J. Kenji López-Alt of Serious Eats is by far my favorite.

2 Make sure your ingredients are at room temperature before you begin. Then, throw the egg yolk, lemon juice, water, and mustard into a narrow blender cup. (Beware: a too-wide blender cup won't work.) Add the oil.

3 Place the head (blade-end) of the hand blender at the very bottom of the cup, and pulse away. As the emulsion forms, carefully lift and tilt the head of the blender so that the mayonnaise blends evenly.

4 Season with salt to taste. Keep your mayo for up to 1 week in the fridge.

HOLD ON ...
WHAT'S SO GREAT ABOUT AVOCADO OIL AND MACADAMIA NUT OIL?

Both avocado oil and macadamia nut oil are healthy, antioxidant-rich fats. They're high in monounsaturated fatty acid content, and studies suggest they help reduce inflammation and improve cardiovascular function, too.

In contrast, canola and soybean oils—used in most store-bought mayonnaise—are among the worst cooking fats. As we discussed on page 34, these oils are unstable and highly prone to oxidation even at room temperature. Heat accelerates this oxidation, which prompts the formation of free radicals that attack the healthy cells in your body.

Health isn't the only reason why I prefer avocado and macadamia nut oils, though—they're also super versatile in the kitchen. Both have high smoke points (over 400°F), which means they're great for everything from stir-fries to baking. And when it comes to making mayo, these mild, buttery oils taste better than olive oil, which can sometimes impart a bitter, pungent quality to your mayonnaise.

I LOVE PALEO MAYO, BUT UNLIKE MICHELLE, I'M TOO LAZY TO MAKE MY OWN. INSTEAD, I TAKE THE EASY WAY OUT: I BUY PALEO-FRIENDLY MAYO MADE WITH GOOD OILS AND NO CHEMICAL ADDITIVES!

THE NEXT RECIPES ARE JUST A COUPLE OF EXAMPLES OF WHAT YOU CAN DO WITH PALEO MAYO!

TONNATO SAUCE

MAKES 2½ CUPS
⏱ **5 MINUTES**

INGREDIENTS:

½   cup Paleo Mayo (page 50)

7   ounces canned tuna packed in olive oil, drained

5   anchovies packed in olive oil, drained

2   tablespoons capers, drained

3   tablespoons fresh lemon juice

½   cup extra-virgin olive oil

Kosher salt

Freshly ground black pepper

INSTRUCTIONS:

① TOSS ALL THE INGREDIENTS INTO A BLENDER.

② BLEND UNTIL SMOOTH, THICK, AND CREAMY.

This classic Italian sauce is typically poured over chilled poached veal and served as a picnic dish. Sadly, I almost never have poached veal lying around the house, so after blitzing a fresh batch of Tonnato Sauce, I like to pour it on crudités, hard-boiled eggs, sliced heirloom tomatoes, poached or *sous vide* chicken, or steamed vegetables.

Or all of the above.

③ PAIR TONNATO SAUCE WITH YOUR FAVORITE PROTEINS OR VEGETABLES, OR SAVE IT FOR UP TO 4 DAYS IN THE REFRIGERATOR.

INSPIRED BY A GORGEOUS SUMMER SALAD AT AVA GENE'S IN PORTLAND, OREGON, I STARTED PAIRING FRESH GARDEN VEGETABLES WITH TONNATO SAUCE. TRY IT!

ROASTED GARLIC MAYONNAISE

MAKES 1 CUP
⏱ 50 MINUTES
(10 MINUTES HANDS-ON)

Truth: Roasted garlic mayo is life.

INGREDIENTS:

- 1   **whole garlic bulb**
- 1   **tablespoon extra-virgin olive oil**
- 1   **tablespoon fresh lemon juice**
- 1   **cup Paleo Mayo (page 50)**
-     **Kosher salt**

INSTRUCTIONS:

1   SET THE OVEN TO 400°F. PEEL OFF THE OUTER SKIN OF THE GARLIC BULB, LEAVING THE SKINS OF THE INDIVIDUAL CLOVES INTACT. CUT ½ INCH OFF THE TOP OF THE CLOVES.

2   PLACE THE GARLIC BULB IN AN OVEN-PROOF CONTAINER. DRIZZLE WITH OLIVE OIL.

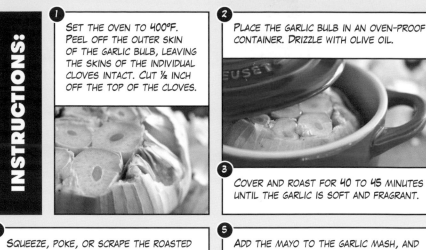

3   COVER AND ROAST FOR 40 TO 45 MINUTES UNTIL THE GARLIC IS SOFT AND FRAGRANT.

4   SQUEEZE, POKE, OR SCRAPE THE ROASTED CLOVES OUT OF THEIR SKINS AND INTO A MEDIUM BOWL. ADD THE LEMON JUICE, AND USE A FORK TO MASH INTO A PASTE.

5   ADD THE MAYO TO THE GARLIC MASH, AND MIX WELL. SEASON TO TASTE WITH SALT. ROASTED GARLIC MAYONNAISE WILL LAST FOR UP TO 1 WEEK IN THE REFRIGERATOR.

SWITCH IT UP:
GARLICKY DEVILS

LONGTIME READERS KNOW THAT I'M MUCH TOO LAZY TO MAKE TRADITIONAL DEVILED EGGS. I PREFER TO JUST TOP HARD-COOKED EGGS WITH WHATEVER I HAVE LYING AROUND. TAKE THESE GARLICKY DEVILS: I SIMPLY CUT UP SOME EGGS, SLATHER ROASTED GARLIC MAYONNAISE ON EACH HALF, AND TOP THEM WITH CHERRY TOMATOES, OLIVES, AND A SPRINKLE OF SALT AND PEPPER. DONE!

NUTTY DIJON VINAIGRETTE

MAKES 1 CUP
⏱ **20 MINUTES**

Have you looked at the ingredient labels on most store-bought salad dressings? Spoiler alert: Many of the components are *no bueno*.

I prefer to make vinaigrettes myself. Often, I just use oil, vinegar, and a bit of mustard as an emulsifier. But when I'm feeling more ambitious, I'll throw in some extra flavor and texture boosters: fragrant toasted nuts, bright green herbs, and a sweet date. The crunch of the nuts holds up best if you add them right before serving, but don't sweat it if you can't.

This dressing is as versatile as it is assertive, which means it matches up incredibly well to everything from hearty game meats to delicate fish and vegetables.

INGREDIENTS:

- ¼ **cup hazelnuts or almonds**
- ¼ **cup finely minced shallots**
- 1 **small garlic clove, minced**
- 2 **tablespoons Dijon-style mustard**
- ¼ **cup sherry vinegar**
- ½ **cup extra-virgin olive oil**
- 1 **large Medjool date, pitted and finely chopped**
- ½ **teaspoon kosher salt**
- ¼ **teaspoon freshly ground black pepper**
- ¼ **cup minced Italian parsley**
- 2 **tablespoons minced chives**

INSTRUCTIONS:

1 In a 325°F oven, toast the nuts on a baking sheet for 10 to 15 minutes or until fragrant. If you're using hazelnuts, rub them with a clean towel to remove some of the skins.

2 Cool the nuts to room temperature, and then coarsely chop them up.

3 In a pint-sized mason jar, combine the shallots, garlic, mustard, vinegar, olive oil, date, salt, and pepper.

4 Screw on the lid and shake the jar vigorously to emulsify the dressing. You can refrigerate the dressing now and finish the recipe when you're ready to eat. Otherwise, keep going!

5 Give the jar another good shake and taste it. If necessary, adjust with a bit more vinegar, oil, salt, or pepper. Stir in the chopped nuts and herbs.

6 Serve this vinaigrette immediately, or refrigerate for up to 4 days.

XO SAUCE

MAKES 2 CUPS
⏱ 8 HOURS
(45 MINUTES HANDS-ON)

Originating in the early 1980s from Hong Kong restaurant kitchens, this chunky hot sauce—deliberately named to evoke the prestige of XO-grade cognac—is a heat-seeking flavor missile. This recipe requires a bit of extra time and effort, but it's worth the wait.

Don't believe me? Add a heaping spoonful of XO Sauce to your stir-fries or toss it with some roasted vegetables, and you'll immediately understand why this umami-packed flavor booster's been hailed as the "Caviar of the East."

INGREDIENTS:

1½ ounces dried scallops

1½ ounces dried shrimp

2 ounces prosciutto, roughly chopped

1 cup avocado oil, divided

4 garlic cloves, minced

1 (4-inch) piece fresh ginger, peeled and finely grated (about ¼ cup)

2 tablespoons red pepper flakes

1 teaspoon kosher salt

1 teaspoon fish sauce

1 teaspoon coconut aminos

NOT SURE WHERE TO FIND DRIED SCALLOPS OR SHRIMP? CHECK YOUR LOCAL ASIAN MARKET OR ONLINE!

USE XO SAUCE TO MAKE THE BLISTERED GREEN BEANS ON PAGE 220!

1 RECONSTITUTE THE DRIED SCALLOPS AND SHRIMP IN A BOWL OF WATER OVERNIGHT. DRAIN AND ROUGHLY CHOP IT ALL INTO SMALL PIECES.

2 PULSE THE SCALLOP AND SHRIMP WITH THE PROSCIUTTO IN A FOOD PROCESSOR...

3 ...UNTIL FINELY SHREDDED BUT NOT PULVERIZED.

4 HEAT HALF OF THE OIL IN A MEDIUM SAUCEPAN OVER MEDIUM HEAT.

5 FRY THE GARLIC AND GINGER IN THE OIL FOR 30 SECONDS OR UNTIL AROMATIC, CRISP, AND GOLDEN. DON'T BURN IT!

6 REMOVE THE CRISPY BITS WITH A SPIDER OR SLOTTED SPOON AND SET ASIDE.

7 ADD THE RED PEPPER FLAKES TO THE HOT OIL, AND COOK FOR 30 SECONDS.

8 CRANK UP THE HEAT TO HIGH, AND ADD THE SCALLOP, SHRIMP, AND PROSCIUTTO MIXTURE TO THE BUBBLING CHILE-INFUSED OIL. GENTLY STIR IN THE SALT, FISH SAUCE, AND COCONUT AMINOS.

9 COOK FOR 1 MINUTE, STIRRING WELL.

10 ADD THE RESERVED GINGER AND GARLIC BACK IN THE PAN, AND STIR TO COMBINE.

11 POUR IN THE REMAINING ½ CUP OF OIL, AND DECREASE THE HEAT TO A SIMMER.

12 COOK, STIRRING FREQUENTLY, FOR ABOUT 30 MINUTES OR UNTIL THE OIL IS INFUSED WITH THE FLAVORS OF THE INGREDIENTS.

13 REMOVE THE SAUCE FROM THE HEAT AND LET IT COOL. THEN, TRANSFER IT TO AN AIRTIGHT CONTAINER. XO SAUCE CAN BE KEPT IN THE FRIDGE FOR UP TO A MONTH.

NOM NOM SRIRACHA

MAKES 2½ CUPS
⏱ **20 MINUTES**

INGREDIENTS:

- 1½ pounds fresh red jalapeño peppers, stemmed, seeded, and roughly chopped
- 8 medium garlic cloves, peeled and smashed
- ¼ cup apple cider vinegar
- 3 tablespoons tomato paste
- 1 large dried Medjool date, pitted
- 2 tablespoons fish sauce
- 1½ teaspoons kosher salt

INSTRUCTIONS:

1 TOSS ALL THE INGREDIENTS INTO A HIGH-SPEED BLENDER OR FOOD PROCESSOR, AND PURÉE UNTIL SMOOTH.

2 POUR THE PURÉE INTO A MEDIUM SAUCE-PAN AND BRING IT TO A BOIL OVER HIGH HEAT. ONCE IT'S BOILING, DECREASE THE HEAT TO LOW AND MAINTAIN A SIMMER FOR 5 TO 10 MINUTES. STIR OCCASIONALLY.

Here it is: my Paleo take on spicy sriracha, known to some as "Asian ketchup" or "The World's Greatest Condiment." I regularly deploy this lip-tingling (and Whole30-friendly) sauce to boost the heat and umami in my dishes. Too lazy to make your own? Go buy sriracha at the grocery store instead—but I'll be giving you major stink-eye.

I'm joking. I can't actually see you.

3 TASTE AND ADJUST FOR SEASONING IF NEEDED. ONCE COOLED, SRIRACHA CAN BE KEPT IN THE FRIDGE FOR UP TO 1 WEEK, OR IN THE FREEZER FOR UP TO 6 MONTHS.

SRIRACHA RANCH DRESSING

MAKES 1 CUP
⏱ **10 MINUTES**

The Paleo-friendly ranch dressing in my first cookbook has always been a hit with my kids, but I enjoy it even more with a punch of heat. So after I've packed lunches for the boys, I'll mix a couple of tablespoons of sriracha into the leftover ranch to serve with Ollie's Cracklin' Chicken (page 278) or Flank Steak Super Salad (page 192). Sriracha Ranch Dressing is great slathered on chicken, fish, or just about anything else.

This versatile dressing can be kept for up to 1 week in the fridge, but I bet you'll run out well before then.

INGREDIENTS:

- ½ cup Paleo Mayo (page 50)
- ¼ cup full-fat coconut milk
- 2 tablespoons Nom Nom Sriracha (page 56) or store-bought sriracha
- 1 tablespoon fresh lemon juice
- 1 tablespoon minced fresh Italian parsley
- 1 tablespoon minced fresh chives
- 1 teaspoon onion powder
- 1 teaspoon minced fresh dill or ½ teaspoon dried dill
- 1 teaspoon kosher salt

NOT A FAN OF SPICY-HOT RANCH? JUST LEAVE OUT THE SRIRACHA FROM THIS RECIPE, AND YOU'LL HAVE A DAIRY-FREE, KID-APPROVED PALEO RANCH DRESSING.

INSTRUCTIONS:

1 TOSS EVERYTHING INTO A MEDIUM BOWL.

2 STIR TOGETHER UNTIL SMOOTH.

3 IF DESIRED, REFRIGERATE FOR A FEW HOURS TO THICKEN A BIT BEFORE SERVING.

4 YOU CAN KEEP SRIRACHA RANCH DRESSING IN THE REFRIGERATOR FOR UP TO 1 WEEK.

I LOVE RAW VEGETABLES A BAZILLION TIMES MORE WHEN THEY COME WITH A SPICY AND CREAMY DIPPING SAUCE!

SPICY THAI NO-NUT SAUCE

MAKES 1 CUP
⏱ **5 MINUTES**

This recipe was inspired by a snack that Henry sometimes whips up at work. When my husband gets hungry, he raids the office pantry and makes a quick sauce of sriracha and nut butter before tossing it with pre-cooked chicken.

My version of this spicy sauce is every bit as tasty and simple, and it's nut-free to boot. And I didn't have to go to the office to make it!

INGREDIENTS:

½ cup sunflower seed butter

3 tablespoons Nom Nom Sriracha (page 56) or store-bought sriracha

   Juice from 2 limes (about ¼ cup)

2 tablespoons water, plus more if needed

1 teaspoon kosher salt

SWITCH IT UP: CHICKEN SATAY SKEWERS

MAKE CHICKEN SATAY SKEWERS WITH THIS SAUCE! WHISK TOGETHER 2 TABLESPOONS FRESH LIME JUICE, 1 TABLESPOON FISH SAUCE, ½ TABLESPOON COCONUT AMINOS, ½ TABLESPOON MINCED FRESH GINGER, ¼ TEASPOON CHILI FLAKES, AND 2 MINCED GARLIC CLOVES. THINLY SLICE 1 POUND OF SKINLESS CHICKEN THIGHS OR BREASTS CROSSWISE INTO LONG STRIPS, AND MARINATE IN THE MIXTURE FOR UP TO 2 HOURS. THEN, THREAD THE CHICKEN ON TO SKEWERS, AND GRILL OVER MEDIUM-HIGH HEAT FOR 3 TO 4 MINUTES PER SIDE UNTIL COOKED THROUGH. SERVE WITH SPICY THAI NO-NUT SAUCE AND SESAME SEEDS!

INSTRUCTIONS:

1 TOSS ALL THE INGREDIENTS INTO A BLENDER CUP.

2 USE AN IMMERSION BLENDER TO PURÉE...

3 ...UNTIL A SMOOTH, THICK SAUCE FORMS. ADD A BIT MORE WATER IF IT'S TOO THICK.

4 USE THIS FIERY SAUCE TO DRESS ZOODLES, SLATHER ONTO BURGERS, OR AS A DIP. IT KEEPS FOR UP TO 1 WEEK IN THE FRIDGE.

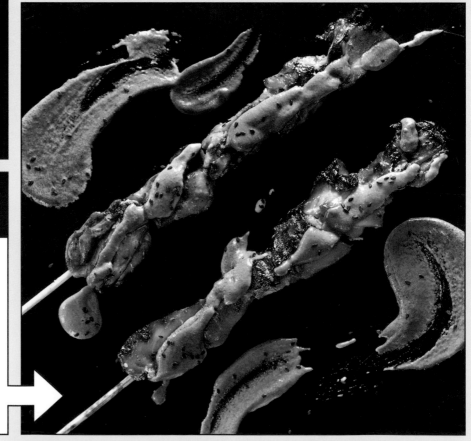

SUNBUTTER HOISIN SAUCE

MAKES ¾ CUP
⏱ **15 MINUTES**

Hoisin sauce—a centuries-old Chinese barbecue sauce—can be hard to pin down. A thick, robust sauce used as a glaze or condiment, hoisin literally means "seafood" in Cantonese, even though the sauce actually contains zero seafood, and isn't typically served with it. In the West, this tangy-sweet sauce is often misidentified as plum sauce or raisin sauce, despite containing neither plums nor raisins. To top it off, there's a dizzying number of hoisin sauce varieties out there, and each one offers a slightly different flavor profile. So which hoisin sauce should you choose?

The answer: this one. After weeks of testing, I've come up with a fantastic version of this rich sauce using Paleo-friendly ingredients. My Sunbutter Hoisin Sauce delivers all the complexity and flavor of the classic, with none of the soy, wheat, sugar, or preservatives.

INGREDIENTS:

- **4 large dried Medjool dates, pitted**
- **¼ cup sunflower butter**
- **¼ cup coconut aminos**
- **¼ cup water**
- **2 tablespoons rice vinegar**
- **1 tablespoon aged balsamic vinegar**
- **½ teaspoon Chinese five-spice powder**
- **½ teaspoon sesame oil**
- **¼ teaspoon kosher salt**

INSTRUCTIONS:

① USING A KNIFE, MINCE AND MASH UP THE DATES UNTIL THEY'RE THE CONSISTENCY OF A THICK, STICKY PASTE.

② IN A SMALL SAUCEPAN OVER MEDIUM HEAT, COMBINE ALL THE INGREDIENTS.

③ COOK, STIRRING, FOR 5 TO 7 MINUTES OR UNTIL THE SAUCE THICKENS AND DARKENS.

④ FOR A SMOOTHER SAUCE, REMOVE THE PAN FROM THE HEAT, AND USE AN IMMERSION BLENDER TO BLITZ AWAY ANY LUMPS.

⑤ COOL AND SERVE. THIS CONDIMENT CAN BE KEPT IN THE FRIDGE FOR UP TO 1 WEEK. (IF IT'S TOO FIRM, JUST STIR IN A TABLESPOON OR TWO OF WATER WHEN YOU'RE REHEATING IT.)

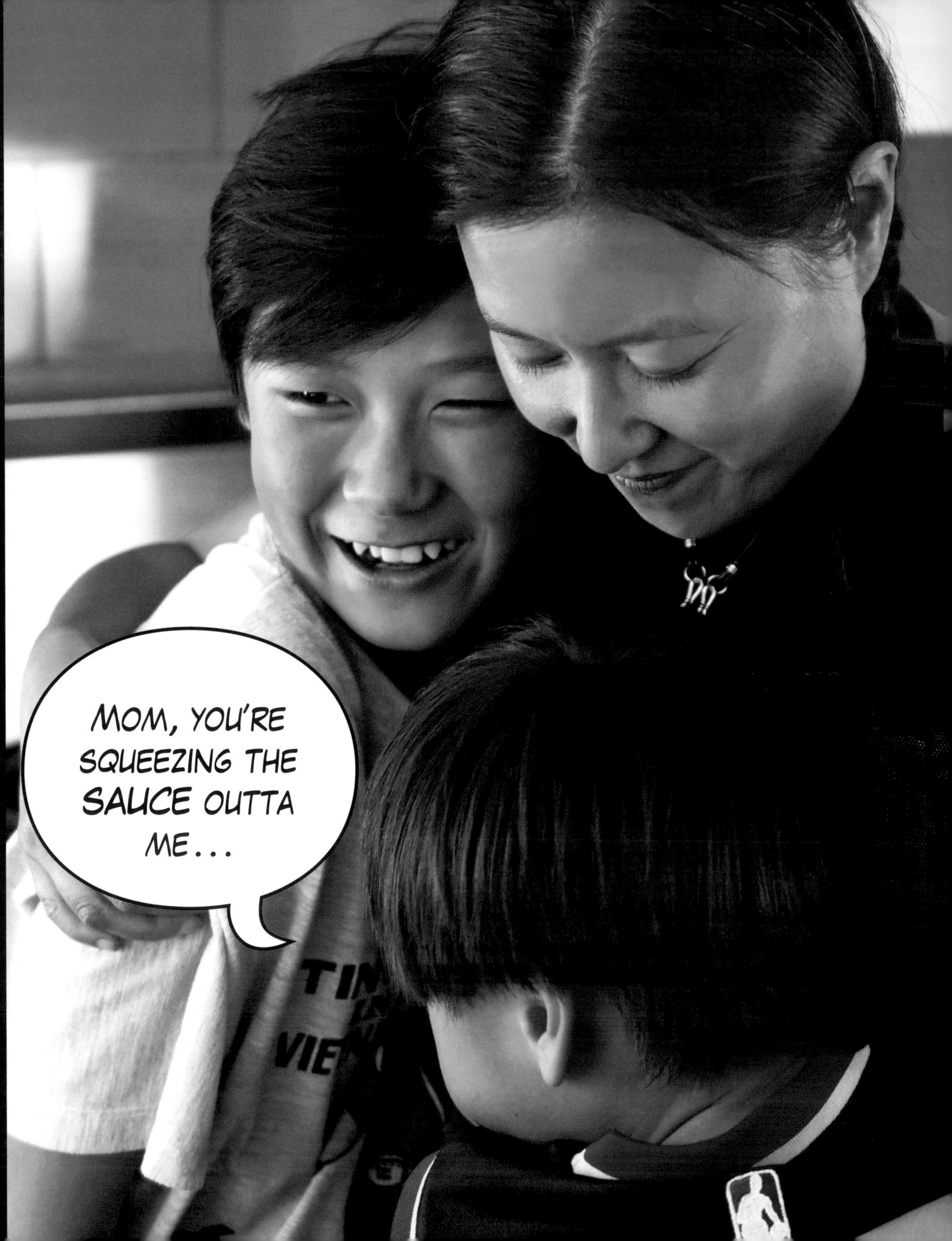
MOM, YOU'RE SQUEEZING THE SAUCE OUTTA ME...

FAUXCHUJANG

MAKES 2 CUPS
⏱ **15 MINUTES**

Gochujang is an aggressively spicy paste that's traditionally made with fermented soybeans, sticky rice, salt, and *gochugaru*—Korean red chile pepper. On your tongue, it explodes with heat, followed by a note of mild sweetness and a wave of brininess and rich umami. *Gochujang* is ubiquitous in Korean cooking; while it can be used as a plain finishing sauce like sriracha, it's more often incorporated into marinades or mixed into the flavors of the dishes themselves.

Finding tubs of *gochujang* at the local Asian market isn't hard, but finding one that uses only Paleo-friendly ingredients is impossible. That's why I've come up with this recipe: a close approximation of *gochujang* that doesn't contain gluten, soy, or refined sugar. And this recipe takes just minutes!

By the way, Fauxchujang isn't just for punching up Korean food. Mix it with some honey to create a barbecue sauce, or use it to marinate steaks before grilling. Squirt some on your tacos, and slather it on your burgers. Your spice-loving mouth will thank you for it!

INGREDIENTS:

½   cup applesauce

¼   cup gochugaru (Korean chili flakes)

2   tablespoons coconut aminos

1   tablespoon honey

2   teaspoons fish sauce

1   teaspoon kosher salt

½   teaspoon rice vinegar

INSTRUCTIONS:

1 COMBINE THE APPLESAUCE, GOCHUGARU, COCONUT AMINOS, HONEY, FISH SAUCE, AND SALT IN A SMALL SAUCEPAN.

2 COOK, STIRRING, OVER MEDIUM HEAT FOR 3 TO 4 MINUTES UNTIL HOT AND BUBBLING.

3 REMOVE THE PAN FROM THE HEAT, AND ADD THE RICE VINEGAR AND **2** TABLESPOONS WATER. STIR WELL, TASTE, AND ADJUST WITH MORE SALT IF NEEDED.

4 BLITZ WITH AN IMMERSION BLENDER FOR A SMOOTHER TEXTURE. (FEEL FREE TO ADD A BIT MORE WATER IF NEEDED.)

5 COOL COMPLETELY.

6 FAUXCHUJANG CAN BE REFRIGERATED FOR UP TO **2** WEEKS, OR FROZEN FOR UP TO **6** MONTHS!

SPICY KIMCHI

&

WIMPCHI

MAKES 1½ QUARTS
⏱ **3 DAYS**
(20 MINUTES HANDS-ON)

I'm obsessed with traditional Korean kimchi, and I try to eat this fermented goodness with anything and everything. For those of you who just can't stand the heat, I've included instructions for making non-spicy white kimchi, too. My buddy Emma dubbed it Wimpchi, 'cause it's kimchi for wimps!

INGREDIENTS:

1   **(2½-pound) Napa cabbage, cut into 2 by 1-inch pieces**

    Kosher salt

6   **scallions, trimmed and cut into 2-inch pieces, greens and whites separated**

1   **(2-inch) piece fresh ginger, peeled and thinly sliced**

1   **medium Asian pear or apple, peeled, cored, and roughly chopped**

2   **teaspoons fish sauce**

2   **tablespoons gochugaru (Korean chili flakes) if making Spicy Kimchi**

1   **large carrot, cut into thin ¼-inch coins**

1   **small red bell pepper, cut into matchsticks**

3   **garlic cloves, peeled and thinly sliced**

2   **teaspoons black sesame seeds (optional)**

FUN FACT: THE AVERAGE SOUTH KOREAN EATS MORE THAN 40 POUNDS OF KIMCHI EACH YEAR!

INSTRUCTIONS:

1 In a large bowl, use your hands to toss the cabbage with **2** tablespoons salt.

2 Set aside to brine for **1** hour.

3 Transfer the cabbage to a colander, and rinse with cool water. Leave the cabbage in the colander to fully drain, or dry it in a salad spinner.

4 Put the scallion whites, ginger, Asian pear, fish sauce, and **2** teaspoons of salt in a blender or food processor.

5 Blitz until smooth.

6 Making Spicy Kimchi? Transfer the paste to a bowl, and stir in the Korean chili flakes. (If Wimpchi is more your style, omit the flakes!)

7 In a large bowl, combine the drained cabbage with the scallion greens, carrot, red bell pepper, and garlic.

8 Pour in the paste, and mix well with your hands. A word to the wise: if you're making Spicy Kimchi, use gloves!

9 Pack the kimchi tightly into two **1**-quart containers, leaving **1** inch of space at the top.

10 Cover the containers tightly...

11 ...and leave them on a rimmed baking sheet at room temperature in a shady spot for **3** to **7** days, depending on how tangy you like your kimchi. (Taste it to see!) Afterwards, keep it in the refrigerator for up to **3** months.

12 If desired, toss on a sprinkle of sesame seeds before eating.

KIMCHI APPLESAUCE

MAKES 2 CUPS
⏱ **5 MINUTES**

Why blend kimchi and applesauce together? 'Cause it's easy to make and tastes amazing. *That's* why.

INGREDIENTS:

- 1½ cups Spicy Kimchi (page 62) or store-bought kimchi
- 1 large Fuji apple, peeled, cored, and diced
- ¼ teaspoon kosher salt

INSTRUCTIONS:

1 MAKE OR BUY SOME KIMCHI. (IF BUYING KIMCHI, LOOK FOR REAL-FOOD INGREDIENTS AND TRY TO AVOID CHEMICAL PRESERVATIVES IF YOU CAN.)

2 THROW EVERYTHING INTO A BLENDER.

3 PURÉE UNTIL SMOOTH.

4 YOU CAN REFRIGERATE YOUR KIMCHI APPLESAUCE IN A BOTTLE FOR UP TO 1 WEEK.

ROMESCO SAUCE

MAKES 1½ CUPS
⏱ 5 MINUTES

INGREDIENTS:

1	small garlic clove
½	cup toasted slivered almonds
1	(12-ounce) jar roasted red peppers, drained
2	tablespoons fresh lemon juice
¼	cup extra-virgin olive oil
1	tablespoon tomato paste
1	teaspoon kosher salt
	Freshly ground black pepper

INSTRUCTIONS:

1 TO TAKE THE BITE OUT OF THE GARLIC, BLANCH IT IN A SMALL SAUCEPAN OF BOILING WATER FOR 30 SECONDS. THEN, SCOOP IT OUT.

2 BLITZ ALL THE INGREDIENTS TOGETHER IN A BLENDER UNTIL SMOOTH.

With roots in the Catalonia region of Spain, Romesco is an almond and red pepper–based sauce that fishermen in northeastern Spain enjoy with seafood. But don't let that stop you from serving my bread-free version of this rich, garlicky sauce on everything from roast chicken to grilled lamb. It makes a fantastic dipping sauce for roasted vegetables, too.

3 IN A SEALED JAR, THIS SAUCE CAN KEEP IN THE REFRIGERATOR FOR UP TO 1 WEEK, AND IN THE FREEZER FOR UP TO 6 MONTHS!

THIS SAUCE IS WHAT MAKES ROASTED CATALAN SHRIMP (PAGE 196) SO GOOD!

GINGER SESAME SAUCE

MAKES 1¼ CUPS
⏱ 15 MINUTES

INGREDIENTS:

- 1   tablespoon sesame seeds or tahini
- ½   cup extra-virgin olive oil
- ¼   cup rice vinegar
- ¼   cup fresh orange juice
- 2   tablespoons coconut aminos
- 2   garlic cloves, minced
- 2   tablespoons peeled and minced ginger
- 1   teaspoon sesame oil
-      Kosher salt

INSTRUCTIONS:

1 TOAST THE SESAME SEEDS FOR 8 TO 10 MINUTES IN A 300°F OVEN, CHECKING FREQUENTLY TO AVOID BURNING. OR JUST USE TAHINI INSTEAD!

2 COMBINE ALL THE INGREDIENTS IN A HIGH-SPEED BLENDER OR FOOD PROCESSOR, AND PURÉE UNTIL SMOOTH.

This creamy dressing was inspired by the stuff that's drizzled on the little chilled plates of vegetables served at my favorite sushi joints—but this sauce doesn't just pair with greens. You can certainly dress up a quick salad with this sauce, but it's equally fantastic when warmed and spooned over roasted meats, poultry, or fish. Don't forget to try it with roasted carrots (page 180)!

3 SEASON TO TASTE WITH SALT. USE IT RIGHT AWAY, OR KEEP IT IN A SEALED JAR IN THE REFRIGERATOR FOR UP TO 1 WEEK.

SWITCH IT UP:
ROASTED GINGER SESAME BROCCOLI

USE GINGER SESAME SAUCE ON BROCCOLI! ON A RIMMED BAKING SHEET, DRIZZLE OLIVE OIL (OR YOUR FAVORITE MELTED FAT) AND SPRINKLE SALT ON SOME BROCCOLI FLORETS. ROAST 'EM IN AN OVEN PREHEATED TO 400°F ON CONVECTION MODE OR 425°F ON REGULAR MODE FOR 20 TO 25 MINUTES OR UNTIL THE FLORETS START TO BROWN. SERVE WITH GINGER SESAME SAUCE AND TOASTED SESAME SEEDS.

POP QUIZ, HOT SHOT: WHAT DO ALL OF THESE QUICK AND EASY STIR-FRIES HAVE IN COMMON?

WHAT?!? NO ONE TOLD ME THERE'D BE A QUIZ!

THE ANSWER:

ALL-PURPOSE STIR-FRY SAUCE

MAKES 2 CUPS
⏱ 10 MINUTES

INGREDIENTS:

½	cup fresh orange juice
1	cup coconut aminos
2	tablespoons rice vinegar
¼	cup fish sauce
2	teaspoons garlic powder
2	teaspoons ginger powder
1	teaspoon sesame oil (optional)

INSTRUCTIONS:

1 COMBINE ALL OF THE INGREDIENTS IN A SMALL JAR.

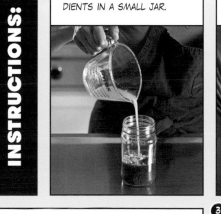

2 COVER IT TIGHTLY WITH A LID, AND SHAKE WELL TO INCORPORATE BEFORE USING.

Having grown up in my mom's kitchen, I'm well aware that Asian stir-fries are among the fastest and easiest meals one can prepare in a pinch. But while my mom can sense by sight and feel how to season her stir-fries, I'm not my mother. As a mere mortal, I prefer to rely on a pre-mixed stir-fry sauce to make spur-of-the-moment cooking as easy as possible.

3 THIS SAUCE KEEPS IN THE REFRIGERATOR FOR UP TO **2** WEEKS. DON'T FORGET TO SHAKE WELL AGAIN BEFORE USING IT!

CRAN-CHERRY SAUCE

MAKES 2 CUPS
⏱ **30 MINUTES
(15 MINUTES HANDS-ON)**

It shouldn't surprise my longtime readers that sweet-and-tart is one of my favorite flavor combinations. After all, it perfectly describes my personality: sweet, but with a side of sour. So even though I'd never before tasted cranberry sauce until I began attending the annual Thanksgiving feast at my in-laws' house, I fell hard for it right away.

Sadly, once I started eating Paleo, I knew I had to skip the cranberry sauce altogether. After all, I knew that most recipes are sweetened with tons and tons of refined sugar.

Needless to say, I was determined to come up with a Paleo-friendly version of cranberry sauce—one inspired by the juice blends from my childhood. By themselves, cranberries can be unpalatably bitter and sour, but by pairing them with cherries and simmering the fruit in apple juice, I was able to counter the mouth-puckering tartness of the cranberries with some natural sweetness. Prefer an even sweeter sauce? Just a touch of honey will do the trick.

INGREDIENTS:

6   ounces frozen cranberries

6   ounces frozen sweet cherries

¾   cup apple juice

½   teaspoon minced ginger

     Kosher salt

2   tablespoons honey (optional)

INSTRUCTIONS:

1. TOSS THE CRANBERRIES AND CHERRIES INTO A SMALL SAUCEPAN.

2. ADD THE APPLE JUICE, GINGER, AND A PINCH OF SALT.

3. BRING THE CONTENTS TO A BOIL OVER HIGH HEAT. THEN, LOWER THE HEAT TO MAINTAIN A SIMMER.

4. COOK FOR 8 TO 10 MINUTES OR UNTIL THE SAUCE THICKENS AND THE FRUIT BREAKS DOWN.

5. REMOVE THE SAUCEPAN FROM THE HEAT. IF YOU PREFER A SMOOTHER TEXTURE, USE AN IMMERSION BLENDER TO PURÉE THE SAUCE TO THE CONSISTENCY YOU WANT.

6. TASTE FOR SWEETNESS AND ADD HONEY IF NEEDED OR DESIRED.

7. COOL TO ROOM TEMPERATURE, AND SERVE WITH ROAST-AHEAD CHICKEN BREASTS (PAGE 84), THANKSGIVING TURKEY BITES (PAGE 206), OR JUST ABOUT ANYTHING ELSE. THIS SAUCE KEEPS FOR UP TO 1 WEEK IN THE FRIDGE OR 6 MONTHS IN THE FREEZER.

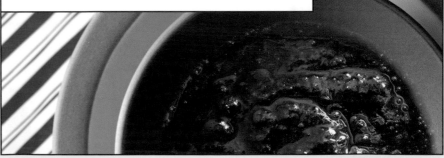

UMAMI GRAVY

MAKES 3 CUPS
⏱ **1½ HOURS**
(30 MINUTES HANDS-ON)

This stuff is pure, unadulterated umami. I recommend freezing some in an ice cube tray so you'll always have individual servings of gravy at the ready. And really: Who doesn't need gravy at all times?

INGREDIENTS:

½ ounce dried porcini mushrooms

2 tablespoons ghee

2 medium yellow onions, diced

1 teaspoon tomato paste

½ teaspoon fish sauce

½ pound cremini mushrooms, sliced

3 garlic cloves, minced

4 cups Bone Broth (page 76) or chicken stock

3 fresh thyme sprigs

Kosher salt

Freshly ground black pepper

INSTRUCTIONS:

1 IN A SMALL BOWL, SOAK THE DRIED MUSHROOMS IN WATER FOR 30 MINUTES OR UNTIL SOFT. TAKE THEM OUT OF THE WATER, ROUGHLY CHOP THEM UP, AND SET ASIDE.

2 IN A MEDIUM SAUCEPAN, MELT THE GHEE OVER MEDIUM HEAT. ADD THE ONIONS AND SAUTÉ FOR 10 TO 15 MINUTES UNTIL SOFT. ADD THE TOMATO PASTE AND FISH SAUCE.

3 STIR TO EVENLY DISTRIBUTE.

4 TOSS IN THE SLICED MUSHROOMS, AND SAUTÉ FOR 8 TO 10 MINUTES OR UNTIL THE MUSHROOM JUICES HAVE RELEASED AND COOKED OFF. ADD THE GARLIC, AND STIR FOR 30 SECONDS UNTIL FRAGRANT.

5 ADD THE RECONSTITUTED MUSHROOMS AND THE BROTH OR CHICKEN STOCK.

6 DROP IN THE THYME SPRIGS. CRANK THE HEAT UP TO HIGH, AND BRING THE GRAVY TO A BOIL.

7 DECREASE THE HEAT TO MEDIUM-LOW TO MAINTAIN A STRONG SIMMER. COOK FOR 30 MINUTES, OR UNTIL THE GRAVY HAS REDUCED BY ABOUT HALF.

8 REMOVE THE SAUCEPAN FROM THE HEAT. DISCARD THE THYME, AND SEASON TO TASTE WITH SALT AND PEPPER. USING A HAND BLENDER OR A REGULAR BLENDER, PURÉE THE GRAVY UNTIL SMOOTH.

9 SERVE OR STORE. THIS GRAVY CAN BE KEPT IN THE FRIDGE FOR UP TO 4 DAYS, OR IN THE FREEZER FOR UP TO 6 MONTHS.

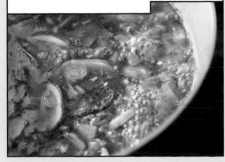

FRUIT + AVOCADO SALSA

MAKES 3 CUPS
⏱ **10 MINUTES**

Admit it: Fruit salad is boring. It's a staple of every office picnic and birthday party—but only because it's cheap and easy. If you ever find yourself picking up a mealy fruit salad tray on the way to a potluck, you know that no one's going to thank you for exerting the absolute minimum amount of effort.

So save yourself the disgrace, and take just 10 minutes out of your day to make a bright, flavorful fruit salsa that'll be the talk of the party. Pick out some sweet, in-season fruit, mix it up with diced avocado, herbs, and seasonings, and watch as the famished hordes descend upon your homemade salsa.

The lesson? Don't be a fruit salad zero. Instead, be a fruit salsa hero.

INGREDIENTS:

- **2** cups diced ripe nectarine, peach, mango, pineapple, or watermelon
- **1** medium Hass avocado, diced
- **½** cup finely diced red onion
- **¼** cup minced fresh cilantro
- **2** tablespoons extra-virgin olive oil
- **Kosher salt**
- **Freshly ground black pepper**
- **¼** teaspoon red pepper flakes
- **Juice from 1 lime**

INSTRUCTIONS:

1. CUT THE FRUIT AND TOSS IT IN A LARGE BOWL. (I USED NECTARINES HERE, BUT FEEL FREE TO MIX IT UP WITH YOUR FAVORITES.)

2. ADD THE AVOCADO, ONION, CILANTRO, AND OLIVE OIL.

3. SEASON WITH A BIG PINCH OF SALT, PEPPER, AND RED PEPPER FLAKES.

4. SQUEEZE IN THE LIME JUICE.

5. STIR TO COMBINE. TASTE AND ADJUST THE SEASONING AS NEEDED.

SWITCH IT UP:
**FRIED GREEN PLANTAINS
WITH NECTARINE SALSA**

THIS ONE'S A NO-BRAINER. MAKE A BATCH OF FRIED GREEN PLANTAINS (PAGE 98) AND SERVE 'EM WITH A BIG BOWL OF NECTARINE SALSA. IT'S A MILLION TIMES BETTER THAN STORE-BOUGHT SALSA AND CHIPS, AND A MILLION TIMES BETTER FOR YOUR HEALTH, TOO.

SALSA AHUMADA

MAKES 1½ CUPS
⏱ **20 MINUTES**

This smoky tomato salsa kicks butt. A dash of this stuff instantly transforms a boring plate of eggs into a spicy scramble, or leftover ground meat into fiery taco filling. Best of all, a single batch of this salsa can be refrigerated for up to 1 week, or frozen in covered ice cube trays for up to 6 months.

INGREDIENTS:

- **2** tablespoons avocado oil or ghee
- **3** medium garlic cloves, peeled
- **1** small yellow onion, roughly chopped
- **6** chiles de arbol, stemmed (pour out the seeds if you prefer a milder salsa)
- **2** tablespoons apple cider vinegar
- **1** (14.5-ounce) can fire-roasted diced tomatoes
- **½** teaspoon kosher salt

INSTRUCTIONS:

1 HEAT THE OIL IN A LARGE SKILLET OVER MEDIUM HEAT. ONCE IT'S SIZZLING HOT, ADD THE GARLIC AND ONIONS.

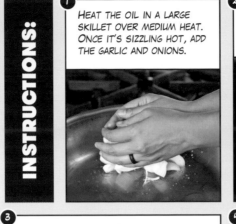

2 COOK THE GARLIC AND ONIONS FOR ABOUT 3 TO 5 MINUTES, STIRRING FREQUENTLY, UNTIL BROWNED IN PARTS AND AROMATIC.

3 TOSS IN THE CHILES. COOK, STIRRING, FOR 1 TO 2 MINUTES. (YOU CAN USE FEWER CHILES IF YOU'RE AFRAID OF THE HEAT.)

4 ADD THE VINEGAR AND DICED TOMATOES WITH THEIR JUICES, AND BRING THE CONTENTS TO A BOIL.

5 LOWER THE HEAT TO MEDIUM-LOW, AND SIMMER UNTIL THE TOMATOES BEGIN TO BREAK DOWN (ABOUT 8 TO 10 MINUTES).

6 TURN OFF THE STOVE, AND TRANSFER THE CONTENTS OF THE SKILLET TO A BLENDER.

7 ADD THE SALT TO THE STUFF IN THE BLENDER.

8 PURÉE EVERYTHING UNTIL SMOOTH. PAUSE TO SCRAPE DOWN THE SIDES OF THE BLENDER IF NECESSARY. TASTE THE SALSA, AND ADJUST WITH MORE SALT IF NEEDED.

9 SERVE THIS SALSA WITH ANYTHING THAT NEEDS AN EXTRA KICK IN THE PANTS.

PESTO POMODORI SECCHI (SUN-DRIED TOMATO PESTO)

MAKES ¾ CUP
⏱ 30 MINUTES
(10 MINUTES HANDS-ON)

Classic green pesto is fantastic, but red's my favorite color. Besides, sun-dried tomatoes are incredibly rich in umami, giving this southern Italian no-cook sauce even more depth. Spoon this goodness onto roasted meats, poultry, or veggies, and you'll see why crimson is my favorite shade of pesto.

INGREDIENTS:

- ½ cup (40 grams) sun-dried tomatoes (not oil-packed)
- ¼ cup toasted pine nuts
- 1 teaspoon dried oregano or marjoram
- 1 tablespoon drained capers
- 1 large garlic clove, peeled
- ¼ teaspoon red pepper flakes
- ½ teaspoon kosher salt
- ½ cup extra-virgin olive oil

> EVEN I LIKE RED PESTO, AND I HATE EVERYTHING!

INSTRUCTIONS:

1 IN A MEDIUM BOWL, SOAK THE SUN-DRIED TOMATOES IN HOT WATER FOR 20 MINUTES OR UNTIL SOFTENED.

2 REMOVE THE TOMATOES FROM THE BOWL, AND SQUEEZE OUT ANY EXCESS WATER.

3 PUT THE REHYDRATED TOMATOES, TOASTED PINE NUTS, OREGANO, CAPERS, GARLIC, RED PEPPER FLAKES, SALT, AND OLIVE OIL IN A BLENDER OR FOOD PROCESSOR.

4 PURÉE THE INGREDIENTS INTO PESTO.

5 THIS PESTO CAN BE REFRIGERATED FOR UP TO 1 WEEK, OR FROZEN FOR UP TO 6 MONTHS.

FRIDGE-PICKLED CUCUMBERS

MAKES 1 CUP
⏱ **35 MINUTES**
(5 MINUTES HANDS-ON)

Spicy pickled cucumber slices are one of my go-to nibbles. This refreshingly tangy and crunchy snack is a total breeze to make, too, so if you have extra vegetables languishing in your crisper, go cut them up and brine 'em already. In a half-hour, you'll have an amazing flavor booster ready for munching.

INGREDIENTS:

- ½   **large English or 1 Persian cucumber, thinly sliced**
- ½   **cup apple juice**
- ½   **cup rice vinegar**
- ½   **teaspoon fish sauce**
- ½   **teaspoon kosher salt**
- ½   **teaspoon red pepper flakes (optional)**

INSTRUCTIONS:

1 PUT THE CUCUMBER SLICES IN A PINT-SIZE JAR.

2 IN A CUP, COMBINE THE APPLE JUICE, RICE VINEGAR, FISH SAUCE, SALT, AND PEPPER FLAKES (IF YOU LIKE YOUR PICKLES SPICY). GIVE IT A GOOD STIR TO MAKE SURE THE SALT COMPLETELY DISSOLVES.

3 POUR THE BRINE INTO THE JAR, MAKING SURE TO SUBMERGE THE PICKLES.

4 COVER AND REFRIGERATE FOR AT LEAST 30 MINUTES AND UP TO **3** WEEKS.

DON'T STOP AT FRIDGE-PICKLED CUCUMBERS. YOU CAN QUICK-PICKLE ALL SORTS OF VEGETABLES, LIKE CARROT AND DAIKON STICKS, WATERMELON RADISH SLICES, AND RED ONIONS!

AREN'T "PICKLED CUCUMBERS" JUST CALLED PICKLES?

5 THESE PICKLES CAN MAKE ANY DISH POP, AND THEY'RE EVEN BETTER THE NEXT DAY.

DUXELLES

MAKES 3 CUPS
⏱ **30 MINUTES**

Did you know that this umami-rich mixture of mushrooms and herbs was named by a 17th-century chef after his employer, the Marquis d'Uxelles? That's right: This flavorful filling for everything from poultry to meatballs was invented as an act of sucking up to the boss.

INGREDIENTS:

2   pounds cremini mushrooms, stemmed, cleaned, and quartered

2   tablespoons ghee or extra-virgin olive oil

½   cup minced shallots

3   medium garlic cloves, minced

1   teaspoon kosher salt

    Freshly ground black pepper

3   fresh thyme sprigs (or 1 teaspoon dried thyme)

2   tablespoons sherry vinegar

¼   cup minced fresh chives or parsley (optional)

THIS MAY LOOK LIKE BROWN MUSH, BUT IT'S AWESOME IN BREAKFAST OMELETS!

INSTRUCTIONS:

1 TOSS HALF OF THE MUSHROOMS INTO A FOOD PROCESSOR.

2 PRESS THE PULSE BUTTON 10 TO 15 TIMES UNTIL THE MUSHROOMS ARE MINCED. TRANSFER TO A BOWL AND REPEAT WITH THE REMAINING MUSHROOMS.

3 MELT THE GHEE IN A LARGE SAUCEPAN OVER MEDIUM HEAT. ADD THE SHALLOTS AND SAUTÉ UNTIL TRANSLUCENT. ADD THE GARLIC AND STIR FOR 30 SECONDS.

4 ADD THE MUSHROOMS, SALT, PEPPER, AND THYME SPRIGS TO THE SKILLET.

5 COOK FOR 15 TO 20 MINUTES, STIRRING FREQUENTLY, UNTIL THE LIQUID'S COOKED OFF.

6 FISH OUT THE THYME. ADD THE VINEGAR AND FRESH HERBS, AND SEASON TO TASTE WITH SALT AND PEPPER. DUXELLES CAN BE STORED IN A SEALED CONTAINER IN THE REFRIGERATOR FOR UP TO 1 WEEK, OR IN THE FREEZER FOR UP TO 6 MONTHS.

BONE BROTH

MAKES 8 CUPS
⏱ 1-24 HOURS
(15 MINUTES HANDS-ON)

Broth, stock, soup, miracle elixir—frankly, I couldn't care less what you want to call it. Just be sure to make some, and keep plenty on hand for sipping or cooking.

Your mom was right: Soup is good for the soul, and this heavenly broth is good for your body, too. Whenever my boys feel down in the dumps, I make some broth for them, and they perk right up. Is it a placebo effect? Perhaps. But as long as it works, who cares?

I add Bone Broth to many of my recipes, but in a pinch, you can use store-bought broth or stock. As always, select those that are made with real, whole food ingredients and without chemical additives and other weirdness. Yes, high-quality broth will cost you more, but that'll just be an added incentive to bookmark this page and make your own Bone Broth. Homemade is always best!

INGREDIENTS:

- **3** pounds assorted beef, chicken, and/or pork bones
- **1** small yellow onion, peeled and halved
- **1** carrot, peeled and halved
- **3** dried shiitake mushrooms, rinsed (optional)
- **1** (1-inch) piece fresh ginger, peeled and cut into thick coins (optional)
- **3** garlic cloves, peeled and smashed (optional)
- **1** tablespoon fish sauce
- Kosher salt

INSTRUCTIONS:

1 GRAB SOME BONES. FOR BEST RESULTS, USE A COMBINATION OF MEATY BONES AND JOINTS. REMEMBER: ALWAYS KEEP EXTRA BONES IN THE FREEZER SO YOU CAN MAKE BONE BROTH AT A MOMENT'S NOTICE.

2 TOSS THE BONES AND VEGETABLES IN A LARGE (AT LEAST 6-QUART) STOCKPOT, SLOW COOKER, OR PRESSURE COOKER.

3 ADD 8 TO 10 CUPS OF WATER TO THE POT, MAKING SURE THE BONES AND VEGETABLES ARE FULLY SUBMERGED. IF YOU'RE USING A PRESSURE COOKER, DON'T FILL IT ABOVE THE MAXIMUM CAPACITY LINE.

4 POUR IN THE FISH SAUCE, AND THEN COOK USING ONE OF THE FOLLOWING METHODS.

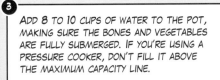

USE A STOCKPOT!

COVER AND BRING TO A BOIL OVER HIGH HEAT. SKIM OFF THE SCUM, AND TURN DOWN THE HEAT TO MAINTAIN A LOW SIMMER. COOK, COVERED, FOR 12 TO 24 HOURS, OR UNTIL THE BONES ARE SOFT. YOU'LL NEED TO MONITOR YOUR BROTH WHILE IT COOKS.

USE A SLOW COOKER!

COVER AND SET TO COOK ON LOW FOR 8 TO 24 HOURS. USING A SLOW COOKER MEANS THAT YOU CAN MAKE BROTH WITHOUT HAVING TO BABYSIT IT, BUT THE DOWNSIDE IS THAT YOU'LL STILL NEED TO BE PATIENT AND WAIT FOR THE BROTH TO COOK.

USE A STOVETOP PRESSURE COOKER!

COOK OVER HIGH HEAT UNTIL HIGH PRESSURE IS REACHED. THEN, IMMEDIATELY TURN THE BURNER DOWN TO THE LOWEST POSSIBLE SETTING THAT WILL STILL MAINTAIN HIGH PRESSURE. COOK THE BROTH FOR AT LEAST 45 MINUTES. THEN, TURN OFF THE BURNER AND REMOVE THE POT FROM THE HEAT. RELEASE THE PRESSURE.

USE AN ELECTRIC PRESSURE COOKER!

COOK UNDER HIGH PRESSURE FOR AT LEAST 45 MINUTES. THE MACHINE'LL TAKE CARE OF THE REST. WHEN THE BROTH IS DONE COOKING, RELEASE THE PRESSURE MANUALLY OR LET IT DROP NATURALLY, DEPENDING ON HOW SOON YOU NEED THE BROTH.

6 STRAIN THE BROTH THROUGH A FINE-MESH SIEVE OR A CHEESECLOTH-LINED COLANDER TO FILTER OUT THE SOLIDS. IF YOU'RE DRINKING THE BROTH STRAIGHT (RATHER THAN COOKING WITH IT), SEASON TO TASTE WITH SALT AND/OR FISH SAUCE.

7 ONCE THE BROTH COOLS, YOU CAN REFRIGERATE IT FOR UP TO 4 DAYS. BETTER YET, FREEZE IT IN CONVENIENT PORTION SIZES. I LIKE TO FREEZE MY BROTH IN SILICONE ICE CUBE TRAYS. FROZEN BROTH CUBES KEEP FOR UP TO 6 MONTHS, AND THEY CAN BE USED AT A MOMENT'S NOTICE.

8 A TIP I LEARNED FROM AMERICA'S TEST KITCHEN: USE FROZEN BROTH CUBES TO COOL OFF SUBSEQUENT POTS OF FRESHLY MADE BROTH. THAT WAY, YOU WON'T HAVE TO WAIT HOURS FOR IT TO COOL BEFORE DOING YOUR POUR 'N' FREEZE THING.

GRAIN-FREE TORTILLAS

MAKES 12 TORTILLAS
⏱ 20 MINUTES

Miss munching on tortillas? Dry those tears, because with cassava flour and arrowroot powder, you can make these versatile wraps at home without flour or corn. That's right, party people: Taco Tuesdays are back on the schedule!

INGREDIENTS:

- **2** cups (270 grams) cassava flour
- **¾** cup (96 grams) arrowroot powder
- **1** teaspoon kosher salt
- **¼** cup ghee, lard, or olive oil
- **1¼** cups hot water

TIP:

Don't confuse cassava flour with tapioca flour. Both come from the cassava root, but cassava flour is made by peeling, drying, and grinding the whole root, while tapioca flour (a.k.a. tapioca starch) is made by drying the starchy liquid extracted from wet cassava root pulp. Tapioca flour is great, but you'll find that it won't work well with this recipe—unless you happen to be a weirdo who loves super-gummy tortillas.

INSTRUCTIONS:

1 IN A LARGE BOWL, COMBINE THE CASSAVA FLOUR, ARROWROOT POWDER, AND SALT. WORK IN THE FAT WITH YOUR FINGERS UNTIL FULLY INCORPORATED. ADD WATER AND KNEAD UNTIL A BALL OF DOUGH IS FORMED.

2 DIVIDE THE DOUGH EQUALLY INTO A DOZEN PIECES. ROLL EACH INTO A BALL, AND COVER THE BOWL SO YOUR BALLS DON'T DRY OUT. KEEP YOUR BALLS MOIST, PEOPLE!

3 ONE BY ONE, FLATTEN EACH BALL BETWEEN PARCHMENT PAPER OR PLASTIC WRAP USING A ROLLING PIN, A TORTILLA PRESS, OR A COUPLE OF HEAVY BOOKS.

4 HEAT A DRY SKILLET OR GRIDDLE OVER MEDIUM-HIGH HEAT. TRANSFER A FLATTENED TORTILLA TO THE HOT SKILLET...

5 ...AND COOK FOR 1 MINUTE OR UNTIL AIR BUBBLES FORM ON THE SURFACE. FLIP THE TORTILLA, AND COOK FOR 1 MINUTE MORE, OR UNTIL EACH SIDE IS LIGHTLY BROWNED.

6 TRANSFER EACH TORTILLA TO A PLATE AS IT FINISHES COOKING, AND COVER WITH A CLEAN TOWEL UNTIL YOU'RE READY TO EAT.

7 FEED YOUR FACE.

8 YOU CAN FREEZE THE TORTILLAS BETWEEN PARCHMENT SHEETS FOR UP TO 6 MONTHS.

NATURE'S TORTILLAS

MAKES 4 SERVINGS
⏱ 1 MINUTE

I'll admit it: This isn't really a recipe. It's my way of reminding you that even though Paleo-friendly tortillas are a fun treat, nothing beats the ease of washing a head of lettuce and using its leaves to wrap up your favorite fillings. Like I always say: K.I.S.S.—keep it simple, silly. Bonus: there's no cooking required, and no dishes to wash.

For sheer wrappability, butter and romaine lettuce work best, but feel free to experiment. For a change of pace, stuff your leftovers inside cabbage leaves, endive spears, cored bell peppers, or even thin slices of roast beef.

INGREDIENTS:

1   head butter lettuce, green leaf lettuce, or romaine lettuce

INSTRUCTIONS:

1 IF YOU'RE USING LETTUCE, SEPARATE THE HEAD INTO LEAVES, AND WASH 'EM. SPIN OR PAT THE LEAVES DRY.

2 WRAP STUFF IN THE LEAVES AND EAT. HERE, I USED SALT + PEPPER FRIED PORK CHOPS (PAGE 124) AS MY FILLING.

3 NATURE'S TORTILLAS CAN TAKE OTHER FORMS. FOR EXAMPLE, I MADE TACOS WITH PRESSURE COOKER SALSA CHICKEN (PAGE 290) STUFFED IN BELL PEPPERS.

OWEN! I HAVE A JOKE FOR YOU: WHAT DID THE DEPRESSED TORTILLA SAY TO HIS THERAPIST?

I HOPE THIS ISN'T AS PAINFULLY BAD AS ALL YOUR OTHER DAD JOKES.

HE SAID: "I REALLY DON'T WANNA TACO 'BOUT IT!"

IS THIS SOME KIND OF PUNISHMENT?

CAULI RICE

MAKES 6 SERVINGS
⏱ 15 MINUTES

Yeah, I'm aware that every other Paleo cookbook out there already contains a cauliflower rice recipe (including my own first book)…so why break with tradition?

Besides, this simple and tasty side dish pairs fantastically with virtually any savory recipe in this book, and it freezes and reheats like a charm.

INGREDIENTS:

1   medium cauliflower head, cut into uniform pieces

2   tablespoons ghee

     Kosher salt

INSTRUCTIONS:

1 PULSE THE CAULIFLOWER IN A FOOD PROCESSOR UNTIL THE SIZE OF RICE GRAINS.

2 IN A LARGE SKILLET, MELT THE GHEE OVER MEDIUM HEAT. ADD THE CAULIFLOWER.

3 COOK, STIRRING, FOR 5 TO 10 MINUTES OR UNTIL SOFT. SEASON WITH SALT TO TASTE.

4 EAT NOW, OR PACK THE "RICE" AWAY FOR LATER. IT CAN BE REFRIGERATED FOR UP TO 4 DAYS, OR FROZEN FOR UP TO 2 MONTHS.

CAULI RICE IS A GREAT ALTERNATIVE TO WHITE RICE, WHICH IS EXCLUDED FROM EARLIER DEFINITIONS OF "PALEO."

BUT THESE DAYS, WHITE RICE AND OTHER "SAFE STARCHES" ARE INCREASINGLY ACCEPTED AS PART OF THE PALEO TEMPLATE.

PERSONALLY, I DO BETTER WITH SOME STARCH IN MY DIET, SO I EAT SOME RICE EVERY NOW AND THEN. HENRY, ON THE OTHER HAND, DOES BETTER ON A LOWER-CARB DIET.

SO IF WHITE RICE DOESN'T SIT WELL WITH YOU, NO WORRIES: MAKE CAULI RICE INSTEAD!

CUMIN CILANTRO LIME RICE

MAKES 6 SERVINGS
⏱ 30 MINUTES

What—is regular old Cauli Rice too ho-hum for you? Need more spice and zing in your fake rice? Then roll up your sleeves and whip up some Cumin Cilantro Lime Rice!

INGREDIENTS:

- **2** tablespoons olive oil or cooking fat of choice
- **1** small yellow or white onion, finely diced
- **3** garlic cloves, minced
- **1** medium cauliflower head, riced (or 20 ounces fresh or frozen riced cauliflower)
- **1½** teaspoons kosher salt
- **1** teaspoon cumin
- **½** cup minced cilantro
- Zest and juice of 2 limes
- Freshly ground black pepper

JUST LIKE WHITE RICE, CAULIFLOWER RICE WILL TAKE ON THE FLAVOR OF ANYTHING YOU ADD TO IT. SO GO CRAZY AND FLAVOR IT UP!

INSTRUCTIONS:

1 POUR THE OLIVE OIL INTO A LARGE SKILLET OVER MEDIUM HEAT. ONCE IT'S SHIMMERING, ADD THE DICED ONIONS.

2 COOK THE ONIONS, STIRRING FREQUENTLY, FOR 8 TO 10 MINUTES OR UNTIL SOFTENED. TOSS IN THE MINCED GARLIC AND STIR FOR 30 SECONDS UNTIL FRAGRANT.

3 ADD THE RICED CAULIFLOWER.

4 SEASON WITH SALT AND CUMIN. STIR WELL.

5 COVER AND COOK FOR 5 MINUTES OR UNTIL TENDER BUT NOT MUSHY.

6 ADD THE CILANTRO, LIME ZEST AND JUICE. TASTE AND ADJUST THE SEASONING WITH SALT AND PEPPER, AND SERVE. EXTRAS CAN BE REFRIGERATED FOR UP TO 4 DAYS OR FROZEN FOR UP TO 2 MONTHS.

NEED TO MAKE HARD-COOKED EGGS WITHOUT A PRESSURE COOKER? STEAM 'EM. POUR AN INCH OF WATER IN A POT, AND PUT A STEAMER INSERT INSIDE. BRING TO A BOIL OVER HIGH HEAT, AND PLACE 6 EGGS ON THE STEAMER INSERT. COVER AND STEAM FOR 12 MINUTES. LASTLY, CHILL THE EGGS IN AN ICE BATH FOR 5 MINUTES BEFORE PEELING.

HARD COOKED EGGS ARE THE EPITOME OF EMERGENCY PROTEIN. I TRY TO ALWAYS KEEP A BUNCH IN MY FRIDGE SO I CAN POP ONE INTO MY BAG IF I'M ON THE GO, OR DIRECTLY INTO MY MOUTH IF I'M STARVING AND TOO BUSY TO COOK A PROPER MEAL.

PRESSURE COOKER HARD "BOILED" EGGS

MAKES 8 EGGS
⏱ **20 MINUTES**
(5 MINUTES HANDS-ON)

In my first book, I showed you how to perfectly hard-boil eggs on the stove. But these days, I prefer to use this (even easier!) pressure cooker method to produce results that are just as flawless.

INGREDIENTS:

8   large eggs

INSTRUCTIONS:

1. POUR 1 CUP OF WATER INTO YOUR PRESSURE COOKER.

2. PLACE A STEAMER INSERT IN THE COOKER.

3. CAREFULLY ARRANGE YOUR EGGS IN A SINGLE LAYER ON THE STEAMER INSERT.

4. COVER AND SEAL THE PRESSURE COOKER.

5. PRESSURE COOK UNDER HIGH PRESSURE FOR 6 MINUTES. IT SHOULD TAKE ABOUT 10 MINUTES FOR A PRESSURE COOKER TO REACH HIGH PRESSURE, AND AN ADDITIONAL 6 MINUTES TO FINISH COOKING.

6. FILL A LARGE BOWL WITH WATER AND ICE.

7. AS SOON AS THE EGGS ARE DONE, MANUALLY RELEASE THE PRESSURE.

8. TAKE OUT THE STEAMER AND DEPOSIT THE EGGS INTO THE ICE BATH. CHILL THEM IN THE ICE BATH FOR AT LEAST 5 MINUTES.

9. YOU CAN STORE THE COOKED EGGS IN THE SHELL FOR ABOUT A WEEK. WHEN YOU'RE READY TO EAT, JUST CRACK AND PEEL. THE SHELLS SHOULD COME OFF PRETTY EASILY.

10. SEE? PERFECTLY YELLOW YOLKS, WITH NO SULFUROUS STINK OR GRAY-GREEN RINGS AROUND THE EDGES!

ROAST-AHEAD CHICKEN BREASTS

MAKES 6 CUPS
⏱ **1 DAY**
(10 MINUTES HANDS-ON)

As a lark, I once tweeted at Bravo TV's Andy Cohen to ask whether he prefers "breasts or thighs"— referring to chicken, of course. He was succinct and unequivocal:

"Breasts."

As a devoted thigh gal myself, I was disappointed, but his reply reminded me that plenty of folks love chicken breasts, and that it's a versatile make-ahead backup protein that can be added to just about any savory soup, salad, wrap, or stir-fry. Try adding shredded chicken to Smoky Chestnut Apple Soup (page 92), Red Pesto Coodles (page 185), Leftacos (page 212), or Persian Cauliflower Rice (page 264)—or toss it on a freshly dressed green salad.

The key to juicy, flavorful breasts is dry-brining, so salt them at least a day in advance of roasting. It's also a good idea to invest in a high-quality instant-read thermometer to make sure your breasts are perfectly cooked.

That said, if Mr. Andy Cohen ever drops by your crib for dinner, I'd be grateful if you'd serve him dry, powdery breasts so that he'll finally see the light and join Team Thighs.

INGREDIENTS:

2   **whole bone-in, skin-on chicken breasts (about 1½ pounds each)**

1   **tablespoon kosher salt**

2   **tablespoons avocado oil or melted fat of choice**

INSTRUCTIONS:

1 ONE TO THREE DAYS BEFORE YOU ROAST THE CHICKEN, RUB THE SALT ALL OVER THE BREASTS, BOTH OVER AND UNDER THE SKIN. PLACE THEM IN A COVERED CONTAINER AND REFRIGERATE FOR 1 TO 3 DAYS.

2 WHEN YOU'RE READY TO COOK, PREHEAT THE OVEN TO 400°F WITH THE RACK IN THE MIDDLE POSITION. TAKE THE BREASTS OUT OF THE REFRIGERATOR AND BLOT THEM DRY WITH PAPER TOWELS.

3 SET THE BREASTS SKIN-SIDE UP ON A WIRE RACK ON TOP OF A RIMMED BAKING SHEET, POINTING IN OPPOSITE DIRECTIONS. BRUSH THE SKIN WITH THE AVOCADO OIL.

4 ROAST THE BREASTS FOR 30 TO 45 MINUTES, ROTATING THE TRAY AT THE HALFWAY POINT. THE CHICKEN IS DONE WHEN THE THICKEST PART OF EACH BREAST REACHES 150°F ON A MEAT THERMOMETER.

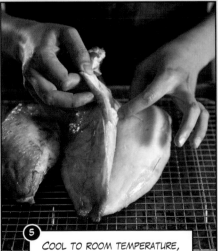

5 COOL TO ROOM TEMPERATURE, AND REMOVE THE SKIN.

6 IF DESIRED, SHRED OR CUT UP THE BREAST MEAT FOR LATER. THE COOKED BREASTS CAN BE KEPT IN A SEALED CONTAINER FOR UP TO 3 DAYS IN THE FRIDGE OR UP TO A MONTH IN THE FREEZER.

A GOOD NUMBER OF THE RECIPES IN THIS BOOK CALL FOR ROASTING OR BAKING FOOD ON A WIRE RACK. WHY? BECAUSE IT ENABLES HOT AIR TO CIRCULATE BENEATH THE FOOD, ENSURING EVEN BROWNING AND COOKING.

NOT SURE WHAT TO DO WITH THESE BUILDING BLOCKS? MIX 'N' MATCH 'EM TO MAKE QUICK AND EASY DISHES!

MEXI-CHICKEN SALAD

Cube or shred up some Roast-Ahead Chicken Breast (page 84), and toss it with diced avocado, a dollop of Salsa Ahumada (page 72), and salad greens. Sprinkle Smoky Lime Pepitas (page 46) on top.

GREEN COBB SALAD

Fill a big platter or salad bowl with chopped salad greens, and then top with rows of diced ripe tomato, crisp bacon bits, diced Roast-Ahead Chicken Breast (page 84), sliced Pressure Cooker Hard "Boiled" Eggs (page 83), and cubed avocado. Drizzle Green Beast Dressing (page 48) over everything.

LUNCHBOX TUNA SALAD

Mix a few tablespoons of Paleo Mayo (page 50) or Roasted Garlic Mayonnaise (page 52) with some diced Fridge-Pickled Cucumbers (page 74), and toss with a can of drained tuna. Mash it all up, season with salt and pepper to taste, and stuff the tuna mixture into halved sweet lunchbox peppers. Garnish with fresh dill and lemon zest.

TONNATO PLATE

Arrange a single layer of thinly sliced roast beef or shredded Roast-Ahead Chicken Breast (page 84) on a platter. Drizzle with Tonnato Sauce (page 51), and top with fresh parsley leaves, celery leaves, shaved fennel, caper berries, thinly sliced radishes, sprinkle of salt, and freshly ground black pepper.

FAUX PHỞ BROTH

Fill a big mug or a soup bowl with piping hot Bone Broth (page 76), and season with a splash of fish sauce to taste. Top with thinly sliced white onions, sliced scallions, Thai basil leaves and/or cilantro, and thinly sliced jalapeños. Stir in a sprinkle of ground cinnamon and a squirt of fresh lime juice.

THAI'D UP + ROLLED UP

Pile roast beef slices on butter lettuce leaves—a.k.a. Nature's Tortillas (page 79)—and top with thinly sliced cucumber, carrots, and avocado. Roll 'em up (and tie up the lettuce rolls with chives if you want). Dip into Thai Citrus Dressing (page 47), and eat.

XO NOODLES

Spiralize a bunch of zucchini or cucumbers, and toss the vegetable noodles with shredded Roast-Ahead Chicken Breast (page 84). Top with warm XO Sauce (page 54) and a generous sprinkle of sliced scallions. Serve immediately.

RED PESTO PRAWNS

Use the cooking method for Roasted Catalan Shrimp (page 196) to roast a tray of shrimp sprinkled with salt and pepper. Toss with Pesto Pomodori Secchi (page 73), and serve over Cauli Rice (page 80).

ROMESCO FISH PACKETS

Chop up some wild mushrooms, and sprinkle salt and pepper on white fish fillets. Using the method for Honey Harissa Salmon on page 272, make and bake parchment packets containing the mushrooms, fish, and Romesco Sauce (page 65).

CHICKEN HASH + GRAVY

In a large skillet, sauté shredded sweet potatoes and leftover Roast-Ahead Chicken Breast (page 84). Season with salt, pepper, and onion powder, and serve with Umami Gravy (page 69). Not in the mood for gravy? Switch things up and enjoy it with Cran-Cherry Sauce (page 68).

ROASTED ONION CHICKEN

Marinate 8 bone-in, skin-on chicken thighs in about 1 cup of Creamy Onion Dressing (page 49), a big pinch of kosher salt, and a small pinch of crushed red pepper flakes for at least 2 hours and up to 24 hours. Then, shake off the excess marinade and bake at 400°F for about 40 minutes or until the skin is golden brown and the meat is cooked through.

SRIRACHA HONEY MARINADE

In a bowl, combine Nom Nom Sriracha (page 56) or Fauxchujang (page 61) with coconut aminos, honey, and fresh lime juice, and use it as a simple marinade for your favorite proteins. I also like to brush this marinade on skewers and ribs.

THAI PORK TENDERLOIN

Sprinkle a pork tenderloin with salt and pepper, and roast it low and slow for about 45 minutes (depending on the size of the pork) in a 250°F oven until the internal temperature (measured with a meat thermometer) reaches 140°F. Then, slather the top with Spicy Thai No-Nut Sauce (page 58) and place it under the broiler for a minute or until browned.

EASY TACOS

In a large skillet, brown a pound of ground beef with a diced onion. Season with salt, pepper, and chili powder. When the meat is no longer pink, add Salsa Ahumada (page 72) and simmer until the flavors meld. Serve with Grain-Free Tortillas (page 78) or Nature's Tortillas (page 79), and top with Fruit + Avocado Salsa (page 70).

ONE OF THE KEYS TO GOOD COOKING IS TASTING AS YOU GO, SO INSTEAD OF GIVING YOU SPECIFIC QUANTITIES FOR THESE RECIPE IDEAS, I WANT YOU TO EXPERIMENT AND CUSTOMIZE THE FLAVORS TO FIT YOUR OWN PALATE!

READY!

PREP-AHEAD RECIPES FOR WHEN YOU HAVE YOUR 💩 TOGETHER

WHAT DOES IT MEAN TO BE
READY?

What do you like to do on weekends? Sleep in? Exercise? Hang out with friends and family? Read a book? Eat something tasty? All of the above?

Me, too—but I also carve out time to cook. Weekends are the perfect time to press "pause," head to the grocery store or farmer's market to load up on fresh supplies, and tend to my favorite creative endeavor: Cooking something insanely delicious.

Weekend cooking can take many forms. Some folks reserve a full day to do all of their cooking for the week (or even the month!), whipping up big batches of multiple meals and dividing them into freezer ready portions. Others focus on more complex, time-intensive recipes—ones they can't ordinarily tackle when trying to feed a hungry household.

The common thread among all these approaches is *readiness*. When we choose to spend the afternoon batch-cooking or experimenting with a new recipe, we're doing it because we're physically and mentally ready to cook. And afterwards, when we step back and admire what we've accomplished in the kitchen, we can feel confident that we're prepared for the week ahead and beyond. We know that when we have time to cook, we can get a delicious, nutrient-packed meal on the dinner table—and with any luck, some extras to stockpile for later, too.

So when you're ready to cook, turn to this section of the cookbook. We've filled its pages with make-ahead meals and spectacular dishes that are worth

the extra elbow grease, and can be stretched and repurposed later in the week. Most of these dishes can be prepared ahead of time, and then finished or reheated when you're ready to chow down.

Compared to the other recipes in this book, these dishes take a smidge longer to prep from start-to-finish, but none take more than an hour of hands-on time. And the reward for all your extra effort? Dishes that'll impress everyone from your finicky in-laws to your new boss.

If you're looking for desserts in this book, this is also where you'll find them. My loyal Nomsters know my stance on sweets: Desserts aren't meant to be an everyday indulgence, so if you're going to make and enjoy a sweet treat, it better knock your socks off. I've included a handful of my favorite desserts here; they require some extra time, but your patience will pay off.

SMOKY CHESTNUT APPLE SOUP

MAKES 6 SERVINGS
⏱ **1 HOUR**
(30 MINUTES HANDS-ON)

Fragrant roasted chestnuts bring me back to childhood evenings at our cozy kitchen table…struggling like crazy to pry off the hot, jagged shells and fuzzy pellicle skin from the tender chestnut flesh. Man, I *hated* peeling those things.

Still, this deliciously creamy cold-weather soup is well worth the trouble—especially if you use packaged, pre-cooked chestnuts instead. Aren't shortcuts great?

INGREDIENTS:

4   slices thick-cut bacon, cut crosswise into ½-inch slices

1   medium fennel bulb, thinly sliced

2   carrots, peeled and sliced into ¼-inch coins

1   medium yellow onion, diced

    Kosher salt

10 ounces roasted chestnuts, chopped

1   medium Braeburn, Cortland, Empire, Fuji, or McIntosh apple, peeled, cored, and chopped

4   cups Bone Broth (page 76) or chicken stock

2   fresh thyme sprigs

    Freshly ground black pepper

2   teaspoons sherry vinegar

    Fennel fronds (as garnish)

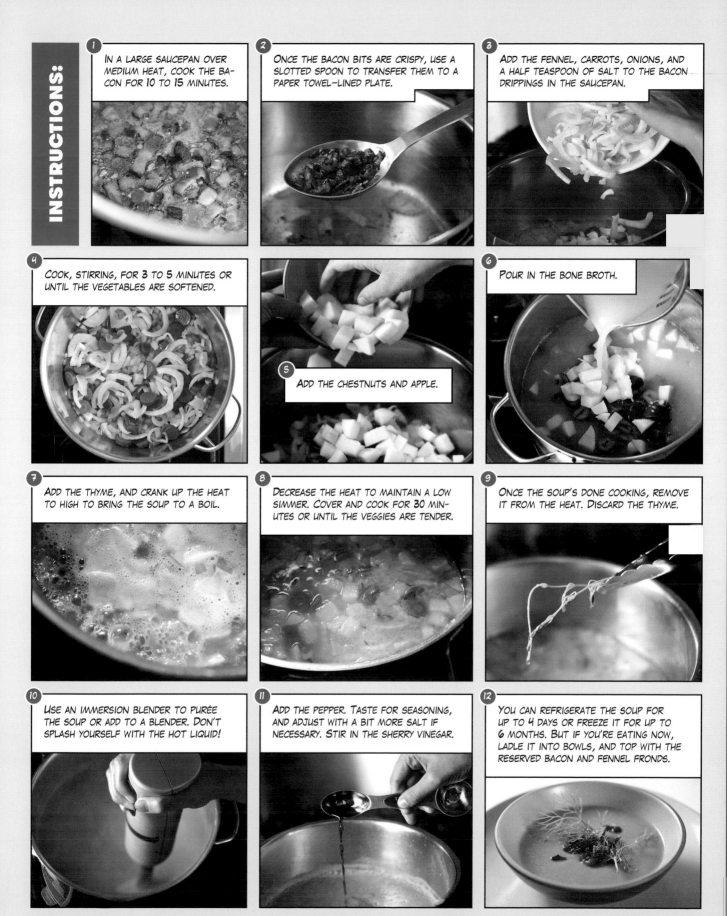

1. IN A LARGE SAUCEPAN OVER MEDIUM HEAT, COOK THE BACON FOR 10 TO 15 MINUTES.

2. ONCE THE BACON BITS ARE CRISPY, USE A SLOTTED SPOON TO TRANSFER THEM TO A PAPER TOWEL–LINED PLATE.

3. ADD THE FENNEL, CARROTS, ONIONS, AND A HALF TEASPOON OF SALT TO THE BACON DRIPPINGS IN THE SAUCEPAN.

4. COOK, STIRRING, FOR 3 TO 5 MINUTES OR UNTIL THE VEGETABLES ARE SOFTENED.

5. ADD THE CHESTNUTS AND APPLE.

6. POUR IN THE BONE BROTH.

7. ADD THE THYME, AND CRANK UP THE HEAT TO HIGH TO BRING THE SOUP TO A BOIL.

8. DECREASE THE HEAT TO MAINTAIN A LOW SIMMER. COVER AND COOK FOR 30 MINUTES OR UNTIL THE VEGGIES ARE TENDER.

9. ONCE THE SOUP'S DONE COOKING, REMOVE IT FROM THE HEAT. DISCARD THE THYME.

10. USE AN IMMERSION BLENDER TO PURÉE THE SOUP OR ADD TO A BLENDER. DON'T SPLASH YOURSELF WITH THE HOT LIQUID!

11. ADD THE PEPPER. TASTE FOR SEASONING, AND ADJUST WITH A BIT MORE SALT IF NECESSARY. STIR IN THE SHERRY VINEGAR.

12. YOU CAN REFRIGERATE THE SOUP FOR UP TO 4 DAYS OR FREEZE IT FOR UP TO 6 MONTHS. BUT IF YOU'RE EATING NOW, LADLE IT INTO BOWLS, AND TOP WITH THE RESERVED BACON AND FENNEL FRONDS.

HONEYDEW LIME GAZPACHO

MAKES 4 SERVINGS
⏱ **4 HOURS**
(20 MINUTES HANDS-ON)

Since ancient times, gazpacho has been made with tomatoes and stale bread. But since when have I ever cared about tradition?

Instead, I've been crushing on this modern variation of this chilled Spanish soup. The combination of sweet honeydew, tangy lime, spicy jalapeño, and fresh mint gives this gazpacho a blast of flavor like no other—and the vivid color makes this soup a treat for the eyes, too.

It takes just a few minutes to blitz up this no-cook recipe. And once this gazpacho is blended, you can keep it in the fridge for up to a couple of days, so you can slurp it down whenever the craving hits.

INGREDIENTS:

- ½ **medium honeydew melon, cubed and seeded (about 2 pounds cubed melon)**
- 2 **medium cucumbers (about 1 pound), peeled, seeded, and roughly chopped**
- ½ **jalapeño pepper, seeded and roughly chopped**
- 1 **large shallot, roughly chopped**
- 2 **tablespoons mint leaves**
- 2 **tablespoons extra-virgin olive oil**
- **Zest and juice from 2 limes**
- 1 **teaspoon kosher salt**
- **Freshly ground black pepper**

INSTRUCTIONS:

1. THROW EVERYTHING EXCEPT THE BLACK PEPPER IN A POWERFUL BLENDER. (USE MORE OR LESS JALAPEÑO PEPPER DEPENDING ON HOW MUCH HEAT YOU PREFER.)

2. BLEND UNTIL SMOOTH. TASTE AND ADJUST FOR SEASONING WITH MORE SALT AND/OR LIME JUICE AS NEEDED.

3. REFRIGERATE IN THE COVERED BLENDER CUP FOR 4 HOURS OR UNTIL FULLY CHILLED (BUT NO LONGER THAN 2 DAYS).

4. THE INGREDIENTS MAY SEPARATE WHILE IN THE FRIDGE, SO JUST PRIOR TO SERVING, QUICKLY BLITZ AGAIN TO RECOMBINE.

5. SEASON TO TASTE WITH BLACK PEPPER. POUR AND SERVE.

ROASTED ONION SOUP

MAKES 4 SERVINGS
⏱ **1½ HOURS**
(15 MINUTES HANDS-ON)

Remember the Creamy Onion Dressing from page 49? When I was testing that recipe, the fragrance of roasted onions and garlic that filled my kitchen was intoxicating. Drunk with the smells, I decided to come up with another way to take advantage of the robust flavors of the roasted aromatics. This inexpensive and hearty soup is the result.

Pro tip: Roasting the onions and garlic can take a while, so you might as well throw extra into the baking dish. That way, you can also make a batch of Creamy Onion Dressing, which doubles as a handy marinade, too. Besides, who doesn't like having extra roasted garlic and onions on hand to flavor up other dishes?

(The correct answer: vampires.)

INGREDIENTS:

- 3   **medium unpeeled yellow onions**
- 6   **unpeeled garlic cloves**
- ¼   **cup olive oil, avocado oil, or melted ghee**
- 2   **cups Bone Broth (page 76) or chicken stock, divided**
- 2   **sprigs fresh thyme**
-    **Kosher salt**
-    **Freshly ground black pepper**
-    **Fresh chives**
-    **Aged balsamic vinegar**
-    **Extra-virgin olive oil**

INSTRUCTIONS:

1 PREHEAT THE OVEN TO 425°F WITH THE RACK IN THE MIDDLE POSITION. PLACE THE ONIONS AND GARLIC IN A BAKING DISH, AND DRIZZLE THE OIL ON TOP.

2 ROAST IN THE OVEN FOR ABOUT 1 HOUR OR UNTIL THE ONIONS AND GARLIC ARE SLIGHTLY CHARRED AND VERY SOFT.

3 PEEL THE ONIONS, TRIMMING OFF THE ROOT ENDS. PEEL THE GARLIC, TOO.

4 ROUGHLY CHOP UP THE ROASTED ONIONS.

5 TOSS THE ONIONS AND GARLIC INTO A BLENDER.

6 ADD ½ CUP OF THE BROTH, AND PURÉE UNTIL SMOOTH.

7 POUR THE PURÉE INTO A LARGE SAUCEPAN.

8 ADD THE THYME AS WELL AS THE REMAINING 1½ CUPS OF BROTH. BRING TO A BOIL OVER HIGH HEAT.

9 LOWER THE HEAT TO MAINTAIN A SIMMER FOR 5 TO 10 MINUTES OR UNTIL THE FLAVORS HAVE DEEPENED. REMOVE THE THYME.

10 SEASON TO TASTE WITH SALT AND PEPPER. LADLE THE SOUP INTO BOWLS, OR KEEP IT IN THE FRIDGE FOR UP TO 4 DAYS OR IN THE FREEZER FOR UP TO 6 MONTHS.

11 BEFORE SERVING, GARNISH WITH FRESH CHIVES, A DRIZZLE OF AGED BALSAMIC VINEGAR, AND A FEW DROPS OF OLIVE OIL.

FRIED GREEN PLANTAINS

MAKES 12 PIECES
⏱ **45 MINUTES**

When we were in Costa Rica, there was one dish we ordered at every restaurant: palm-sized fried green plantains (also known as *patacones* or *tostones*). Satisfyingly crunchy from end-to-end, our favorite fried green plantains were served at Restaurant Los Almendros in Esterillos. While some folks brine their plantains before frying them, and others make them smaller and thicker, I like my *patacones* the Los Almendros way: no brine, pounded thin, and double-fried.

Patacones are great as-is, but they're even better as a substitute for tortillas or bread. Check out the Jíbaritos on page 210 to see how to use 'em to make sandwiches!

INGREDIENTS:

4   **cups coconut oil, avocado oil, ghee, lard, or tallow**

4   **green plantains (2 pounds)**

Kosher salt

EVEN IN SPANISH-SPEAKING COUNTRIES, FRIED GREEN PLANTAINS GO BY MANY DIFFERENT NAMES. IN PUERTO RICO, GUATEMALA, HONDURAS, AND NICARAGUA (AND IN SOME PARTS OF THE DOMINICAN REPUBLIC, CUBA, AND VENEZUELA), THEY'RE KNOWN AS TOSTONES. BUT THEY'RE CALLED PATACONES IN COLOMBIA, PANAMA, PERU, VENEZUELA, COSTA RICA AND ECUADOR, TACHINOS IN CUBA, AND FRITOS VERDES IN THE DOMINICAN REPUBLIC.

BE SURE TO USE SUPER-GREEN PLANTAINS. IF YOU SPOT ONLY RIPE, SPLOTCHY, YELLOW-BROWN PLANTAINS AT THE MARKET, ASK YOUR FRIENDLY PRODUCE GUY OR GAL IF THEY HAVE SOME GREEN ONES IN THE BACK. THEY OFTEN DO.

≈CRUNCH!≈

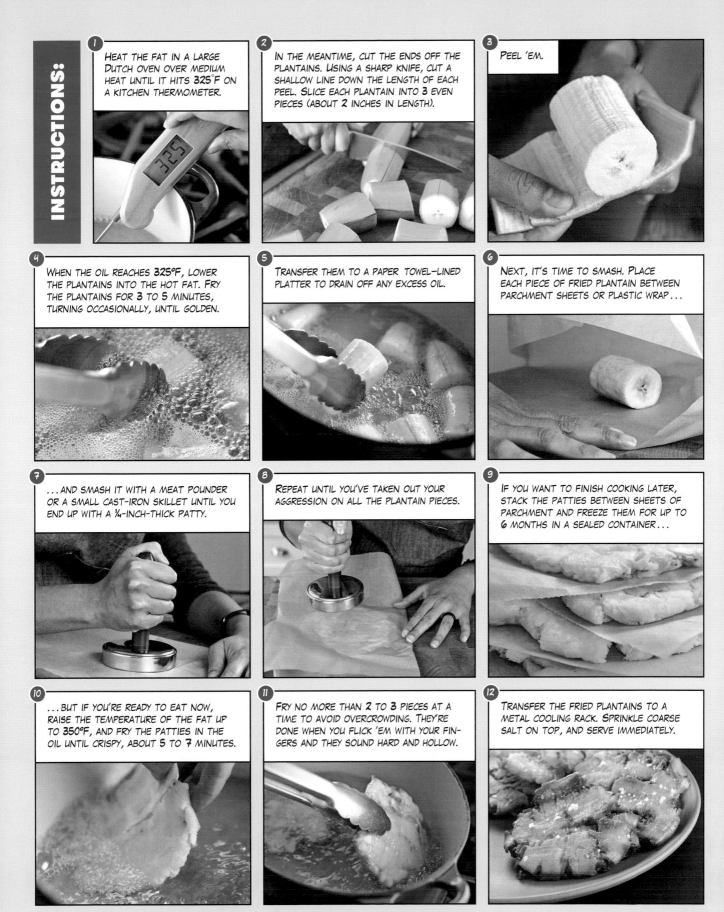

1 HEAT THE FAT IN A LARGE DUTCH OVEN OVER MEDIUM HEAT UNTIL IT HITS **325°F** ON A KITCHEN THERMOMETER.

2 IN THE MEANTIME, CUT THE ENDS OFF THE PLANTAINS. USING A SHARP KNIFE, CUT A SHALLOW LINE DOWN THE LENGTH OF EACH PEEL. SLICE EACH PLANTAIN INTO **3** EVEN PIECES (ABOUT **2** INCHES IN LENGTH).

3 PEEL 'EM.

4 WHEN THE OIL REACHES **325°F**, LOWER THE PLANTAINS INTO THE HOT FAT. FRY THE PLANTAINS FOR **3** TO **5** MINUTES, TURNING OCCASIONALLY, UNTIL GOLDEN.

5 TRANSFER THEM TO A PAPER TOWEL–LINED PLATTER TO DRAIN OFF ANY EXCESS OIL.

6 NEXT, IT'S TIME TO SMASH. PLACE EACH PIECE OF FRIED PLANTAIN BETWEEN PARCHMENT SHEETS OR PLASTIC WRAP . . .

7 . . . AND SMASH IT WITH A MEAT POUNDER OR A SMALL CAST-IRON SKILLET UNTIL YOU END UP WITH A ¼-INCH-THICK PATTY.

8 REPEAT UNTIL YOU'VE TAKEN OUT YOUR AGGRESSION ON ALL THE PLANTAIN PIECES.

9 IF YOU WANT TO FINISH COOKING LATER, STACK THE PATTIES BETWEEN SHEETS OF PARCHMENT AND FREEZE THEM FOR UP TO **6** MONTHS IN A SEALED CONTAINER . . .

10 . . . BUT IF YOU'RE READY TO EAT NOW, RAISE THE TEMPERATURE OF THE FAT UP TO **350°F**, AND FRY THE PATTIES IN THE OIL UNTIL CRISPY, ABOUT **5** TO **7** MINUTES.

11 FRY NO MORE THAN **2** TO **3** PIECES AT A TIME TO AVOID OVERCROWDING. THEY'RE DONE WHEN YOU FLICK 'EM WITH YOUR FINGERS AND THEY SOUND HARD AND HOLLOW.

12 TRANSFER THE FRIED PLANTAINS TO A METAL COOLING RACK. SPRINKLE COARSE SALT ON TOP, AND SERVE IMMEDIATELY.

BUFFALO CAULIFLOWER THINGS

MAKES 4 SERVINGS
⏱ 1 HOUR
(15 MINUTES HANDS-ON)

I sometimes get the feeling that my non-Paleo friends think my diet consists of nothing but red meat, yet nothing could be further from the truth. I love vegetables, and cram them into my mouth at every opportunity. Even when there's a perfectly good meat recipe available, I'll often vegetarianize it—for kicks, but also to make sure my kids actually get their share of plant-based foods. Case in point: these wonderfully spicy-tangy bites made with battered and baked cauliflower. They're perfect as a vegetable side—or as a substitute for Buffalo Wings (page 102) when you feel like switching things up.

INGREDIENTS:

1   medium cauliflower head (about 2½ pounds), cut into uniform-sized florets

2   large egg whites

½   cup arrowroot powder or tapioca flour

1   teaspoon garlic powder

¾   teaspoon kosher salt

• BUFFALO SAUCE •

¼   cup ghee

½   cup cayenne pepper sauce (I like Frank's Red Hot Sauce)

1½   tablespoons apple juice

1   tablespoon fresh lemon juice

INSTRUCTIONS:

1 SET THE OVEN TO 400°F ON CONVECTION MODE WITH A RACK IN THE MIDDLE. IF YOUR OVEN DOESN'T HAVE A CONVECTION MODE, PREHEAT IT TO 425°F, AND ROTATE THE TRAY OF CAULIFLOWER MORE FREQUENTLY DURING THE COOKING PROCESS.

2 IN A LARGE BOWL, WHISK THE EGG WHITES UNTIL FROTHY.

3 ADD THE ARROWROOT POWDER, GARLIC POWDER, AND SALT. CONTINUE WHISKING UNTIL A SMOOTH, STICKY BATTER FORMS.

4 DUMP THE CAULIFLOWER INTO THE BATTER. TOSS WITH YOUR HANDS TO COAT WELL.

5 SHAKE OFF THE EXCESS BATTER. PLACE THE FLORETS ON A WELL-GREASED WIRE RACK PLACED ON A RIMMED BAKING SHEET.

6 BAKE FOR 20 MINUTES. FLIP THE FLORETS OVER, AND ROTATE THE TRAY. CONTINUE COOKING FOR 15 TO 20 MINUTES MORE OR UNTIL GOLDEN BROWN AND CRISPY.

7 WHILE THE FLORETS ARE BAKING, MAKE THE SAUCE. MELT THE GHEE IN A SMALL SAUCEPAN OVER LOW HEAT. WHISK IN THE HOT SAUCE, APPLE JUICE, AND LEMON JUICE. REMOVE THE PAN FROM THE HEAT.

8 WHEN THE FLORETS ARE FINISHED COOKING, TOSS WITH THE SAUCE.

9 SERVE!

BUFFALO WINGS

MAKES 4 SERVINGS
⏱ **1 HOUR**
(30 MINUTES HANDS-ON)

Now that you've made my Buffalo Cauliflower Things, don't you think it's time to make the real deal?

INGREDIENTS:

1	tablespoon cream of tartar
2	teaspoons kosher salt
2	teaspoons baking soda
1	teaspoon arrowroot powder or tapioca flour
4	pounds chicken wings and/ or drummettes
	Ghee for greasing the rack

• SAUCE •

½	cup ghee
¾	cup cayenne pepper sauce (like Frank's Red Hot Sauce)
3	tablespoons apple juice
2	tablespoons fresh lemon juice

• RANCH DRESSING •

½	cup Paleo Mayo (page 50)
¼	cup full-fat coconut milk
1	tablespoon fresh lemon juice
1	tablespoon minced fresh Italian parsley
1	tablespoon minced chives
1	teaspoon onion powder
1	teaspoon minced fresh dill or ½ teaspoon dried dill
1	teaspoon kosher salt

HANKERING FOR A SPICIER DIPPING SAUCE? MAKE SRIRACHA RANCH DRESSING (PAGE 57) INSTEAD.

HOW CAN BUFFALOES FLY WITH SUCH LITTLE WINGS?

SHEER WILLPOWER AND JET ENGINES IN THEIR BUTTS. OBVIOUSLY.

MOK MOK WINGS

MAKES 4 SERVINGS
⏱ 1 HOUR
(30 MINUTES HANDS-ON)

If you love the intense brininess of fish sauce as much as I do, you'll love these sweet and sticky wings. Here's a tip: While you can certainly bake these wings in a standard 425°F oven, this Thai-inspired recipe works best when cooked at 400°F on convection mode. The circulating heated air ensures crisp, uniformly golden skin.

INGREDIENTS:

2 tablespoons ghee, divided

4 pounds chicken wings and/or drummettes

1 tablespoon cream of tartar

2 teaspoons kosher salt

2 teaspoons baking soda

1 teaspoon arrowroot powder or tapioca flour

• SAUCE •

1 tablespoon ghee

1 large shallot, minced

2 garlic cloves, minced

½ teaspoon red pepper flakes

¼ cup honey

¼ cup fish sauce

  Juice from 1 lime

• GARNISH •

2 tablespoons toasted sesame seeds

¼ cup sliced scallions

INSTRUCTIONS:

1 PREHEAT THE OVEN TO 400°F ON CONVECTION MODE (OR 425°F STANDARD) WITH A RACK IN THE UPPER MIDDLE POSITION AND ANOTHER IN THE LOWER MIDDLE POSITION.

2 IN SMALL BOWL, COMBINE THE CREAM OF TARTAR, SALT, BAKING SODA, AND ARROWROOT POWDER.

3 PLACE THE WINGS AND/OR DRUMMETTES IN A LARGE MIXING BOWL, AND POUR THE DRY MIXTURE ONTO THE CHICKEN PIECES.

4 USE YOUR HANDS TO SPREAD THE MIXTURE EVENLY ON THE CHICKEN.

5 ARRANGE THE CHICKEN ON **2** GREASED WIRE RACKS PLACED ON **2** RIMMED BAKING SHEETS. (CRAMMING ALL THE CHICKEN ONTO A SINGLE RACK WON'T WORK 'CAUSE OVERCROWDED WINGS WON'T GET CRISPY.)

6 PLACE A TRAY OF CHICKEN ON EACH RACK IN THE OVEN, AND BAKE FOR **20** MINUTES.

7 FLIP EACH CHICKEN WING OVER, AND SWAP THE TOP TRAY WITH THE BOTTOM ONE.

8 BAKE FOR **20** TO **25** MINUTES MORE OR UNTIL THE SKIN IS CRISP AND GOLDEN.

9 WHILE THE CHICKEN'S COOKING, MAKE THE SAUCE. HEAT THE GHEE IN A SMALL SAUCEPAN OVER MEDIUM HEAT. ADD THE SHALLOTS AND SAUTÉ UNTIL SOFTENED, ABOUT **3** TO **5** MINUTES.

10 ADD THE GARLIC AND RED PEPPER. STIR FOR **30** SECONDS OR UNTIL FRAGRANT.

11 ADD THE HONEY AND FISH SAUCE, AND BRING TO A BOIL.

12 LOWER THE HEAT AND SIMMER THE SAUCE FOR **8** TO **10** MINUTES UNTIL IT THICKENS.

13 REMOVE THE SAUCEPAN FROM THE HEAT, AND ADD THE LIME JUICE.

14 TRANSFER THE SAUCE TO A LARGE MIXING BOWL, AND ADD THE CRISPY BAKED WINGS.

15 TOSS TO COAT THE WINGS WITH THE SAUCE.

16 TOP WITH SESAME SEEDS AND SCALLIONS.

ROASTED DIJON TARRAGON CHICKEN

MAKES 8 SERVINGS
⏱ **1½ HOURS**
(20 MINUTES HANDS-ON)

If you're planning to roast one chicken, you might as well throw two in the oven. That way, you'll have enough for tonight's supper and more for when your hunger pangs strike again. After all, you're not going to be satisfied with just one meal of this flavorful roast chicken. The herby, mustardy marinade keeps the meat tender and aromatic—which is key to transforming lowly leftovers into incredible bestovers. One more tip: When you're done, save both chicken carcasses to make Bone Broth (page 76).

INGREDIENTS:

1	**cup Dijon-style mustard**
¼	**cup extra-virgin olive oil**
2	**tablespoons minced fresh tarragon leaves**
12	**garlic cloves, minced**
1	**tablespoon kosher salt**
2	**(4-pound) whole chickens, with giblets removed**

↻ SWITCH IT UP: ORANGE DIJON CHICKEN

NO TARRAGON ON HAND? MAKE ORANGE DIJON CHICKEN! IN A BOWL, WHISK TOGETHER ¾ CUP DIJON-STYLE MUSTARD, ¼ CUP FRESH ORANGE JUICE, 2 TABLESPOONS EXTRA-VIRGIN OLIVE OIL, 1 TABLESPOON KOSHER SALT, AND 6 MINCED GARLIC CLOVES. THEN, CONTINUE WITH THE RECIPE AT STEP 2.

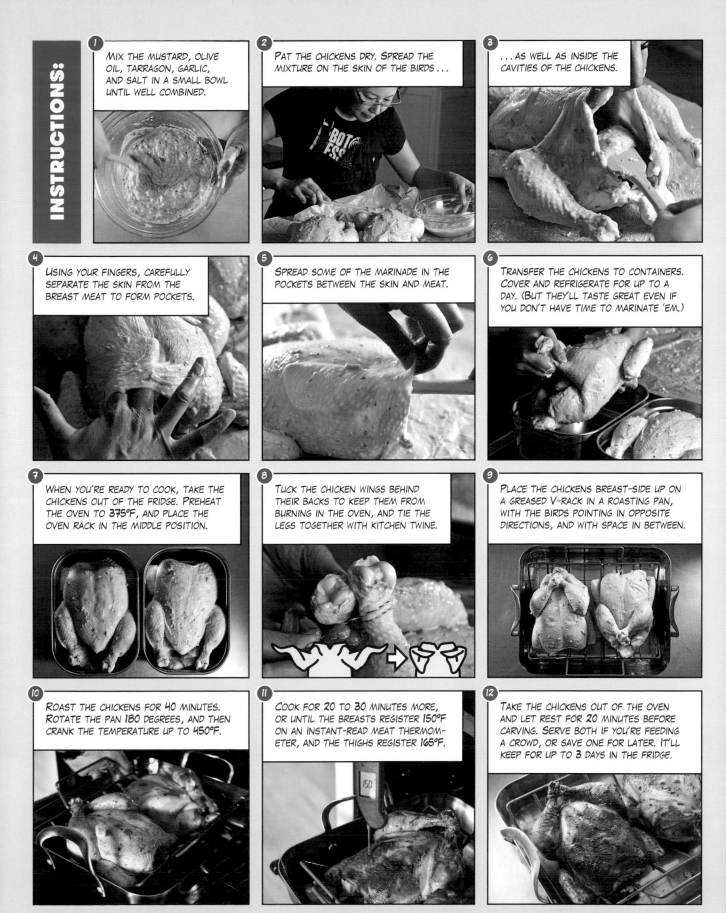

1. MIX THE MUSTARD, OLIVE OIL, TARRAGON, GARLIC, AND SALT IN A SMALL BOWL UNTIL WELL COMBINED.

2. PAT THE CHICKENS DRY. SPREAD THE MIXTURE ON THE SKIN OF THE BIRDS ...

3. ...AS WELL AS INSIDE THE CAVITIES OF THE CHICKENS.

4. USING YOUR FINGERS, CAREFULLY SEPARATE THE SKIN FROM THE BREAST MEAT TO FORM POCKETS.

5. SPREAD SOME OF THE MARINADE IN THE POCKETS BETWEEN THE SKIN AND MEAT.

6. TRANSFER THE CHICKENS TO CONTAINERS. COVER AND REFRIGERATE FOR UP TO A DAY. (BUT THEY'LL TASTE GREAT EVEN IF YOU DON'T HAVE TIME TO MARINATE 'EM.)

7. WHEN YOU'RE READY TO COOK, TAKE THE CHICKENS OUT OF THE FRIDGE. PREHEAT THE OVEN TO 375°F, AND PLACE THE OVEN RACK IN THE MIDDLE POSITION.

8. TUCK THE CHICKEN WINGS BEHIND THEIR BACKS TO KEEP THEM FROM BURNING IN THE OVEN, AND TIE THE LEGS TOGETHER WITH KITCHEN TWINE.

9. PLACE THE CHICKENS BREAST-SIDE UP ON A GREASED V-RACK IN A ROASTING PAN, WITH THE BIRDS POINTING IN OPPOSITE DIRECTIONS, AND WITH SPACE IN BETWEEN.

10. ROAST THE CHICKENS FOR 40 MINUTES. ROTATE THE PAN 180 DEGREES, AND THEN CRANK THE TEMPERATURE UP TO 450°F.

11. COOK FOR 20 TO 30 MINUTES MORE, OR UNTIL THE BREASTS REGISTER 150°F ON AN INSTANT-READ MEAT THERMOMETER, AND THE THIGHS REGISTER 165°F.

12. TAKE THE CHICKENS OUT OF THE OVEN AND LET REST FOR 20 MINUTES BEFORE CARVING. SERVE BOTH IF YOU'RE FEEDING A CROWD, OR SAVE ONE FOR LATER. IT'LL KEEP FOR UP TO 3 DAYS IN THE FRIDGE.

CHICKEN BREASTS WITH GINGER SCALLION PESTO

MAKES 4 SERVINGS
⏱ **1 HOUR**
(30 MINUTES HANDS-ON)

INGREDIENTS:

- ¼ cup softened duck fat, ghee, or fat of choice

- ½ cup thinly sliced scallions (about 3 scallions)

- 1 tablespoon grated ginger
  Kosher salt

- 4 bone-in, skin-on chicken breasts (10-12 ounces each)

- 1 tablespoon melted duck fat, ghee, or fat of choice

CHICKEN BREASTS OFTEN TURN OUT DRY AND POWDERY, BUT THIS RECIPE PRODUCES TENDER, JUICY CHICKEN EVERY TIME!

1. PREHEAT THE OVEN TO 450°F WITH THE RACK IN THE MIDDLE POSITION.

2. IN A SMALL BOWL, ADD THE FAT, SCALLIONS, GINGER, AND 2 TEASPOONS OF SALT.

3. MIX WELL.

4. USING YOUR FINGERS, CAREFULLY SEPARATE THE SKIN OF EACH CHICKEN BREAST AWAY FROM THE MEAT TO FORM A POCKET.

5. ADD 1 TABLESPOON OF THE PESTO UNDER THE SKIN OF EACH BREAST.

6. CAREFULLY PRESS AND MASSAGE THE SKIN TO EVENLY DISTRIBUTE THE PESTO.

7. AT THIS POINT, YOU CAN PROCEED WITH COOKING THE CHICKEN, OR REFRIGERATE IT FOR UP TO A DAY AND ROAST IT LATER.

8. PUT THE CHICKEN SKIN-SIDE UP ON A WIRE RACK ATOP A FOIL-LINED BAKING SHEET.

9. BRUSH THE MELTED FAT ON THE CHICKEN BREASTS, AND SEASON WITH MORE SALT.

10. OVEN-ROAST FOR 30 TO 35 MINUTES OR UNTIL AN INSTANT-READ THERMOMETER INSERTED INTO THE THICKEST PART OF THE CHICKEN BREAST REGISTERS 150°F.

11. REST THE CHICKEN FOR 5 TO 10 MINUTES BEFORE DE-BONING, SLICING AND SERVING. IF YOU HAVE LEFTOVERS, THEY CAN BE KEPT IN THE FRIDGE FOR UP TO 3 DAYS.

BACON-WRAPPED CHICKEN
+
LEMON-DATE SAUCE

MAKES 6 SERVINGS
⏱ 1 HOUR
(45 MINUTES HANDS-ON)

This recipe is inspired by a special on the menu at Odys + Penelope, a Brazilian *churrascaria* on La Brea in Los Angeles. After just one bite of the restaurant's succulent, sweet-and-savory bacon-wrapped chicken, I was intent on making my own version. Try as I might, I simply couldn't stop thinking about the tender chicken underneath the smoky, crisp ribbon of bacon. So as soon as I got home, I started tinkering. The result? A startlingly delicious, crave-worthy dish.

INGREDIENTS:

12   boneless and skinless chicken thighs

      Kosher salt

      Freshly ground black pepper

12   slices bacon

1   large shallot, sliced

1   tablespoon minced ginger

3   garlic cloves, minced

1   cup Bone Broth (page 76) or chicken stock

5   large Medjool dates, pitted and cut into strips, divided

3   tablespoons fresh lemon juice

¼   cup chopped Italian parsley

GOT SOME LEFTOVER BACON-WRAPPED CHICKEN IN THE FRIDGE? WHEN YOU'RE READY TO CHOW DOWN AGAIN, SLICE 'EM CROSSWISE INTO MEDALLIONS, AND PAN-FRY THEM IN A SKILLET OVER MEDIUM-HIGH HEAT. SERVE ON A BED OF GREENS WITH WHATEVER SAUCE YOU HAVE ON HAND.

1 SET THE OVEN TO 400°F WITH THE RACK IN THE MIDDLE.

2 GENEROUSLY SPRINKLE SALT AND PEPPER ON THE THIGHS.

3 ROLL EACH THIGH INTO A CIGAR SHAPE, AND WRAP A STRIP OF BACON AROUND IT. SECURE THE BACON WITH A TOOTHPICK.

4 HEAT A LARGE, HEAVY-BOTTOMED SKILLET OVER MEDIUM-HIGH HEAT. CAREFULLY PLACE 6 OF THE BACON-WRAPPED THIGHS ON THE SKILLET'S SURFACE TO COOK.

5 COOK ABOUT 5 MINUTES PER SIDE OR UNTIL BROWNED.

6 LEAVING THE DRIPPINGS IN THE SKILLET, MOVE THE THIGHS TO A WIRE RACK ATOP A FOIL-LINED BAKING SHEET. REPEAT THE PROCESS TO COOK THE REMAINING CHICKEN.

7 OVEN-ROAST FOR 25 TO 30 MINUTES OR UNTIL THE THIGHS REGISTER 165°F ON A MEAT THERMOMETER. TRANSFER THE THIGHS TO A PLATE, AND TENT WITH FOIL.

8 WHILE THE CHICKEN IS COOKING, MAKE THE SAUCE. LOWER THE HEAT ON THE STOVE TO MEDIUM. ADD THE SHALLOTS TO THE BACON DRIPPINGS IN THE SKILLET. SAUTÉ FOR 2 TO 3 MINUTES OR UNTIL SOFTENED.

9 TOSS IN THE GINGER AND GARLIC. COOK FOR 30 SECONDS OR UNTIL FRAGRANT.

10 POUR IN THE BROTH, AND TOSS IN 3 OF THE SLICED DATES.

11 BRING THE SAUCE TO A BOIL OVER HIGH HEAT. THEN, DECREASE THE HEAT TO MEDIUM-LOW. SIMMER FOR 5 MINUTES OR UNTIL THE SAUCE THICKENS SLIGHTLY AND THE DATES HAVE SOFTENED. SEASON TO TASTE WITH SALT AND PEPPER.

12 TRANSFER THE SAUCE TO A BLENDER OR IMMERSION BLENDER CUP. ADD THE LEMON JUICE AND PURÉE UNTIL SMOOTH. TASTE AND ADJUST THE SAUCE FOR SEASONING.

13 SLICE THE CHICKEN. SERVE WITH THE SAUCE, ITALIAN PARSLEY, AND THE REST OF THE SLICED DATES. LEFTOVERS CAN BE REFRIGERATED FOR UP TO 3 DAYS.

CHINESE CHICKEN IN A POT

MAKES 4 SERVINGS
⏱ 2 HOURS
(30 MINUTES HANDS-ON)

When I lived with my grandmother, she'd occasionally cook a whole chicken in a broth infused with aromatics like green scallions, ginger, and shiitake mushrooms. She didn't cook very often, so whenever she made her perfectly tender, never overcooked chicken, I savored it. Sadly, I didn't get my grandmother's recipe before she passed, but with persistence and some elbow grease, I've managed to replicate and even concentrate the flavors of her chicken dish.

INGREDIENTS:

- 1 **(4-pound) whole chicken, with giblets removed**
- 2 **teaspoons kosher salt**
- ¼ **teaspoon freshly ground black pepper**
- 1 **tablespoon ghee**
- ¼ **pound fresh shiitake mushrooms, stemmed and quartered**
- 3 **scallions, trimmed and cut into 2-inch segment**
- 3 **medium garlic cloves, peeled and trimmed**
- 1 **(1-inch) piece fresh ginger, peeled and cut into ¼-inch coins**
  Juice from 1 lime
- ½ **teaspoon sesame oil**
- ¼ **cup fresh cilantro or sliced scallions**

INSTRUCTIONS:

1. PREHEAT THE OVEN TO 250°F WITH THE RACK IN THE LOWEST POSITION. PAT THE CHICKEN DRY, AND SPRINKLE SALT AND PEPPER ALL OVER THE BIRD, INSIDE AND OUT.

2. HEAT THE GHEE IN A LARGE POT OR DUTCH OVEN OVER MEDIUM HEAT. TOSS IN THE MUSHROOMS AND SCALLIONS, AND COOK FOR 1 TO 2 MINUTES OR UNTIL SOFTENED.

3. ADD THE GARLIC AND GINGER, AND SAUTÉ FOR 30 SECONDS OR UNTIL FRAGRANT. PUSH THE VEGETABLES TO THE SIDES OF THE POT, LEAVING THE MIDDLE CLEAR.

4. TUCK THE CHICKEN'S WINGS BEHIND ITS BACK. CAREFULLY PLACE THE CHICKEN, BREAST-SIDE DOWN, IN THE CENTER OF THE POT AND COOK FOR 5 MINUTES OR UNTIL THE BREAST IS LIGHTLY BROWNED.

5. FLIP THE CHICKEN BREAST-SIDE UP, AND COOK FOR ANOTHER 6 TO 8 MINUTES OR UNTIL THE VEGGIES ARE WELL BROWNED.

6. REMOVE THE POT FROM THE HEAT. PUT A LARGE SHEET OF FOIL OVER THE TOP OF THE POT, COVER WITH THE LID, AND CRIMP THE FOIL UP OVER THE EDGES OF THE LID.

7. BAKE FOR 60 TO 75 MINUTES, OR UNTIL AN INSTANT-READ THERMOMETER REGISTERS 150°F WHEN INSERTED IN THE BREAST AND 165°F IN THE THIGH. LARGER CHICKENS CAN TAKE UP TO 90 MINUTES.

8. TRANSFER THE BIRD TO A PLATE, TENT IT WITH FOIL, AND REST IT FOR 10 MINUTES.

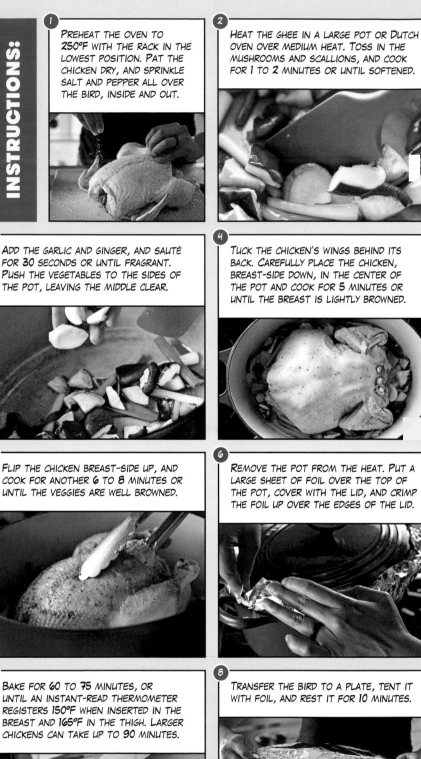

9 MEANWHILE, PICK OUT THE MUSHROOMS FROM THE POT, AND SET THEM ASIDE.

10 PASS THE JUICES FROM THE POT THROUGH A FINE-MESH STRAINER, PRESSING ON THE SOLIDS TO SQUEEZE OUT THE LIQUID.

11 DISCARD THE SOLIDS, AND POUR THE JUS INTO A SAUCEPAN. BRING THE LIQUID TO A SIMMER OVER LOW HEAT.

12 STIR IN THE LIME JUICE AND SESAME OIL.

13 ADD THE RESERVED MUSHROOMS.

14 CARVE UP THE CHICKEN.

15 GARNISH WITH CILANTRO OR SCALLIONS, AND SERVE WITH THE MUSHROOMS AND JUS.

LEFTOVERS CAN BE KEPT IN THE REFRIGERATOR FOR UP TO 3 DAYS.

SWITCH IT UP:
CHINESE CHICKEN IN A SLOW COOKER

YOU CAN ALSO MAKE THIS RECIPE IN A SLOW COOKER! JUST USE A SKILLET TO COOK THE VEGETABLES IN STEPS 2 AND 3, AND ARRANGE THE VEGGIES AROUND THE BREAST-SIDE DOWN CHICKEN IN A SLOW COOKER. COOK FOR 4 TO 6 HOURS ON LOW OR UNTIL THE CHICKEN IS COOKED THROUGH, AND THEN CONTINUE WITH THE RECIPE AT STEP 8.

CHINESE CHICKEN IN A PRESSURE COOKER

MAKES 4 SERVINGS
⏱ 1 HOUR
(30 MINUTES HANDS-ON)

Now that you know how to prepare my Chinese Chicken in the oven and in a slow cooker, I might as well share my pressure cooker instructions for this recipe, too.

Important note: Stick with a chicken that weighs 4 pounds or less, or you'll risk undercooking your bird. Salmonella is not your friend.

INGREDIENTS:

- 2   teaspoons kosher salt
- ¼   teaspoon freshly ground black pepper
- 1   (4-pound) whole chicken, with giblets removed
- 2   tablespoons ghee, divided
- ¼   pound fresh shiitake mushrooms, stemmed and quartered
- 3   scallions, trimmed and cut into 2-inch segments
- 3   medium garlic cloves, peeled and trimmed
- 1   (1-inch) piece fresh ginger, peeled and cut into ¼-inch coins
  Juice from 1 lime
- ½   teaspoon sesame oil
- ¼   cup fresh cilantro or sliced scallions

INSTRUCTIONS:

1 SPRINKLE SALT AND PEPPER ALL OVER THE CHICKEN, BOTH INSIDE AND OUT.

2 TUCK THE WINGS BEHIND THE BACK.

3 ADD 1 TABLESPOON OF THE GHEE TO THE PRESSURE COOKER, AND HIT THE "SAUTÉ" FUNCTION ON YOUR ELECTRIC PRESSURE COOKER. (IF USING A STOVETOP PRESSURE COOKER, COOK OVER MEDIUM-HIGH HEAT.)

4 WHEN THE FAT IS SHIMMERING, TOSS IN THE MUSHROOMS AND SCALLIONS. COOK FOR ABOUT 1 TO 2 MINUTES OR UNTIL THE VEGETABLES HAVE SOFTENED.

5 ADD THE GARLIC AND GINGER, AND SAUTÉ FOR 30 SECONDS OR UNTIL FRAGRANT.

6 PUSH THE VEGETABLES TO THE SIDES OF THE POT, LEAVING THE MIDDLE CLEAR. ADD THE REMAINING TABLESPOON OF GHEE TO THE EXPOSED SURFACE IN THE CENTER.

7 SEAR THE CHICKEN BREAST-SIDE DOWN IN THE CENTER OF THE POT FOR 5 MINUTES OR UNTIL LIGHTLY BROWNED.

8 FLIP THE BIRD (HA HA!) BREAST-SIDE UP. COOK FOR ANOTHER 5 MINUTES OR UNTIL WELL BROWNED. TURN OFF THE SAUTÉ FUNCTION (OR TURN OFF THE STOVE IF YOU'RE USING A STOVETOP COOKER).

9 Transfer the chicken to a plate. Then, pour ½ cup of water into the pot, scraping up any browned bits.

10 Add a steamer insert to the bottom of the pressure cooker, and lay the bird on top of it, breast-side up.

11 Cover and pressure-cook on high for **20** minutes. Then, turn off the electric pressure cooker (or remove the stovetop cooker from the heat), and immediately release the pressure.

12 Open the lid and transfer the chicken to a plate or carving board. Tent it with foil, and rest it for 10 minutes.

13 Pass the juices from the pot through a fine-mesh strainer. Pick out and set aside the mushrooms. Press down on the solids to extract any liquid.

14 Scoop the fat off the top of the sauce. Stir in the lime juice and sesame oil, and adjust the seasoning to taste. Add the reserved mushrooms.

15 Garnish with cilantro or scallions, and serve with the mushrooms and jus. The chicken will keep for up to **3** days in the fridge.

EASY CHICKEN TINGA

MAKES 8 SERVINGS
⏱ **50 MINUTES**
(30 MINUTES HANDS-ON)

Want a simple pantry dinner? My Easy Chicken Tinga recipe calls for chipotle chili powder and canned tomatoes instead of harder-to-find fresh peppers and ripe tomatoes. These kitchen shortcuts make this classic Mexican dish a breeze to make—without compromising any of the authentic flavors. With tender chicken and onions simmered in a lip-tingling chipotle sauce, this one-pot dish packs a spectacularly delicious punch—and can be on the table in less than an hour.

INGREDIENTS:

- **3** pounds boneless, skinless chicken thighs
- **½** teaspoon freshly ground black pepper

  Kosher salt
- **2** tablespoons ghee or lard
- **1** small white onion, finely chopped
- **1** tablespoon tomato paste
- **6** medium garlic cloves, minced
- **2** teaspoons dried oregano (preferably Mexican)
- **2** teaspoons chipotle chili powder
- **2** bay leaves
- **1** (28-ounce) can fire-roasted diced tomatoes, drained
- **2** tablespoons apple cider vinegar
- **2** cups Bone Broth (page 76 or chicken stock

> WANNA GET *FANCY?* GARNISH YOUR CHICKEN TINGA WITH FRESH CILANTRO, FINELY DICED WHITE ONION, THIN SLICES OF RADISH, OR AVOCADO.

> OR JUST DRESS UP LIKE A DRAGON!

1 IN A LARGE BOWL, TOSS THE CHICKEN THIGHS WITH PEPPER AND **2** TEASPOONS OF SALT.

2 MELT THE FAT IN A LARGE POT OVER MEDIUM HEAT. ONCE THE FAT IS SHIMMERING HOT, ADD THE ONIONS, TOMATO PASTE, AND ½ TEASPOON OF SALT. COOK, STIRRING, UNTIL THE ONIONS HAVE SOFTENED.

3 TOSS IN THE GARLIC, OREGANO, CHIPOTLE POWDER, AND BAY LEAVES. STIR FOR ABOUT **30** SECONDS OR UNTIL FRAGRANT.

4 ADD THE DRAINED TOMATOES AND APPLE CIDER VINEGAR, AND POUR IN THE BROTH.

5 STIR WELL TO COMBINE, AND THEN ADD THE CHICKEN. INCREASE THE HEAT TO HIGH, AND BRING EVERYTHING TO A BOIL.

6 LOWER THE HEAT TO A SIMMER. COVER AND COOK FOR **15** TO **20** MINUTES OR UNTIL THE THIGHS ARE COOKED THROUGH.

7 TRANSFER THE COOKED THIGHS TO A PLATE AND SET IT ASIDE. CRANK THE STOVE UP TO HIGH AND BRING THE SAUCE TO A BOIL.

8 WHILE THE SAUCE IS COOKING, SHRED THE CHICKEN THIGHS. (BE CAREFUL: IT'S HOT!)

9 ONCE THE SAUCE REDUCES BY HALF (WHICH TAKES ABOUT **10** MINUTES), TURN OFF THE HEAT, AND FISH OUT THE BAY LEAVES.

10 WITH AN IMMERSION BLENDER, PURÉE THE SAUCE UNTIL SMOOTH. TASTE AND ADJUST WITH SALT AND PEPPER IF NECESSARY.

11 ADD THE CHICKEN BACK INTO THE POT AND STIR TO COMBINE.

12 SERVE THE TINGA IN LETTUCE CUPS OR GRAIN-FREE TORTILLAS (PAGE **78**). IT KEEPS IN THE FRIDGE FOR UP TO **4** DAYS, OR IN THE FREEZER FOR UP TO **6** MONTHS.

DUCK CONFAUX

MAKES 4 SERVINGS
⏱ **1 DAY**
(30 MINUTES HANDS-ON)

The centuries-old French method for preparing duck confit can be daunting: It involves salt-curing duck for a couple of days, and then submerging and slowly poaching the meat in fat. The duck is then packed in fat until it's ready for crisping and eating.

But who has the time and patience for *that*—and who has a quarter-gallon of duck fat sitting around? My version of this classic recipe gets right to the point: meltingly tender duck with crisp, golden skin—all without having to spend a fortune on duck fat or babysit the duck while it's cooking.

INGREDIENTS:

- **4 duck legs, patted dry**
- **1½ teaspoons kosher salt**
- **Zest from 1 orange, peeled with a vegetable peeler**
- **1 teaspoon black peppercorns, roughly crushed**
- **1 teaspoon juniper berries, roughly crushed**
- **4 medium garlic cloves, smashed and peeled**
- **4 fresh thyme sprigs**
- **2 dried bay leaves, torn in half**
- **2 tablespoons duck fat, melted**
- **2 teaspoons duck fat for frying**

INSTRUCTIONS:

1. RUB THE DUCK LEGS WITH SALT, AND ARRANGE THEM IN A SINGLE LAYER ON A PLATTER. TOP EACH LEG WITH ORANGE ZEST, PEPPERCORNS, JUNIPER BERRIES, GARLIC, THYME, AND BAY LEAVES.

2. COVER THE PLATTER WITH PLASTIC WRAP AND REFRIGERATE FOR 12 TO 24 HOURS.

3. WHEN YOU'RE READY TO COOK, POUR THE MELTED FAT INTO THE SLOW COOKER. PLACE THE DUCK SKIN-SIDE DOWN IN A SINGLE LAYER IN THE COOKER, ALONG WITH THE TOPPINGS. (YOU MAY HAVE TO PLAY DUCK LEG TETRIS TO MAKE IT ALL FIT.)

4. COVER THE SLOW COOKER, AND PROGRAM IT TO COOK ON LOW FOR 8 HOURS.

5. TRANSFER THE LEGS TO A PLATE (BUT NOT THE TWIGS AND BERRIES). AT THIS POINT, YOU CAN EITHER FINISH COOKING OR SAVE THE DUCK IN A SEALED CONTAINER FOR LATER. IT CAN BE REFRIGERATED FOR UP TO 4 DAYS OR FROZEN UP TO 6 MONTHS.

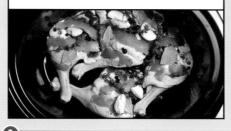

6. HEAT A HEAVY SKILLET ON MEDIUM-HIGH. WHEN THE PAN IS HOT, ADD 2 TEASPOONS OF DUCK FAT. CAREFULLY PLACE 2 LEGS SKIN-SIDE DOWN IN THE SIZZLING FAT.

7. COOK UNDISTURBED (OR YOU'LL RISK TEARING THE SKIN) FOR ABOUT 2 MINUTES OR UNTIL CRISPY AND GOLDEN BROWN. THEN, FLIP THE DUCK LEGS AND COOK ON THE OTHER SIDE FOR ANOTHER 2 MINUTES.

8. TRANSFER THE DUCK LEGS TO A WIRE RACK TO MAKE SURE THE SKIN STAYS CRISPY.

9. REPEAT STEPS 6 THROUGH 8 WITH THE REMAINING DUCK LEGS, AND PLATE 'EM UP.

I SERVED THESE CRISPY DUCK LEGS ON TOP
OF BOWLS OF SAUTÉED BABY SPINACH, BUT
THEY'RE JUST AS TASTY ON SALADS, CAULI
RICE (PAGE 80), SPIRALIZED ZUCCHINI (A.K.A.
ZOODLES), OR ROASTED ROOT VEGETABLES.

SLOW COOKER KABOCHA + GINGER PORK

MAKES 8 SERVINGS
⏱ 10 HOURS
(15 MINUTES HANDS-ON)

This comforting meal of succulent pork and Japanese pumpkin has a prime spot on my list of make-ahead meals. It freezes and re-heats beautifully, and the leftovers taste even better the next day.

INGREDIENTS:

- 1   **tablespoon ghee**
- 3   **pounds boneless pork shoulder, cut into 2-inch cubes**
- 1   **teaspoon kosher salt**
- ½   **teaspoon freshly ground black pepper**
- ¼   **pound shiitake mushrooms, stemmed and cut in half**
- 4   **cups peeled and seeded kabocha squash, cut into 1-inch pieces**

• SAUCE •

- 1   **teaspoon ghee**
- 1   **small shallot, minced (about ¼ cup)**
- 3   **garlic cloves, minced**
- 1   **tablespoon grated ginger**
- ½   **cup fresh orange juice**
- ¼   **cup coconut aminos**
- 2   **tablespoons rice vinegar**
- 1   **teaspoon fish sauce**

• GARNISH •

- 2   **scallions, thinly sliced**

> KABOCHA IS A JAPANESE WINTER SQUASH WITH THE TEXTURE OF ROASTED CHESTNUTS AND THE SWEETNESS OF SWEET POTATOES!

SWITCH IT UP:
PRESSURE COOKER KABOCHA + GINGER PORK

FEELING IMPATIENT? WELL, YOU'RE IN LUCK, PROVIDED YOU HAVE A PRESSURE COOKER. FOLLOW STEPS 1 THROUGH 9 ON THE OPPOSITE PAGE, BUT TOSS THE INGREDIENTS INTO A PRESSURE COOKER INSTEAD. THEN, IN STEP 10, COVER AND COOK THE PORK UNDER HIGH PRESSURE FOR 45 MINUTES.

INSTRUCTIONS:

1 HEAT THE GHEE IN A SKILLET OVER HIGH HEAT. TOSS THE PORK CUBES WITH SALT AND PEPPER, AND SEAR THEM OFF IN BATCHES, BROWNING EACH SIDE FOR 1 TO 2 MINUTES.

2 TRANSFER THE PORK TO A SLOW COOKER.

3 TOSS THE MUSHROOMS INTO THE EMPTY SKILLET, AND LOWER THE HEAT TO MEDIUM-HIGH.

4 COOK, STIRRING, FOR 3 TO 5 MINUTES OR UNTIL THE MOISTURE IS RELEASED.

5 TRANSFER THE MUSHROOMS TO THE SLOW COOKER.

6 ADD THE KABOCHA SQUASH, TOO.

7 TO MAKE THE SAUCE, MELT A TEA-SPOON OF GHEE IN A SMALL SAUCEPAN OVER MEDIUM HEAT. COOK AND STIR THE SHALLOT, GARLIC, AND GINGER UNTIL FRAGRANT, ABOUT 30 SECONDS.

8 POUR IN THE JUICE, COCONUT AMINOS, RICE VINEGAR, AND FISH SAUCE. BRING TO A SIMMER AND REMOVE FROM THE HEAT.

9 POUR THE SAUCE OVER THE MUSHROOMS, KABOCHA, AND PORK IN THE SLOW COOKER.

10 COVER AND COOK ON LOW FOR 8 TO 10 HOURS OR UNTIL TENDER.

11 GARNISH WITH SCALLIONS, AND SERVE. YOU CAN REFRIGERATE EXTRAS FOR UP TO 4 DAYS OR FREEZE FOR UP TO 6 MONTHS.

BACON APPLE SMOTHERED PORK CHOPS

MAKES 4 SERVINGS
🕐 **1 HOUR**
(30 MINUTES HANDS-ON)

This Creole-inspired dish is comfort food at its heartiest: tender, flavorful pork chops covered with a blanket of sautéed onions and a thick layer of savory gravy. The sweetness of the fruit and onions strikes the perfect counterbalance to the smoky richness of the gravy. And let's get real: Nothing goes better with pork chops than apples. An apple a day keeps the doctor away—and it also takes these chops from good to great.

STOP SMOTHERING ME!

INGREDIENTS:

3	slices thick-cut bacon, cut crosswise into ¼-inch slices
2	tablespoons arrowroot powder
1½	cups Bone Broth (page 76) or chicken stock
1	teaspoon fish sauce
5	(¾-inch-thick) bone-in pork chops
	Kosher salt
	Freshly ground black pepper
1	tablespoon ghee
1	large yellow onion, thinly sliced
1	medium apple, peeled, cored, and thinly sliced
2	medium garlic cloves, minced
2	fresh thyme sprigs
¼	cup minced Italian parsley

INSTRUCTIONS:

1 START BY RENDERING THE BACON DRIPPINGS. FRY UP THE BACON IN A SAUCEPAN OVER MEDIUM-LOW HEAT.

2 ONCE THE BACON BITS ARE CRUNCHY, SPOON THEM OUT AND SET THEM ASIDE ON A PAPER TOWEL–LINED DISH TO DRAIN.

3 THERE SHOULD BE ABOUT 2 TABLESPOONS OF DRIPPINGS LEFT IN THE SAUCEPAN. OVER MEDIUM-LOW HEAT, WHISK THE ARROWROOT POWDER INTO THE DRIPPINGS TO FORM A SMOOTH ROUX (WHICH IS JUST A FANCY FRENCH TERM FOR A FLOUR-AND-FAT MIXTURE USED TO THICKEN SAUCES).

4 KEEP WHISKING AS YOU COOK. ONCE THE ROUX TURNS GOLDEN BROWN...

5 ...POUR IN THE BROTH AND FISH SAUCE, AND STIR UNTIL WELL INCORPORATED. CRANK UP THE HEAT TO MEDIUM-HIGH, AND BRING THE SAUCE TO A BOIL.

6 COOK, STIRRING OCCASIONALLY, UNTIL THE GRAVY IS THICKENED (ABOUT 3 MINUTES). TASTE AND ADJUST FOR SEASONING. COVER THE SAUCEPAN AND SET IT ASIDE.

7 TO KEEP THE PORK FROM CURLING UP AT THE SIDES DURING THE COOKING PROCESS, SNIP A SMALL INCISION IN THE BORDER OF FAT AROUND THE OUTSIDE OF THE CHOPS.

8 GENEROUSLY SPRINKLE SALT AND PEPPER ON BOTH SIDES OF THE PORK CHOPS.

9 HEAT THE GHEE IN A LARGE SKILLET OVER MEDIUM-HIGH HEAT. ADD THE CHOPS AND COOK ON EACH SIDE FOR 1 MINUTE OR UNTIL GOLDEN BROWN. COOK IN BATCHES TO AVOID OVERCROWDING THE PORK CHOPS.

10 TRANSFER THE CHOPS TO A PLATE, AND TOSS THE ONIONS, APPLE, AND A SPRINKLE OF SALT INTO THE NOW-EMPTY SKILLET.

11 COOK, STIRRING CONSTANTLY, UNTIL THE ONIONS ARE BROWNED ON THE EDGES, ABOUT 5 MINUTES. SCRAPE UP AS MUCH OF THE BROWNED PORKY BITS ON THE BOTTOM OF THE SKILLET AS POSSIBLE.

12 ADD THE MINCED GARLIC AND SAUTÉ FOR ABOUT 30 SECONDS OR UNTIL FRAGRANT.

13 TRANSFER THE CHOPS (AND ANY JUICES) BACK INTO THE SKILLET. SMOTHER THEM WITH THE COOKED ONIONS AND APPLE.

14 POUR THE RESERVED SAUCE ON THE CHOPS.

15 ADD THE THYME SPRIGS. BRING THE SAUCE TO A BOIL OVER HIGH HEAT. THEN, LOWER THE HEAT TO LOW, AND COVER THE SKILLET. SIMMER FOR ABOUT 30 MINUTES OR UNTIL THE PORK CHOPS ARE FORK-TENDER.

16 DISCARD THE THYME. PLATE THE CHOPS, AND TOP WITH THE GRAVY, RESERVED BACON BITS, AND ITALIAN PARSLEY.

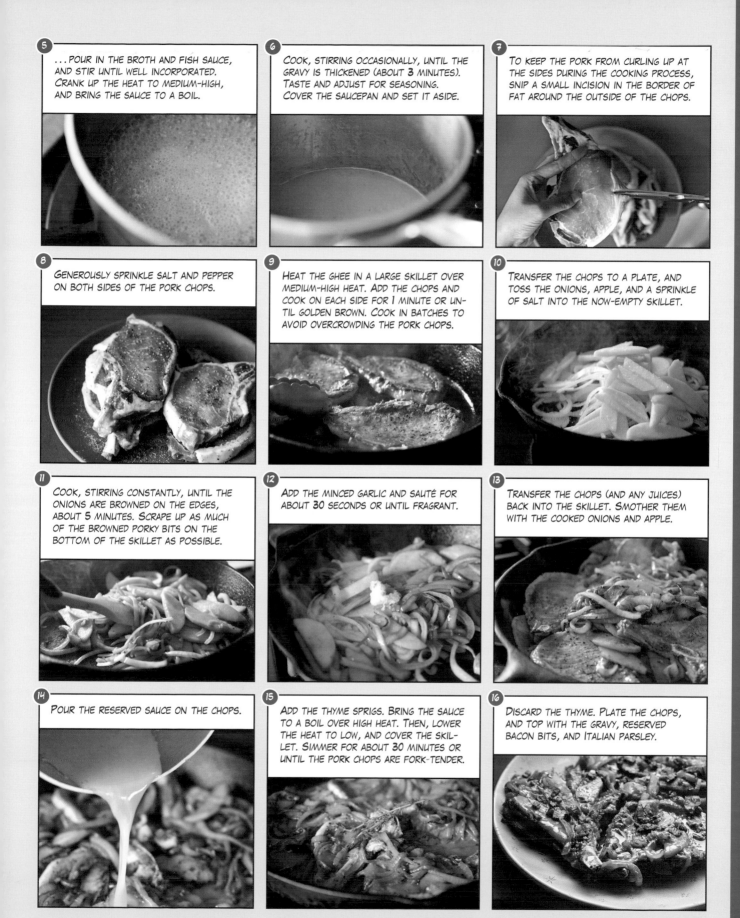

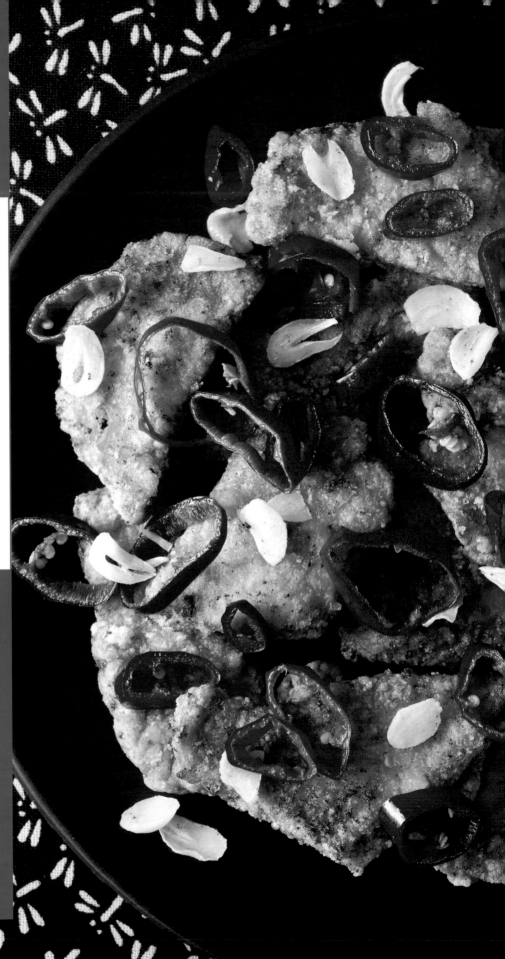

SALT + PEPPER FRIED PORK CHOPS

MAKES 4 SERVINGS
⏱ **1 HOUR**

Tossed in a spicy coating and shallow-fried to golden perfection, thinly sliced salt and pepper pork chops are heaven on a plate. My trick to getting a crisp, light crust on the chops? Instead of the traditional breading of all-purpose flour and cornstarch, I use potato starch.

Yes, I said the "P" word. As I explained way back on page 16, potatoes are real, wholesome root vegetables that fit into my approach to Paleo. Potatoes and potato starch are even approved for the Whole30 dietary reset. If you're still stridently anti-potato, you can use arrowroot powder in this recipe instead, but beware: The crust on the chops won't turn out as crisp. And isn't the whole point of frying pork chops to get that perfectly satisfying crunch?

INGREDIENTS:

8	thin-cut, boneless pork chops (about 1½ pounds)
2½	tablespoons coconut aminos
1½	cups lard, duck fat, ghee, or coconut oil
½	cup potato starch
1	teaspoon kosher salt
¼	teaspoon ground white pepper or freshly ground black pepper
3	garlic cloves, thinly sliced
4	hot peppers, thinly sliced crosswise

1 USING KITCHEN SHEARS OR A KNIFE, TRIM THE FAT FROM THE PORK CHOPS. THEN, CUT EACH CHOP IN HALF.

2 SMASH THE CHOPS WITH A MEAT POUNDER UNTIL THEY'RE EACH ABOUT ¼-INCH THICK.

3 TRANSFER THE PORK TO A MEDIUM BOWL, AND ADD THE COCONUT AMINOS. COAT THE CHOPS WELL, AND LET THEM MARINATE FOR AT LEAST 10 MINUTES OR UP TO 1 DAY.

4 ADD THE COOKING FAT TO A HIGH-SIDED POT OR FRYING PAN. (IT SHOULD REACH ABOUT ½-INCH UP THE SIDES.) COOK OVER MEDIUM HEAT UNTIL THE FAT REACHES 375°F ON A MEAT THERMOMETER.

5 MEANWHILE, MIX TOGETHER THE POTATO STARCH, WHITE PEPPER, AND 1 TEASPOON OF SALT IN A LARGE, SHALLOW BOWL.

6 TOSS A FEW PIECES OF PORK IN THE POTATO STARCH MIXTURE TO COAT, SHAKING OFF ANY EXCESS.

7 WHEN THE OIL IS HOT, CAREFULLY ADD THE POWDER-COATED CHOPS, MAKING SURE NOT TO OVERCROWD THEM. TO MAKE SURE YOUR PORK GETS CRISPY, DON'T COAT EACH CHOP UNTIL IMMEDIATELY BEFORE FRYING.

8 FRY THE CHOPS FOR 2 TO 3 MINUTES ON EACH SIDE OR UNTIL THEY'RE CRISPY, GOLDEN BROWN, AND COOKED THROUGH.

9 GENTLY BLOT THE CHOPS WITH A PAPER TOWEL, AND THEN TRANSFER THEM TO A WIRE RACK. REPEAT STEPS 6 THROUGH 8 TO FRY UP THE REMAINING PORK CHOPS.

10 TURN DOWN THE HEAT TO MEDIUM-LOW, AND ADD THE SLICED GARLIC AND HOT PEPPERS TO THE OIL.

11 FRY FOR 1 MINUTE OR UNTIL THE GARLIC TURNS A LIGHT GOLDEN BROWN AND THE PEPPERS ARE BRIGHTLY COLORED. USE A SLOTTED SPOON TO REMOVE THE FRIED GARLIC AND PEPPERS FROM THE HOT OIL.

12 TOP THE CHOPS WITH THE FRIED GARLIC AND PEPPERS, AND SERVE.

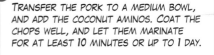

BRAISED PORK IN COCONUT WATER

MAKES 6 SERVINGS
⏱ 2 HOURS
(30 MINUTES HANDS-ON)

Thit kho tàu—caramelized pork belly braised in coconut water—is a Vietnamese dish traditionally served during Tết, the celebration of the Lunar New Year. But why enjoy the rich flavors of this hearty stew just once a year? Here's a stripped-down, weeknight version that you can enjoy all year round.

THIS BRAISED PORK GOES GREAT WITH CAULI RICE (PAGE 80)!

INGREDIENTS:

- 1 tablespoon coconut oil or ghee
- 2 pounds boneless pork shoulder, cut into 2-inch cubes
- 1 teaspoon kosher salt
- ¼ cup thinly sliced shallots
- 3 carrots, peeled and cut into 2-inch pieces
- ¼ pound shiitake mushrooms, stemmed and cut in half (or into quarters if large)
- 3 coin-sized slices peeled fresh ginger
- 4 garlic cloves, smashed and peeled
- 2 cups coconut water
- ¼ cup fish sauce
- ½ cup fresh cilantro leaves
- 3 scallions, thinly sliced

SWITCH IT UP:
SLOW / PRESSURE COOKER PORK IN COCONUT WATER

USING A SLOW COOKER OR A PRESSURE COOKER? DECREASE THE AMOUNT OF COCONUT WATER TO 1 CUP. THEN, EITHER COOK FOR 8 HOURS ON LOW IN A SLOW COOKER, OR FOR 40 MINUTES UNDER HIGH PRESSURE IN A PRESSURE COOKER, RELEASING THE PRESSURE NATURALLY. IF USING A PRESSURE COOKER, DON'T SALT IN STEP 1. WAIT 'TIL THE END.

1. IN A LARGE POT, HEAT THE OIL OVER MEDIUM-HIGH HEAT. TOSS THE PORK WITH SALT.

2. ONCE THE OIL IS SHIMMERING, BROWN A COUPLE OF THE SIDES OF THE PORK CUBES IN THE SKILLET. (DO THIS IN BATCHES.)

3. TRANSFER THE PORK TO A PLATTER AND SET ASIDE.

4. LOWER THE HEAT TO MEDIUM, AND TOSS THE SHALLOTS, CARROTS, AND SHIITAKE MUSHROOMS INTO THE NOW-EMPTY POT.

5. COOK FOR 3 TO 5 MINUTES OR UNTIL THE SHALLOTS HAVE SOFTENED.

6. ADD THE GINGER AND GARLIC, AND TOSS FOR 30 SECONDS OR UNTIL FRAGRANT.

7. RETURN THE PORK TO THE POT ALONG WITH ANY ACCUMULATED JUICES ON THE PLATTER.

8. POUR IN THE COCONUT WATER. (IDEALLY, IT SHOULD REACH ABOUT TWO-THIRDS OF THE WAY UP THE SIDES OF THE PORK CUBES.)

9. ADD THE FISH SAUCE.

10. TURN THE HEAT UP TO HIGH, AND BRING THE CONTENTS OF THE POT TO A BOIL.

11. THEN, LOWER THE HEAT UNTIL JUST HIGH ENOUGH TO MAINTAIN A SIMMER. COVER AND SIMMER UNTIL THE PORK IS TENDER, ABOUT 1½ HOURS. (CHECK PERIODICALLY TO MAKE SURE IT CONTINUES TO SIMMER.)

12. TASTE AND ADD SALT IF NEEDED. THE PORK CAN BE REFRIGERATED FOR UP TO 4 DAYS OR FROZEN FOR UP TO 6 MONTHS. WHEN YOU'RE READY TO REHEAT AND EAT, TOP WITH FRESH CILANTRO AND SCALLIONS.

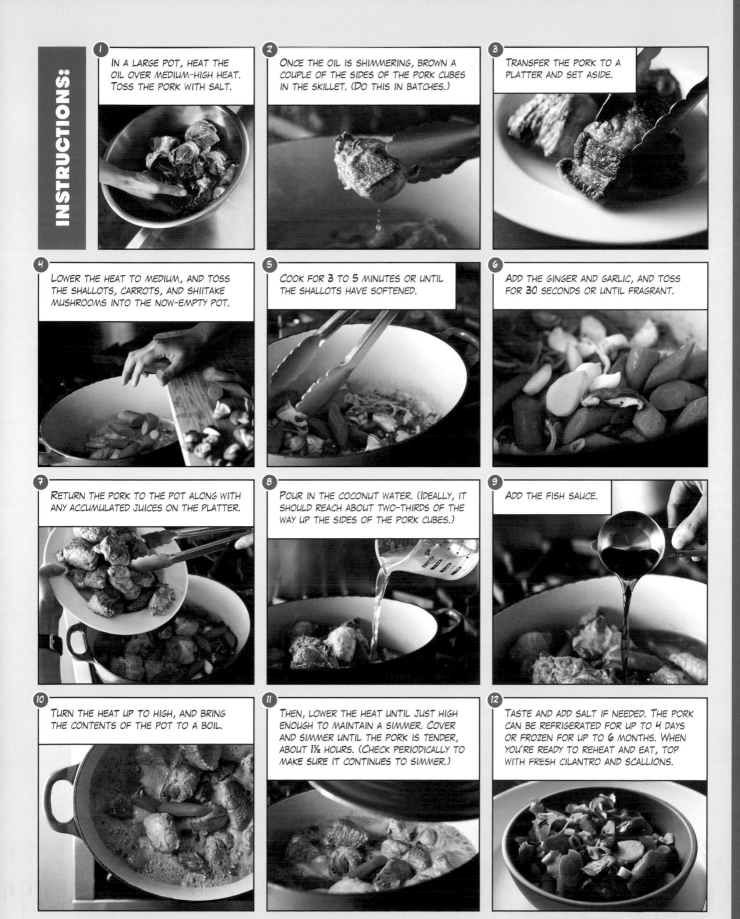

PRESSURE COOKER KALUA PIG

MAKES 8 SERVINGS
⏱ 2 HOURS
(15 MINUTES HANDS-ON)

I've been making kalua pig in a slow cooker for years. The simple, classic Hawaiian flavors of salted, slowly cooked pork never fail to bring me back to my tropical home away from home—but truth be told, the 9-hour cooking time always drove me bonkers. Even the traditional method of cooking kalua pig in a giant hole dug out of the ground takes less time.

Enter the pressure cooker. After a lot of delicious experimentation, I've come up with a kalua pig recipe that takes just a fraction of the time—and tastes even better than my slow cooker version. This method requires a pressure cooker (obviously), so if you don't have one, it's time to invest in this time-saving, life-changing tool.

Always make extra kalua pig—it keeps for up to 4 days in the fridge or up to 6 months in the freezer.

INGREDIENTS:

3   slices thick-cut bacon

1   (5-pound) bone-in pork shoulder roast

5   peeled garlic cloves (optional)

1½   tablespoons coarse Alaea red Hawaiian sea salt (or ¾ tablespoon fine Alaea red Hawaiian sea salt)

1   cabbage, cored, and cut into 6 wedges

SWITCH IT UP:
SLOW COOKER KALUA PIG

NO PRESSURE COOKER? MAKE THIS IN A SLOW COOKER. LINE THE BOTTOM OF YOUR SLOW COOKER WITH 3 SLICES OF BACON, AND THEN FOLLOW STEPS 3 THROUGH 6. DON'T ADD LIQUID. SLOW-COOK ON LOW FOR 8 TO 10 HOURS OR UNTIL THE PORK IS FALL-APART TENDER. THEN, TRANSFER THE MEAT TO A LARGE BOWL AND SHRED IT. TASTE AND ADJUST FOR SEASONING USING THE COOKING LIQUID LEFT IN THE COOKER.

1 LINE THE BOTTOM OF THE PRESSURE COOKER WITH THE THICK-CUT BACON STRIPS.

2 IF YOU'RE USING AN ELECTRIC COOKER, USE THE SAUTÉ FUNCTION TO COOK THE BACON FOR 5 MINUTES, FLIPPING ONCE HALFWAY THROUGH. IF YOU'RE FRYING THE BACON IN A STOVETOP PRESSURE COOKER INSTEAD, COOK THE STRIPS OVER MEDIUM HEAT.

3 IN THE MEANTIME, CUT THE PORK INTO 3 EQUAL PIECES.

4 WITH A SHARP PARING KNIFE, MAKE A FEW SLITS IN EACH PIECE OF PORK, AND TUCK THE GARLIC CLOVES INTO THESE SLITS.

5 SEASON THE PORK WITH ALAEA SALT.

6 ARRANGE THE PORK IN A SINGLE LAYER ON TOP OF THE BACON IN THE COOKER.

7 POUR IN 1 CUP OF WATER.

8 COVER AND COOK UNDER HIGH PRESSURE FOR 90 MINUTES. IF YOU'RE USING A STOVETOP COOKER, COOK ON HIGH HEAT UNTIL HIGH PRESSURE IS REACHED. THEN, LOWER THE HEAT TO MAINTAIN HIGH PRESSURE FOR 75 MINUTES. ONCE IT'S DONE, REMOVE THE COOKER FROM THE HEAT.

9 LET THE PRESSURE RELEASE NATURALLY, WHICH WILL TAKE ABOUT 15 MINUTES. THE MEAT SHOULD BE FALL-APART TENDER, BUT IF NOT, COOK THE PORK UNDER HIGH PRESSURE FOR ANOTHER 5 TO 10 MINUTES.

10 TRANSFER THE COOKED PORK TO A LARGE BOWL. TASTE THE REMAINING LIQUID IN THE POT, AND ADJUST THE SEASONING WITH MORE WATER OR SALT AS NEEDED.

11 ADD THE CABBAGE TO THE LIQUID.

12 COVER AND COOK UNDER HIGH PRESSURE FOR 3 TO 5 MINUTES. THEN, ACTIVATE THE QUICK RELEASE VALVE TO DEPRESSURIZE.

13 SHRED THE PORK, DIVIDE IT INTO SERVING BOWLS, TOP WITH CABBAGE, AND SERVE.

ONE OF THE BEST WAYS TO HEAT UP LEFTOVER KALUA PIG IS TO CRISP IT UP IN A MEDIUM-HOT SKILLET FOR 5 TO 8 MINUTES OR UNTIL GOLDEN BROWN!

PRESSURE COOKER BO SSÄM

MAKES 6 SERVINGS
⏱ **12 HOURS**
(30 MINUTES HANDS-ON)

If you're feeling porky, I've got just the thing. *Bo ssäm* is a traditional Korean dish that'll both impress your guests and stuff you silly.

From the moment David Chang launched Momofuku Ssäm Bar in the East Village, his amazing take on *bo ssäm* captured the hearts of foodies—and for good reason. *Bo ssäm* isn't just a big hunk of cured, spiced, and roasted meat. It's the entire package: slow-cooked meat with a crunchy exterior, spicy sauce, kimchi, pickles, and rice—all wrapped in lettuce leaves. In fact, *bo ssäm* literally means "wrapped" or "packaged." The caramelized crust of the pork shoulder and bright and spicy tang of the condiments are in wonderful balance.

But there's only one Momofuku Ssäm Bar. If you're not in New York City or don't have hundreds of dollars to spend on dinner—or if you're just looking for a Paleo-friendly version of *bo ssäm*—try my shortcut version on for size. By making *bo ssäm* in a pressure cooker, you'll minimize your prep time and still end up with an epic feast that'll make your head spin.

INGREDIENTS:

- 1 (3½-pound) boneless pork shoulder roast, tied with butcher's twine
- 1 tablespoon kosher salt
- 1 tablespoon coconut sugar
- 1 tablespoon ghee or lard
- 3 scallions, trimmed and cut into 3-inch segments
- 6 garlic cloves, peeled
- 1 (1-inch) piece fresh ginger, peeled and cut into ¼-inch coins
- 2 heads butter, green leaf, or romaine lettuce, washed and spun dry, and separated into leaves
- 2 cups Cauli Rice (page 80)
- 1 cup Spicy Kimchi (page 62) and/or Wimpchi (page 62)
- 1 cup Fridge-Pickled Cucumbers (page 74)
- ½ cup Fauxchujang (page 61)

SWITCH IT UP: SLOW COOKER BO SSÄM

TO MAKE THIS IN A SLOW COOKER INSTEAD, SEAR THE ROAST IN A LARGE CAST-IRON SKILLET OVER MEDIUM-HIGH HEAT. THEN, COOK IT IN A SLOW COOKER ON LOW WITH THE SCALLIONS, GINGER, AND GARLIC (NO LIQUID NEEDED!) FOR 9 TO 12 HOURS OR UNTIL THE PORK IS FORK-TENDER. FINALLY, CONTINUE WITH THE RECIPE AT STEP 12.

INSTRUCTIONS:

1 PAT THE PORK ROAST DRY.

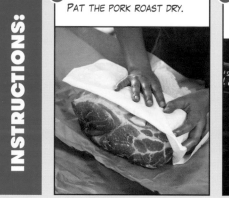

2 MIX TOGETHER THE SALT AND COCONUT SUGAR IN A SMALL BOWL.

3 RUB THE SALT-AND-SUGAR MIXTURE ALL OVER THE PORK SHOULDER. GET IT IN ALL THE NOOKS AND CREVICES.

4 PLOP THE ROAST IN A LARGE BOWL. REFRIGERATE THE MEAT, UNCOVERED, FOR AT LEAST 8 HOURS OR UP TO 3 DAYS.

5 WHEN YOU'RE READY TO COOK, TAKE THE PORK OUT OF THE FRIDGE AND PAT IT DRY.

6 ADD 1 TABLESPOON OF GHEE TO YOUR ELECTRIC PRESSURE COOKER, AND HIT THE "SAUTÉ" FUNCTION. (IF YOU'RE USING A STOVETOP PRESSURE COOKER, COOK THE GHEE OVER MEDIUM-HIGH HEAT.)

7 ONCE THE FAT IS SHIMMERING, SEAR THE ROAST ON 3 SIDES (ABOUT 2 MINUTES UNDISTURBED ON EACH SIDE), LEAVING THE TOP (SKIN- OR FAT-SIDE) UNBROWNED.

8 ADD THE SCALLIONS, GARLIC, GINGER, AND ½ CUP WATER. COVER AND PRESSURE-COOK ON HIGH FOR 2 HOURS. (IF YOU'RE USING A STOVETOP PRESSURE COOKER INSTEAD, ADD 1 CUP WATER, AND COOK UNDER HIGH PRESSURE FOR 1½ HOURS.)

9 THEN, TURN OFF THE ELECTRIC COOKER (OR REMOVE THE STOVETOP COOKER FROM THE HEAT), AND LET THE PRESSURE RELEASE NATURALLY. IF THE PRESSURE STILL HASN'T COME DOWN AFTER 15 MINUTES, MANUALLY RELEASE THE PRESSURE.

10 UNCOVER THE COOKER, AND CHECK THAT THE ROAST IS FORK-TENDER. (IF IT'S NOT, COOK FOR ANOTHER 30 MINUTES UNDER HIGH PRESSURE, AND THEN RELEASE THE PRESSURE ACCORDING TO STEP 9.)

11 TURN ON THE BROILER TO HIGH, AND POSITION THE OVEN RACK IN THE LOWER MIDDLE SPOT. PLACE A WIRE RACK ON TOP OF A FOIL-LINED RIMMED BAKING SHEET.

12 CAREFULLY TAKE THE ROAST OUT OF THE PRESSURE COOKER, REMOVE THE BUTCHER'S TWINE, AND PLACE THE PORK SKIN- OR FAT-SIDE UP ON THE WIRE RACK.

13 POUR OUT THE LIQUID FROM THE COOKER INTO A LARGE CUP...

14 ...AND SKIM OFF THE TOP LAYER OF FAT. AFTERWARDS, YOU SHOULD BE LEFT WITH APPROXIMATELY 2 CUPS OF PORK JUS.

15 BROIL THE ROAST FOR 5 TO 10 MINUTES...

16 ...BASTING THE ROAST PERIODICALLY WITH THE PORK JUS...

17 ...UNTIL NICELY BROWNED. TRANSFER THE PORK ROAST TO A SERVING PLATTER.

18 SHRED THE PORK, AND POUR SOME MORE OF THE JUS ON THE MEAT.

EXTRAS CAN BE REFRIGERATED FOR UP TO 4 DAYS OR FROZEN FOR UP TO 6 MONTHS.

19 SERVE WITH LETTUCE LEAVES, CAULI RICE, KIMCHI, PICKLES, AND FAUXCHUJANG.

20 TO EAT, PILE SOME SHREDDED PORK, CAULI RICE, KIMCHI, AND PICKLES ON A LETTUCE LEAF. SPOON SOME FAUXCHUJANG ON TOP, WRAP IT ALL UP, AND CHOW DOWN.

SOUVLAKI

MAKES 8 SKEWERS
⏱ **1 HOUR**

Souvlaki—which literally translates to "little skewer"—is classic Greek fast food at its best. For thousands of years, these marinated, flame-kissed meat kababs have been the highlight of impromptu summer barbecues. But to be honest, even gloomy weather won't stop me from making souvlaki. I just pull out my trusty grill pan!

Souvlaki's usually made with pork, but it's fantastic with lamb and chicken, too. Some recipes call for tons of herbs and spices in the marinade, but I prefer to keep the flavors clean and uncluttered. With the sweetness of charred red onions and the refreshing zing of lemon, these portable meat sticks will never disappoint.

INGREDIENTS:

½ cup fresh lemon juice

¾ cup extra-virgin olive oil

4 garlic cloves, minced

1 tablespoon dried oregano or dried marjoram

2 teaspoons kosher salt

½ teaspoon freshly ground black pepper

3 pounds boneless pork loin or shoulder roast, leg of lamb, or skinless chicken thighs, cut into 1½-inch cubes

1 medium red onion, cut into 1½-inch cubes

Ghee or fat of choice (for greasing the grill)

2 lemons, cut into quarters

INSTRUCTIONS:

1 In a large bowl, whisk together the lemon juice, olive oil, garlic, oregano, salt, and pepper.

2 Add the meat and coat well. Cover and marinate in the fridge for at least 20 minutes or up to 12 hours.

3 Heat your grill pan or outdoor grill to medium. In the meantime, evenly divide the meat among 8 skewers, with the onions threaded between each chunk of meat.

4 Brush some melted fat on the grill grates, and then put the skewers on.

5 Cook the skewers for 3 to 5 minutes on each of the 4 sides or until the onions are softened and meat is cooked to the desired doneness.

6 SERVE WITH LEMON WEDGES. LEFTOVERS CAN BE REFRIGERATED FOR UP TO 4 DAYS OR FROZEN FOR UP TO 3 MONTHS.

IS THERE ANYTHING MORE PALEO THAN GRILLED MEAT ON A STICK?

WHAT ABOUT PALEO DONUTS?

BANGIN' BABY BACK RIBS

MAKES 4 SERVINGS
⏱ 8 HOURS
(30 MINUTES HANDS-ON)

Why are these ribs so bangin'?

To begin with, baby back ribs are shorter and meatier than side ribs, making them a bit quicker to cook and tastier to eat. Each bite yields a fiery punch, and the sticky-sweet sauce will have you coming back for seconds and thirds. You don't even need to bust out your backyard grill or smoker for this recipe—an oven is all you need.

Making ribs ahead of time? You can season these baby back ribs for up to 3 days in advance. Once they're cooked, you can refrigerate them for up to 4 more days. My Chinese-style barbecue sauce can be made up to 1 week ahead, too. When you're ready to eat, reheat the ribs in a 300°F oven for 20 minutes before brushing on the sauce and broiling to finish.

To stay Paleo-friendly, make sure you use jam that's sweetened with just fruit juice—not refined sugar or chemical preservatives.

RIBS CAN BE KEPT IN A SEALED CONTAINER IN THE REFRIGERATOR FOR UP TO 4 DAYS OR IN THE FREEZER FOR UP TO 4 MONTHS.

INGREDIENTS:

• DRY RUB •

1½ tablespoons kosher salt

1 teaspoon onion powder

1 teaspoon garlic powder

1 teaspoon paprika

½ teaspoon freshly ground black pepper

• RIBS •

2 racks pork back ribs (approximately 2½ pounds per rack)

• BARBECUE SAUCE •

½ cup apricot jam (sweetened with just fruit juice)

2 tablespoons coconut aminos

¼ cup Nom Nom Sriracha (page 56), store-bought sriracha, or Fauxchujang (page 61)

2 tablespoons tomato paste

1 teaspoon minced fresh ginger

IF YOU HAVE A LITTLE BROTHER WHO CAN'T STAND THE HEAT, JUST USE A SINGLE TABLESPOON OF SRIRACHA!

INSTRUCTIONS:

1 IN A SMALL BOWL, COMBINE THE DRY RUB INGREDIENTS AND MIX WELL.

2 PAT THE PORK RIBS DRY WITH A PAPER TOWEL.

3 IF YOUR BUTCHER DIDN'T REMOVE THE SILVERSKIN ON THE BONE SIDE OF THE RIBS, PULL THIS THIN MEMBRANE OFF WITH YOUR HANDS OR WITH A PAPER TOWEL.

4 SPRINKLE THE DRY RUB ALL OVER BOTH RIB RACKS, AND RUB IT IN WITH YOUR HANDS.

5 PLACE THE SEASONED RACKS ON A RIMMED BAKING SHEET, AND COVER THEM LOOSELY WITH PLASTIC WRAP.

6 REFRIGERATE FOR AT LEAST **2** HOURS OR UP TO **24** HOURS.

7 WHEN YOU'RE READY TO COOK THE RIBS, PREHEAT THE OVEN TO **300°F** WITH THE RACK PLACED IN THE MIDDLE POSITION.

8 TAKE THE RIBS OUT OF THE FRIDGE, AND PAT THEM DRY WITH PAPER TOWELS. WRAP EACH RACK IN FOIL OR PARCHMENT PAPER.

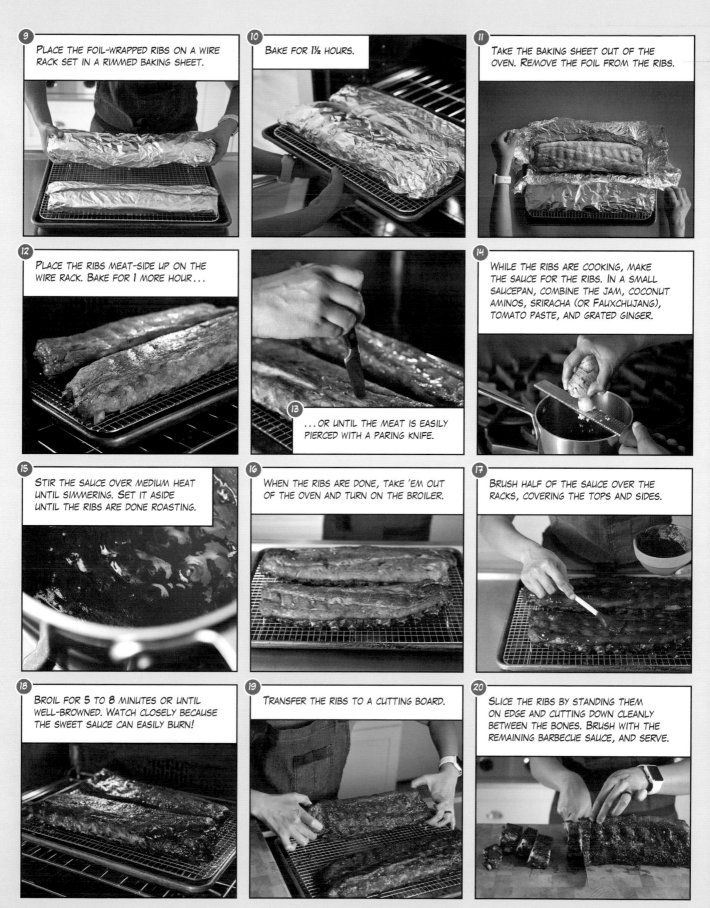

9 PLACE THE FOIL-WRAPPED RIBS ON A WIRE RACK SET IN A RIMMED BAKING SHEET.

10 BAKE FOR 1½ HOURS.

11 TAKE THE BAKING SHEET OUT OF THE OVEN. REMOVE THE FOIL FROM THE RIBS.

12 PLACE THE RIBS MEAT-SIDE UP ON THE WIRE RACK. BAKE FOR 1 MORE HOUR...

13 ...OR UNTIL THE MEAT IS EASILY PIERCED WITH A PARING KNIFE.

14 WHILE THE RIBS ARE COOKING, MAKE THE SAUCE FOR THE RIBS. IN A SMALL SAUCEPAN, COMBINE THE JAM, COCONUT AMINOS, SRIRACHA (OR FAUXCHUJANG), TOMATO PASTE, AND GRATED GINGER.

15 STIR THE SAUCE OVER MEDIUM HEAT UNTIL SIMMERING. SET IT ASIDE UNTIL THE RIBS ARE DONE ROASTING.

16 WHEN THE RIBS ARE DONE, TAKE 'EM OUT OF THE OVEN AND TURN ON THE BROILER.

17 BRUSH HALF OF THE SAUCE OVER THE RACKS, COVERING THE TOPS AND SIDES.

18 BROIL FOR 5 TO 8 MINUTES OR UNTIL WELL-BROWNED. WATCH CLOSELY BECAUSE THE SWEET SAUCE CAN EASILY BURN!

19 TRANSFER THE RIBS TO A CUTTING BOARD.

20 SLICE THE RIBS BY STANDING THEM ON EDGE AND CUTTING DOWN CLEANLY BETWEEN THE BONES. BRUSH WITH THE REMAINING BARBECUE SAUCE, AND SERVE.

PRESSURE COOKER CARNE MECHADA

MAKES 6 SERVINGS
⏱ **1 HOUR**
(15 MINUTES HANDS-ON)

Like *ropa vieja* ("old clothes"), a dish named for its resemblance to a mess of colorful rags, this Latin American stew of boiled and shredded flank steak usually takes hours to prepare. But patience isn't one of my virtues, so I made a pressure cooker version that cuts the cooking time in half—but tastes just as fabulous.

INGREDIENTS:

- 3 pounds flank steak, cut against the grain into 2-inch strips
- 1½ tablespoons chili powder

  Kosher salt
- 1 tablespoon ghee
- 1 medium yellow onion, diced
- 2 medium carrots, diced
- 1 red bell pepper, diced
- 2 tablespoons tomato paste
- 6 garlic cloves, peeled and smashed
- 1 (14-ounce) can diced roasted tomatoes, drained
- ½ cup Bone Broth (page 76) or chicken stock
- 2 teaspoons fish sauce
- 2 teaspoons dried oregano
- 2 dried bay leaves

  Freshly ground black pepper
- ½ cup fresh cilantro leaves

🔄 SWITCH IT UP: **SLOW COOKER CARNE MECHADA**

NO PRESSURE COOKER? USE A SKILLET FOR STEPS 2 THROUGH 4, AND THEN COOK THIS IN A SLOW COOKER SET ON LOW FOR 8 HOURS.

1. IN A LARGE BOWL, TOSS THE BEEF WITH CHILI POWDER AND **2** TEASPOONS OF SALT. MIX WITH YOUR HANDS TO INCORPORATE. SET ASIDE.

2. HEAT THE GHEE IN A PRESSURE COOKER. (DO IT OVER MEDIUM-HIGH HEAT IF YOU'RE USING A STOVETOP COOKER.) ADD THE ONIONS, CARROTS, BELL PEPPERS, AND A SPRINKLE OF SALT. SAUTÉ THE VEGGIES FOR **3** TO **5** MINUTES OR UNTIL SOFTENED.

3. ADD THE TOMATO PASTE AND GARLIC. STIR FOR **30** SECONDS OR UNTIL FRAGRANT.

4. POUR IN THE CANNED TOMATOES, STOCK, AND FISH SAUCE. STIR IN THE DRIED OREGANO AND BAY LEAVES.

5. ADD THE BEEF.

6. STIR TO MIX WELL.

7. COVER AND COOK UNDER HIGH PRESSURE FOR **20** MINUTES. (IF USING A STOVETOP COOKER, COOK ON HIGH HEAT UNTIL YOU REACH HIGH PRESSURE. THEN, TURN DOWN THE STOVE TO LOW TO MAINTAIN HIGH PRESSURE FOR ABOUT **18** MINUTES.)

8. WHEN THE STEW'S DONE, LET THE PRESSURE RELEASE NATURALLY (WHICH TAKES ABOUT **15** MINUTES). REMOVE THE LID, AND TRANSFER THE BEEF TO A SERVING BOWL.

9. SHRED THE MEAT WITH TWO FORKS.

10. BRING THE SAUCE TO A BOIL IN THE PRESSURE COOKER, AND SKIM OFF ANY EXCESS OIL. TASTE THE SAUCE IN THE POT, AND SEASON TO TASTE WITH SALT AND PEPPER.

11. REMOVE AND DISCARD THE BAY LEAVES. LADLE THE SAUCE ON TOP OF THE MEAT.

12. GARNISH WITH CILANTRO AND SERVE. (OR REFRIGERATE THE BEEF FOR UP TO **4** DAYS OR FREEZE IT FOR UP TO **4** MONTHS.)

TEX-MEX BEEF AND RICE CASSEROLE

MAKES 4 SERVINGS
⏱ **1 HOUR**
(30 MINUTES HANDS-ON)

You're gonna get a big, spicy kick out of this beefy, one-skillet casserole. Eat it now, or slice it up and toss it in the fridge for the coming week's pack-and-go lunches.

INGREDIENTS:

1	pound riced cauliflower
1	pound ground beef
1	small yellow onion, diced
1	red bell pepper, diced
3	garlic cloves, minced
1½	cups store-bought roasted tomato salsa or Salsa Ahumada (page 72)
1	teaspoon dried oregano
1	tablespoon chili powder
	Kosher salt
	Freshly ground black pepper
4	large eggs, whisked
6	cherry tomatoes, cut in half
1	jalapeño or serrano pepper, thinly sliced crosswise (optional)
¼	cup fresh cilantro, lightly packed

NOT A FAN OF FIERY FOODS? DE-SEED THE JALAPEÑO OR SERRANO PEPPER BEFORE YOU USE IT IN STEP 8, OR JUST LEAVE IT OUT. ON THE OTHER HAND, IF YOU WANT TO CRANK UP THE HEAT EVEN MORE, USE A HABANERO OR GHOST PEPPER INSTEAD.

INSTRUCTIONS:

1 GOT RICED CAULIFLOWER? IF NOT, CUT UP A SMALL CAULIFLOWER INTO UNIFORM-SIZE PIECES, AND PULSE 'EM IN A FOOD PROCESSOR UNTIL THE SIZE OF RICE GRAINS.

2 PREHEAT THE OVEN TO 350°F WITH THE RACK IN THE MIDDLE. HEAT A LARGE, OVEN-PROOF SKILLET OVER MEDIUM-HIGH HEAT. ADD THE BEEF WHEN THE PAN IS HOT.

3 BREAK UP THE MEAT WITH A SPATULA. COOK, STIRRING, FOR 5 TO 7 MINUTES OR UNTIL IT'S NO LONGER PINK.

4 ADD THE ONION AND BELL PEPPER. COOK FOR 5 MINUTES UNTIL SOFTENED.

5 ADD THE RICED CAULIFLOWER AND STIR TO COMBINE. STIR IN THE MINCED GARLIC AND COOK FOR 1 MINUTE OR UNTIL FRAGRANT.

6 POUR IN THE SALSA, AND ADD THE OREGANO AND CHILI POWDER. SEASON TO TASTE WITH SALT AND PEPPER.

7 REMOVE THE SKILLET FROM THE HEAT, AND POUR IN THE WHISKED EGGS. GENTLY STIR TO INCORPORATE, AND SMOOTH THE TOP OF THE CASSEROLE WITH A SPATULA.

8 TOP WITH THE SLICED TOMATOES (CUT-SIDE UP) AND HOT PEPPER, IF USING. PUT THE SKILLET IN THE OVEN.

9 COOK FOR 40 TO 45 MINUTES OR UNTIL THE EGGS ARE SET AND BROWNED ON THE EDGES. REST FOR 5 MINUTES, AND TOP WITH CILANTRO. SLICE AND SERVE.

EXTRAS CAN BE REFRIGERATED FOR UP TO 4 DAYS OR FROZEN FOR UP TO 4 MONTHS.

PRIMETIME RIB ROAST

MAKES 10 SERVINGS
🕐 **1 DAY**
(30 MINUTES HANDS-ON)

Prime rib is pricey, so you don't want to mess it up—especially if you're trying to dazzle your boss, your neighbors, or your in-laws. So when the occasion calls for it, use this simple recipe for perfect prime rib. A mash-up of techniques from J. Kenji López-Alt and the nerds at *Cook's Illustrated*—two of my favorite and most trusted cooking resources—this method produces perfectly cooked prime rib every single time, and requires very little hands-on work. Even if you have no special guests to impress, this totally butt-kicking prime rib roast will have you patting your own back (and your satisfied belly, too).

INGREDIENTS:

1   (9-pound) prime rib roast
    Kosher salt
    Freshly ground black pepper

> TECHNICALLY, PRIME RIB'S A **ROAST**, NOT A STEAK. BUT IF YOU SLICE IT INTO INDIVIDUAL RIBS BEFORE COOKING, THEY BECOME **RIB EYE STEAKS!**

INSTRUCTIONS:

1 USING A SHARP KNIFE, CUT THE BONES OFF THE RIB ROAST. (BETTER YET, HAVE YOUR BUTCHER DO THIS FOR YOU.) SET THE BONES ASIDE.

2 IN A SMALL BOWL, MEASURE OUT ABOUT ¾ TEASPOON KOSHER SALT PER POUND OF MEAT. MIX IN FRESHLY CRACKED PEPPER.

3 USE THE SALT AND PEPPER MIXTURE TO SEASON ALL SIDES OF THE NOW-BONELESS ROAST.

4 PLACE THE ROAST BACK ON TOP OF THE RIBS. THIS WILL HELP THE ROAST COOK MORE EVENLY, AND YOU WON'T HAVE TO CARVE THE MEAT OFF THE BONES LATER.

5 THE ROAST SHOULD REST ON THE RIBS THE SAME WAY AS BEFORE. THE CUT SIDE OF THE ROAST SHOULD BE DOWN, WITH THE FAT CAP FACING UP.

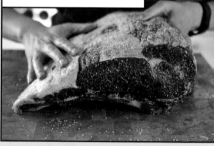

6 SECURE THE ROAST TO THE BONES WITH KITCHEN TWINE, AND PLACE IT ON A TRAY.

7 LEAVE THE ROAST UNCOVERED IN THE REFRIGERATOR FOR AT LEAST 1 DAY OR UP TO 4 DAYS. THE PRE-SALTING AND AIR-DRYING WILL ENSURE A DELICIOUS ROAST WITH A BROWNED, BEEFY CRUST.

8 Take the roast out of the fridge at least 3 hours before you plan to cook. About 15 minutes before cooking, set the oven to 250°F with the rack in the lower middle position.

9 Place the roast on a roasting rack in a roasting tray. (Yes, I just used the word "roast" 3 times in a sentence.)

10 Cook for 4 to 5 hours in the oven until the meat's internal temperature registers 125 to 130°F for medium rare, or 135 to 140°F for medium.

11 Take out the roast, and tent it with foil. Preheat the oven to its highest temperature (500 to 550°F). Use convection mode if your oven has it.

12 When you're ready to eat, remove the foil from the roast, and put it back in the oven. Cook for 8 to 10 minutes or until the meat's surface is crisp and well-browned (but not burnt).

13 Take the roast out of the oven. Snip off the twine, and lift the roast off the bones.

14 Place the roast on a cutting board, and carve the meat into slices.

15 Serve with Umami Gravy (page 69) if you have it. Keep leftovers in the fridge for up to 4 days or freeze 'em for up to 3 months.

SUNDAY GRAVY

MAKES 10 SERVINGS
⏱ 5 HOURS
(45 MINUTES HANDS-ON)

If I were your *nonna*, I'd feed you this meaty Italian-American classic every Sunday night. But I'm not, so you'll have to make it yourself.

INGREDIENTS:

1   tablespoon extra-virgin olive oil

1   pound sweet and/or hot Italian sausage

1   small yellow onion, diced

2   medium carrots, diced

2   celery stalks, diced

     Kosher salt

6   garlic cloves, minced

¼   cup tomato paste

1   cup Bone Broth (page 76) or chicken stock

3   (28-ounce) cans whole San Marzano tomatoes

1   (1½-pound) flank steak, cut in half crosswise

2   pounds boneless pork country-style ribs from the shoulder

2   dried bay leaves

1   teaspoon dried oregano

¼   teaspoon freshly ground black pepper

¼   teaspoon red pepper flakes

½   cup chopped fresh basil

¼   cup chopped fresh Italian parsley

INSTRUCTIONS:

1 PREHEAT THE OVEN TO 300°F WITH THE RACK IN THE LOWER MIDDLE POSITION. HEAT THE OLIVE OIL IN AN 8-QUART HEAVY-BOTTOMED POT OVER MEDIUM HEAT.

2 ONCE THE OIL IS HOT, BROWN THE SAUSAGES IN THE POT, ABOUT 5 MINUTES PER SIDE. TRANSFER THEM TO A PLATTER.

3 TOSS THE ONIONS, CARROTS, AND CELERY INTO THE EMPTY POT, AND ADD A SPRINKLE OF SALT. SAUTÉ FOR 10 TO 12 MINUTES OR UNTIL SOFTENED. ADD THE GARLIC. STIR FOR 30 SECONDS OR UNTIL FRAGRANT.

4 ADD THE TOMATO PASTE. STIR FOR 2 TO 3 MINUTES UNTIL THE COLOR DEEPENS.

5 ADD THE BROTH, AND SCRAPE UP THE TASTY BROWNED BITS AT THE BOTTOM.

6 POUR THE CANNED TOMATOES INTO A LARGE MIXING BOWL. CRUSH THEM WITH YOUR FINGERS OR PURÉE WITH AN IMMERSION BLENDER, AND ADD 'EM TO THE POT.

7 NESTLE THE SAUSAGES, FLANK STEAK, AND COUNTRY-STYLE RIBS INTO THE SAUCE.

8 ADD THE BAY LEAVES, 1½ TEASPOONS SALT, OREGANO, PEPPER, AND RED PEPPER FLAKES. CRANK UP THE HEAT TO HIGH, AND BRING EVERYTHING TO A BOIL.

(BONUS: FOR EXTRA UMAMI, ADD 1 OUNCE OF DRIED PORCINI MUSHROOMS, TOO.)

9 CAREFULLY TRANSFER THE POT TO THE OVEN. PLACE THE LID ON THE POT AT A SLIGHT ANGLE, LEAVING A 1-INCH VENT.

10 COOK FOR 3 TO 4 HOURS IN THE OVEN OR UNTIL THE MEAT IS FORK-TENDER AND THE SAUCE HAS REDUCED BY ABOUT A QUARTER.

11 DISCARD THE BAY LEAVES. TRANSFER THE MEAT FROM THE POT TO A LARGE BOWL, AND CUT THE SAUSAGE LINKS INTO THIRDS.

12 BREAK UP THE RIB MEAT WITH 2 FORKS. DISCARD ANY GRISTLE AND EXCESS FAT.

13 CUT THE FLANK STEAK PIECES IN HALF CROSSWISE, AND THEN SHRED THEM, TOO. DISCARD ANY TENDONS OR GRISTLE.

14 IF DESIRED, SKIM THE EXCESS FAT FROM THE SURFACE OF THE SAUCE. THEN, PUT THE SHREDDED MEAT BACK IN THE POT, AND STIR TO INCORPORATE. ADJUST THE SEASONING OF THE SAUCE TO YOUR TASTE.

15 TOSS IN THE FRESH BASIL AND PARSLEY, AND SERVE. LEFTOVERS WILL KEEP IN A COVERED CONTAINER IN THE FRIDGE FOR UP TO 4 DAYS OR IN THE FREEZER FOR UP TO 6 MONTHS. IF YOU'RE GOING TO FREEZE THE LEFTOVERS, PORTION IT OUT INTO SMALLER CONTAINERS SO YOUR FUTURE SELF WON'T HAVE TO THAW A GIANT BLOCK OF SUNDAY GRAVY WHEN YOU FEEL LIKE MAKING MONDAY FRITTATA (PAGE 218) OR STUFFED SUNDAY PEPPERS (PAGE 217).

SWITCH IT UP: PRESSURE COOKER / SLOW COOKER SUNDAY GRAVY

TO MAKE SUNDAY GRAVY IN A PRESSURE COOKER OR A SLOW COOKER, YOU'LL NEED LESS LIQUID, SO ADD JUST ½ CUP OF BROTH IN STEP 5. ALSO, IN STEP 6, DRAIN THE CANNED TOMATOES BEFORE SMUSHING OR PURÉEING THEM. INSTEAD OF POPPING EVERYTHING IN THE OVEN, COOK THE SUNDAY GRAVY IN A PRESSURE COOKER UNDER HIGH PRESSURE FOR 50 MINUTES, OR IN A SLOW COOKER SET ON LOW FOR 8 TO 10 HOURS. THEN, CONTINUE WITH THE RECIPE AT STEP 11.

Sunday Gravy is traditionally served on a heaping bowl of pasta, but in case you forgot, this is a Paleo cookbook. Toss raw spiralized zucchini noodles (a.k.a. zoodles) with hot Sunday Gravy, allotting 1 medium zucchini per person. There's no need to cook the zoodles because they'll soften in the warm sauce without getting overly watery and soggy. Top with fresh herbs, and serve.

READY FOR SOMETHING SWEET?

MICHELLE: Ah, desserts. Is there anything more controversial than desserts in the world of Paleo?

HENRY: It sometimes seems like *everything* about Paleo is controversial—but desserts are definitely a source of a lot of debate in caveman circles. On one end of the spectrum, there are Paleo eaters who firmly believe that because refined sugar is addictive, promotes obesity, and is bad for metabolic health, desserts are the devil: They're an evil temptation.

MICHELLE: On the opposite end of the spectrum, there are those who think that as long as you make desserts out of Paleo-friendly ingredients, you can keep scarfing down sweets just like before.

HENRY: And not just desserts, but other treats as well, like Paleo pancakes, Paleo breads, and Paleo breakfast muffins.

MICHELLE: I think we can safely toss Paleo breakfast pastries into the dessert category, because pastries are just desserts you eat when you wake up.

HENRY: Wouldn't you say, though, that most Paleo eaters are somewhere in the middle of the spectrum we just described?

MICHELLE: Sure. First of all, I think it's pretty extreme to never consume anything sweet. In fact, it's almost impossible for anyone to completely avoid eating anything sweet—even for people who don't really have much of a sweet tooth.

HENRY: Like me and Owen.

OWEN: Yeah. I don't even like desserts. When you guys order dessert at restaurants, I usually don't get anything, because I just want some watermelon when I get home.

MICHELLE: Yes—but even fruit is sweet. All humans are wired biologically to prefer calorie-rich sweet foods, but scientists have found that this is especially true in growing kids like you, Owen. So even if you're not a big fan of ice cream or cake, humans in general are predisposed to liking sweet things.

OLLIE: I love sweet things. I *only* love sweet things.

MICHELLE: I know exactly how you feel, Ollie. I felt the same way growing up.

HENRY: Yeah—as we were writing our first cookbook, I went through all your childhood photo albums, and found that just about *every single photograph* taken of you as a child shows you staring intently at birthday cakes. Other people in the photos are smiling and looking at the camera, but not you. Your gaze was locked on the cake, like you were going to devour it with your eyeballs.

MY SISTER MINI-ME

MICHELLE: True, but let's not get too carried away. We're talking about the 1970s, before the modern age of digital cameras, so my parents tended to take photographs only on special occasions like birthdays. And what else was I supposed to look at when there's a big frosting-covered birthday cake sitting right in front of me? Besides, as I just pointed out, kids have a biological preference for sweets.

HENRY: Yeah, but you didn't just *prefer* sweets. You have to admit you went a little overboard.

MICHELLE: Are you referring to the fact that I used to sneak little sandwich bags filled with sugar-packed, powdery drink mix into bed so that I could lick my fingers, dip them into the bag of sugar powder, and

then stick my fingers in my mouth as I drifted off to sleep? Or are you talking about the fact that my favorite birthday present of all time was a huge bag of Japanese candy that was the size of my head?

HENRY: Both, probably. I'm amazed you never got any cavities while growing up.

MICHELLE: Anyway, my point is that people are hard-wired to love sweets, so it's unreasonable to expect that Paleo eaters will completely avoid sugar forever unless there's a medical reason to do so. Very few people can go cold turkey for a sustainable period of time. That's probably one of the reasons why folks who embark on nutritional resets to temporarily eliminate all gluten, dairy, soy, and sugar from their diets don't remain that strict indefinitely. It's not impossible, but it's certainly not easy. And for most people, it's not necessary, either.

HENRY: What about the other end of the spectrum? What about those who think that "anything goes" as long as desserts are made from Paleo ingredients?

MICHELLE: That's pretty extreme, too. I mean, I get that for a lot of people who are accustomed to eating highly processed desserts made with unhealthy, low quality ingredients, replacing the worst components in these treats is clearly a better choice. For people with gluten issues like me, replacing the flour in cookies with gluten-free or grain-free substitutes will make them feel better. So I don't mean to say that grain-free desserts aren't helpful.

HENRY: But helpful isn't the same as healthful.

MICHELLE: Right. Paleo-izing desserts might be a step in the right direction, but they're not going to get you to your intended destination.

HENRY: I think it's pretty much a given that eating massive quantities of desserts isn't on the roadmap to a healthy lifestyle.

MICHELLE: Which is why it's frustrating sometimes when I see people assuming that it's fine to regularly eat sweet Paleo treats. I'm not saying that there isn't a place for Paleo dessert recipes, but I worry that some folks have lost sight of the fact that dessert is meant to be a special-occasion food, and not an everyday food. Sure, I was staring at cakes in all my childhood photos, but it wasn't every day that my mom would bust out a cake. It was only for birthdays, and our entire family probably celebrated fewer than a dozen birthdays a year, which meant an average of one slice of cake per month. But these days, you can have cake pretty much every single day, in the form of cupcakes and muffins. Cake isn't a once-in-a-while food anymore.

HENRY: Part of it has to do with the way we now associate treats with not just celebrations, but with day-to-day expressions of love and affection. Do you remember those old PSAs that would come on during the commercial breaks when you watched cartoons as a kid?

MICHELLE: Not really. I didn't watch a lot of cartoons. I preferred daytime soap operas and talk shows.

HENRY: Well, anyway, there were a lot of PSAs that told kids how to eat. Not all of them were good. But I remember a PSA that wasn't actually targeted at children at all—it was directed at adults who were feeding their kids. This particular PSA pointed out that a lot of grown-ups think that a great way to show affection for their children is to hand them sweets.

MICHELLE: That's 'cause it works. When I was a kid, if someone gave me candy, they were guaranteed a checkmark in the awesome column.

HENRY: It's a good thing no stranger ever offered you candy, then.

MICHELLE: Yeah. I totally dodged a bullet there.

HENRY: This particular PSA reminded people that there are tons of ways to show your love for your kids. You can play with them, hug them, or frankly, just tell them how much you love them. You don't actually have to ply them with sugar.

MICHELLE: But as a parent, it's an incredibly easy trap to fall into. When Ollie gets hurt at school and asks for something sweet to make him feel better, I know it's not actually going to physically heal him, but I also know that giving him a treat feels special.

HENRY: And it's not like I think parents should never give treats to their kids. *We* certainly do it. It's just that it's a good reminder that there are other ways to express love—including just spending time with your kids. Sugar isn't a substitute.

MICHELLE: I should emphasize that occasional treats aren't the problem—as long as they're occasional. That means dessert shouldn't automatically follow dinner. Unless dessert consists of orange slices.

HENRY: Which is also why we didn't load up this book with dessert recipes.

MICHELLE: Here's the thing: The food that shows up on my blog, cookbooks, app, and social media reflects the way I actually cook for my family. And to be perfectly honest, I rarely whip up sugary treats—Paleo or otherwise. It's not that I suddenly stopped loving sweets, but after I started eating Paleo, I found that the constant, low-level sugar craving was gone. I didn't feel like I physically needed it anymore. But I also knew that if I started backsliding into bad habits and took up sweets again, I wouldn't stop.

HENRY: You definitely have a binary switch when it comes to certain things.

MICHELLE: Get me started on desserts, and you'll have a hard time keeping me from stuffing my face with sweets all the time. That's why I rarely indulge in sweet treats these days. Desserts are the exception, not the rule. In fact, we've implemented a rule about sweets at our house: We generally don't have desserts except on "S" days. Owen, do you want to explain what "S" days are?

OWEN: "S" days are days of the week that start with the letter "S." That means Saturday and Sunday.

OLLIE: And Suesday and Sursday.

OWEN: You just made those up, Ollie.

OLLIE: Maybe. Maybe not.

HENRY: But for you, Michelle, dark chocolate's in a category by itself, right?

MICHELLE: Yeah—to me, it's actually a health food! I really enjoy having a little nibble of it. A square or two every day of 85 percent cacao chocolate has barely any sugar in it, and it contains a bunch of good stuff, too, like magnesium, zinc, and healthy fats. Besides, it makes me happy, and happiness is a big part of a healthy lifestyle. Too many people are so crazy-strict about their food choices that they undermine the whole point of Paleo, which is to get healthier.

HENRY: I love that you've found a way to justify eating chocolate as a health choice.

MICHELLE: Well, I figure there are a lot worse things I could be eating.

OWEN: Like cotton candy. Or a cheesecake burrito!

OLLIE: Or hairballs! Or cardboard! Or dirt!

NOT DIRT

VANILLA ALMOND MILK

MAKES 3 CUPS
⏱ **1 DAY**
(10 MINUTES HANDS-ON)

Recently, one of my old college pals posed an interesting question: What would the 1990s version of me think of my current incarnation as a modern-day caveperson? I knew the answer immediately: "I would've hated the current me."

It's the truth. Despite spending my grunge-era college years among the unwashed masses at Berkeley, '90s-me would have a field day mocking my current hobbies: home-brewing kombucha, collecting bones for broth, and soaking almonds to make dairy-free milk. I hate to admit it, but '90s-me was a self-righteous know-it-all.

Call me an aging hippie—I don't care. If I could, I'd tell '90s-me to stop wolfing down gut-irritating foods, turn off the TV, and make some almond milk already. After all, a frosty glass of this stuff never fails to hit the spot.

She'd listen to me, too. After all, almond milk is incredibly easy to make, and if there's one thing that '90s-me has in common with present-day-me, it's laziness.

INGREDIENTS:

1   cup organic raw almonds

2½ cups water, plus extra for soaking

1   teaspoon vanilla extract (optional, but if you leave it out, you can't call it Vanilla Almond Milk)

     Sea salt

PIÑA COLADA TAPIOCA PUDDING

MAKES 6 SERVINGS
⏱ **5 HOURS**
(40 MINUTES HANDS-ON)

Need a recipe for a fancy treat that'll please even your toughest critics? Then try this tropical dessert, which combines creamy tapioca pudding, tangy pineapple ice, and toasted coconut flakes.

Inspired by *très* innovative desserts at ultra-modern, white-tablecloth Vietnamese joints, this after-dinner treat has quickly become a family favorite. Even my nitpicky mother asks for seconds, so you know this tapioca pudding's the real deal.

INGREDIENTS:

• PUDDING •

½ cup small pearl tapioca

2 cups coconut water

1 (14-ounce) can full-fat coconut milk

2 tablespoons honey

Kosher salt

½ vanilla bean pod

½ cup toasted coconut flakes

• GRANITA •

1 (14-ounce) can pineapple chunks in pineapple juice with no added sugar

½ vanilla bean pod

1 tablespoon honey (optional)

Juice from ½ lime

Kosher salt

INSTRUCTIONS:

1 RINSE THE TAPIOCA IN A STRAINER UNDER COLD WATER FOR 15 TO 20 SECONDS.

2 IN A SMALL SAUCEPAN OVER HIGH HEAT, BRING THE COCONUT WATER TO A BOIL.

3 ADD THE TAPIOCA. LOWER THE HEAT TO MAINTAIN A LOW SIMMER, AND COOK FOR 10 TO 12 MINUTES, STIRRING FREQUENTLY. DON'T LET THE PEARLS STICK TO THE PAN!

4 COOK UNTIL THE LIQUID THICKENS AND THE PEARLS ARE MOSTLY TRANSLUCENT.

5 CUT THE VANILLA BEAN POD IN HALF LENGTHWISE AND SCRAPE OUT THE SEEDS.

6 STIR IN HALF A VANILLA BEAN POD AND HALF OF THE SCRAPED-OUT VANILLA SEEDS. ADD THE COCONUT MILK, HONEY, AND A PINCH OF SALT.

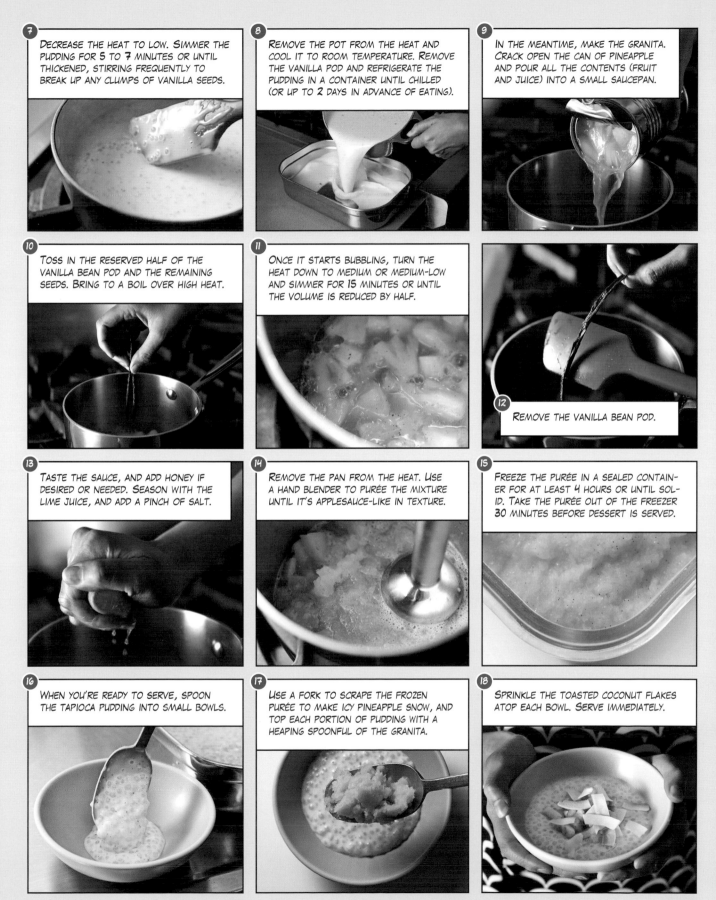

7 DECREASE THE HEAT TO LOW. SIMMER THE PUDDING FOR 5 TO 7 MINUTES OR UNTIL THICKENED, STIRRING FREQUENTLY TO BREAK UP ANY CLUMPS OF VANILLA SEEDS.

8 REMOVE THE POT FROM THE HEAT AND COOL IT TO ROOM TEMPERATURE. REMOVE THE VANILLA POD AND REFRIGERATE THE PUDDING IN A CONTAINER UNTIL CHILLED (OR UP TO 2 DAYS IN ADVANCE OF EATING).

9 IN THE MEANTIME, MAKE THE GRANITA. CRACK OPEN THE CAN OF PINEAPPLE AND POUR ALL THE CONTENTS (FRUIT AND JUICE) INTO A SMALL SAUCEPAN.

10 TOSS IN THE RESERVED HALF OF THE VANILLA BEAN POD AND THE REMAINING SEEDS. BRING TO A BOIL OVER HIGH HEAT.

11 ONCE IT STARTS BUBBLING, TURN THE HEAT DOWN TO MEDIUM OR MEDIUM-LOW AND SIMMER FOR 15 MINUTES OR UNTIL THE VOLUME IS REDUCED BY HALF.

12 REMOVE THE VANILLA BEAN POD.

13 TASTE THE SAUCE, AND ADD HONEY IF DESIRED OR NEEDED. SEASON WITH THE LIME JUICE, AND ADD A PINCH OF SALT.

14 REMOVE THE PAN FROM THE HEAT. USE A HAND BLENDER TO PURÉE THE MIXTURE UNTIL IT'S APPLESAUCE-LIKE IN TEXTURE.

15 FREEZE THE PURÉE IN A SEALED CONTAINER FOR AT LEAST 4 HOURS OR UNTIL SOLID. TAKE THE PURÉE OUT OF THE FREEZER 30 MINUTES BEFORE DESSERT IS SERVED.

16 WHEN YOU'RE READY TO SERVE, SPOON THE TAPIOCA PUDDING INTO SMALL BOWLS.

17 USE A FORK TO SCRAPE THE FROZEN PURÉE TO MAKE ICY PINEAPPLE SNOW, AND TOP EACH PORTION OF PUDDING WITH A HEAPING SPOONFUL OF THE GRANITA.

18 SPRINKLE THE TOASTED COCONUT FLAKES ATOP EACH BOWL. SERVE IMMEDIATELY.

TANGERINE DREAM TART

MAKES 8 SERVINGS
⏱ **5 HOURS**
(40 MINUTES HANDS-ON)

Inspired by the Lemon Cream Tart at San Francisco's Tartine Bakery, this dairy-free tart holds a perfectly creamy custard with a sweet, citrusy tang. Make this already.

INGREDIENTS:

• CRUST •

2   cups (224 grams) finely ground almond flour

2   tablespoons arrowroot powder

3   tablespoons chilled ghee or coconut oil

2   tablespoons raw honey

Kosher salt

• FILLING •

½   teaspoon powdered gelatin

¾   cup fresh tangerine juice

2   tablespoons fresh lime juice

1   large egg

3   large egg yolks

¼   cup raw honey

Kosher salt

1   cup chilled refined coconut oil or chilled ghee

Zest from 1 tangerine

↻ SWITCH IT UP:
ORANGE CREAM TART

PEAK TANGERINE SEASON LASTS FROM FALL TO SPRING, BUT IF YOU CAN'T FIND ANY, YOU CAN ALWAYS MAKE AN ORANGE CREAM TART. JUST USE ORANGE JUICE AND ORANGE ZEST INSTEAD.

1. POUR THE ALMOND FLOUR AND ARROWROOT POWDER INTO A FOOD PROCESSOR. ADD THE CHILLED GHEE, HONEY, AND A PINCH OF SALT.

2. PULSE TO COMBINE. THE DOUGH WILL LOOK CRUMBLY, BUT IT SHOULD STICK TOGETHER WHEN YOU PRESS IT WITH YOUR FINGERS.

3. PRESS THE DOUGH INTO THE BOTTOM AND SIDES OF A 9½-INCH TART PAN. PACK IT DOWN FIRMLY TO FORM A THIN SHELL. USE A STRAIGHT-SIDED, ROUND MEASURING CUP TO SMOOTH OUT AND FURTHER COMPACT THE BOTTOM AND SIDES OF THE SHELL.

4. PREHEAT THE OVEN TO 325°F. BAKE FOR 20 TO 25 MINUTES OR UNTIL BROWNED AND FIRM. LEAVE THE BAKED SHELL IN THE TART PAN AND COOL IT ON A WIRE RACK.

5. IN A SMALL BOWL, SPRINKLE THE GELATIN OVER 2 TABLESPOONS OF WATER. SET THE BOWL ASIDE FOR 5 MINUTES OR UNTIL THE GELATIN HYDRATES AND BLOOMS.

6. FILL A MEDIUM SAUCEPAN WITH WATER TO A DEPTH OF ABOUT 2 INCHES, AND BRING TO A SIMMER OVER MEDIUM HEAT.

7. IN A STAINLESS STEEL BOWL (ONE THAT CAN SIT ON TOP OF THE RIM OF THE SIMMERING SAUCEPAN), WHISK TOGETHER THE TANGERINE JUICE, LIME JUICE, WHOLE EGG, EGG YOLKS, HONEY, AND A PINCH OF SALT.

8. PLACE THE BOWL OVER THE SAUCEPAN. ADD THE GELATIN TO THE MIXTURE, AND WHISK FOR 8 TO 10 MINUTES UNTIL THE MIXTURE THICKENS AND REGISTERS 180°F ON AN INSTANT-READ THERMOMETER.

9. TAKE THE BOWL OFF THE SAUCEPAN, AND TURN OFF THE HEAT. COOL THE MIXTURE TO 140°F, STIRRING OCCASIONALLY.

10. USE AN IMMERSION OR COUNTERTOP BLENDER TO GRADUALLY BLEND IN THE CHILLED COCONUT OIL A TABLESPOON OR SO AT A TIME. MAKE SURE EACH BIT OF COCONUT OIL IS WELL INCORPORATED BEFORE BLENDING IN THE NEXT TABLESPOON.

11. POUR THE THICKENED MIXTURE INTO THE COOLED CRUST. CHILL IN THE FRIDGE FOR AT LEAST 4 HOURS (UNTIL THE TART SETS UP) OR UP TO 3 DAYS.

12. TAKE THE TART OUT OF THE REFRIGERATOR 15 MINUTES BEFORE SERVING. GARNISH IT WITH A SPRINKLE OF TANGERINE ZEST. POP THE TART OUT OF THE PAN, AND SERVE.

RUSTIC CHOCOLATE CAKE

MAKES 8 SERVINGS
⏱ **8 HOURS**
(30 MINUTES HANDS-ON)

After seeing pastry maven Liz Prueitt's gorgeous grain-free chocolate cake on Instagram, I knew I had to make a Paleo version. The result: a light, fluffy delight that reminds me of the treats I made as a kid using boxed cake mix.

INGREDIENTS:

Ghee or coconut oil to grease the pan

2 cups (224 grams) almond flour

½ cup (48 grams) cocoa powder

¼ teaspoon salt

½ teaspoon baking soda

2 large eggs

½ cup (100 grams) coconut sugar

¾ cup full-fat coconut milk

1 teaspoon apple cider vinegar

1 teaspoon vanilla extract

• TOPPING •

1 (14-ounce) can full-fat coconut milk, refrigerated overnight

1 tablespoon coconut sugar (optional)

½ teaspoon vanilla extract

1 tablespoon cocoa powder

½ cup fresh raspberries

INSTRUCTIONS:

1 BEFORE GETTING STARTED, REMEMBER TO LEAVE A CAN OF COCONUT MILK IN THE REFRIGERATOR SO YOU CAN MAKE THE WHIPPED COCONUT CREAM LATER IN STEP 12.

2 WHEN YOU'RE READY TO BAKE, PREHEAT THE OVEN TO 350°F WITH THE RACK IN THE MIDDLE POSITION.

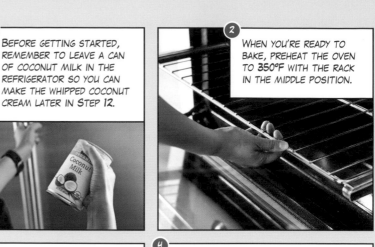

3 GREASE THE BOTTOM AND SIDES OF AN 8-INCH ROUND CAKE PAN WITH GHEE OR COCONUT OIL. PLACE A PARCHMENT ROUND ON THE BOTTOM OF THE GREASED PAN.

4 IN A LARGE MIXING BOWL, WHISK TOGETHER THE ALMOND FLOUR, COCOA POWDER, SALT, AND BAKING SODA.

5 IN A SEPARATE BOWL, USE AN ELECTRIC MIXER TO WHIP THE EGGS TOGETHER WITH THE COCONUT SUGAR UNTIL SMOOTH. THE COLOR SHOULD BRIGHTEN TO LIGHT-BEIGE.

6 POUR IN THE COCONUT MILK, APPLE CIDER VINEGAR, AND VANILLA EXTRACT. (DON'T USE THE COCONUT MILK YOU LEFT IN THE FRIDGE. SAVE IT FOR STEP 12.) MIX WELL.

7 ADD THE WET INGREDIENTS TO THE DRY INGREDIENTS...

8 ...AND BEAT ON LOW TO COMBINE.

9 POUR THE BATTER INTO THE CAKE PAN, AND SMOOTH THE TOP WITH A SPATULA.

10 BAKE FOR ABOUT 25 MINUTES OR UNTIL THE TOP SPRINGS BACK WHEN YOU GENTLY PRESS ON IT. A TOOTHPICK INSERTED IN THE MIDDLE SHOULD COME OUT CLEAN.

11 COOL THE CAKE FOR 20 MINUTES ON A WIRE RACK. THEN, POP IT OUT OF THE PAN AND COOL IT COMPLETELY ON THE RACK.

12 MEANWHILE, MAKE THE WHIPPED COCONUT CREAM. TAKE THE CAN FROM THE FRIDGE AND USE A CAN OPENER TO CUT 2 SLITS ON THE BOTTOM. ALLOW THE WATERY LIQUID TO DRAIN OUT, LEAVING ONLY THE THICK COCONUT CREAM LAYER IN THE CAN.

13 OPEN THE CAN, AND TRANSFER THE CREAM TO THE CHILLED BOWL. ADD 1 TABLESPOON OF COCONUT SUGAR (IF YOU SO DESIRE) AND ½ TEASPOON VANILLA EXTRACT. WHISK VIGOROUSLY UNTIL MEDIUM PEAKS FORM.

14 TOP THE CAKE WITH WHIPPED COCONUT CREAM (OR REGULAR WHIPPED CREAM IF YOU'RE OKAY WITH DAIRY). USE A SIFTER TO DUST THE TOP WITH COCOA POWDER.

15 GARNISH WITH RASPBERRIES, AND SERVE. LEFTOVERS CAN BE REFRIGERATED IN A SEALED CONTAINER FOR UP TO 4 DAYS.

CHERRY CHOCOLATE CHIP ICE CREAM

MAKES 6 SERVINGS
⏱ 4 HOURS
(15 MINUTES HANDS-ON)

When you're hankering for a fancy banana split with all the fixin's, make this dessert. It includes everything you love about the classic dessert—including the bananas, which are frozen and blended in as the creamy base.

Remember to freeze any ripe bananas that you don't get around to eating. That way, you'll always be able to whip up this dairy-free, no-ice-cream-maker-required treat.

INGREDIENTS:

3   frozen medium bananas, peeled and cut into ½-inch coins

2½ cups (340 grams) frozen pitted dark sweet cherries

½   cup cherry juice

1   teaspoon vanilla extract

    Kosher salt

½   cup dark chocolate chips

½   cup toasted almond slices

• GANACHE •

½   cup full-fat coconut milk

4   ounces dark chocolate, chopped

    Kosher salt

INSTRUCTIONS:

1 TOSS THE FROZEN BANANA AND CHERRIES, CHERRY JUICE, VANILLA EXTRACT, AND A PINCH OF SALT INTO A FOOD PROCESSOR.

2 PULSE UNTIL THE FRUIT IS UNIFORMLY CHOPPED. THEN, BLITZ FOR 1 TO 2 MINUTES UNTIL THE MIXTURE TAKES ON THE TEXTURE OF SOFT SERVE ICE CREAM.

3 ADD THE CHOCOLATE CHIPS AND PULSE 3 TO 5 TIMES OR UNTIL COMBINED.

4 POUR THE MIXTURE INTO AN AIRTIGHT CONTAINER. COVER AND FREEZE FOR AT LEAST 4 HOURS AND UP TO 2 WEEKS.

(FEELING IMPATIENT? GO AHEAD AND EAT IT NOW. JUST TELL YOUR GUESTS IT'S CHERRY CHOCOLATE CHIP SOFT SERVE.)

5 WHEN YOU'RE READY TO SERVE, TAKE THE ICE CREAM OUT OF THE FREEZER TO SOFTEN A BIT. YOU CAN EAT IT AS-IS...

6 ...OR YOU CAN GO ALL-OUT AND MAKE GANACHE TO SERVE WITH IT. IN A SMALL SAUCEPAN, WARM THE COCONUT MILK OVER MEDIUM HEAT UNTIL IT SIMMERS.

7 PUT THE CHOCOLATE IN A BIG BOWL. ADD THE HOT COCONUT MILK AND A PINCH OF SALT. LET IT SIT FOR 1 TO 2 MINUTES.

8 THEN, STIR AS THE HOT COCONUT MILK MELTS THE CHOCOLATE. KEEP STIRRING UNTIL SMOOTH AND WELL COMBINED.

9 SCOOP THE ICE CREAM INTO SERVING BOWLS. TOP WITH GANACHE AND SLICED ALMONDS, AND SERVE IMMEDIATELY.

STRAWBERRY ALMOND SEMIFREDDO + BERRY BALSAMIC SAUCE

MAKES 6 SERVINGS
⏱ 10 HOURS
(1 HOUR HANDS-ON)

Traditionally, Italian *semifreddo*—an elegant hybrid of ice cream and custard—is made by carefully folding a *zabaglione* into a fluffy cloud of meringue and whipped cream, and then freezing it. Needless to say, *semifreddo* ain't easy to make, which is why I held off until I finally spied a simple method by *Cook's Illustrated*. I adapted that technique to make my own Paleo-ish *semifreddo*, and lo and behold: It works like a charm.

In fact, it may work a little *too* well. While writing this cookbook, I kept coming up with excuses to make (and taste-test) batch after batch of light and airy *semifreddo*.

In the end, my non-stop testing actually yielded some useful lessons. For example, I discovered that *semifreddo* can be made with just a hand mixer, though it's much easier with a stand mixer. I found that quickly and gently folding the ingredients together produced the best texture. And of course, both the *semifreddo* and sauce can be made in advance, eliminating the stress of last-minute dessert prep.

I also learned that even a simplified *semifreddo* recipe calls for more effort and care than most of the other dishes in this book—and that's a good thing. It keeps lazy ex-sugar fiends like me from making this decadent treat every day.

INGREDIENTS:

- 1 cup coconut cream, chilled overnight
- ½ cup grade A light amber maple syrup
- ½ lemon, cut crosswise
- 3 large egg whites, room temperature
- 1 teaspoon vanilla extract
- ½ cup (90 grams) fresh strawberries, finely diced
- ¼ cup toasted almonds, chopped

• SAUCE •

- ¼ cup balsamic vinegar
- 2 cups (340 grams) thinly sliced hulled strawberries
- 3 tablespoons raw honey
- 1 tablespoon fresh lemon juice
- 1 teaspoon vanilla extract
- ¼ teaspoon salt

• GARNISH •

- ¼ cup sliced fresh strawberries
- ¼ cup toasted almonds, chopped
- 2 tablespoons fresh mint leaves

INSTRUCTIONS:

1 LINE A 9 BY 5 BY 3-INCH LOAF PAN WITH PLASTIC WRAP WITH THE ENDS OVER-HANGING THE SIDES. SET THE PAN ASIDE.

2 IN A LARGE MIXING BOWL, USE A WHISK OR ELECTRIC MIXER TO BEAT THE COCONUT CREAM UNTIL SMOOTH AND LIGHT. COVER AND PLACE THE CREAM IN THE FRIDGE.

3 POUR THE MAPLE SYRUP INTO A SMALL SAUCEPAN, BUT DON'T TURN ON THE STOVE YET. THE NEXT 4 STEPS WILL COME FAST AND FURIOUS, SO BE PREPARED TO GET THROUGH 'EM IN QUICK SUCCESSION.

4 WIPE THE INSIDE OF A LARGE MIXING BOWL OR THE BOWL OF YOUR STAND MIXER WITH THE CUT SIDE OF THE LEMON. (I'M GOING TO DEMONSTRATE THIS RECIPE USING A HAND MIXER, BUT FOR THE SAKE OF EASE, USE A STAND MIXER IF YOU'VE GOT ONE.)

5 ADD THE EGG WHITES TO THE BOWL, AND BEAT ON MEDIUM SPEED FOR 2 MINUTES OR UNTIL SOFT (BUT NOT STIFF) PEAKS FORM. SET THE BOWL OF WHITES ASIDE.

6 AS SOON AS THE WHITES FORM PEAKS, HEAT THE MAPLE SYRUP OVER MEDIUM FOR ABOUT 3 MINUTES OR UNTIL IT REGISTERS 238 TO 242°F ON A CANDY THERMOMETER.

7 GRAB YOUR BOWL OF WHIPPED EGG WHITES. WITH THE MIXER RUNNING AT MEDIUM-HIGH SPEED, SLOWLY DRIZZLE IN THE HOT MAPLE SYRUP. DON'T LET THE STREAM TOUCH THE BEATERS OR THE BOWL.

8 INCREASE THE SPEED TO HIGH, AND WHIP FOR 4 TO 5 MINUTES UNTIL STIFF, GLOSSY PEAKS FORM. ADD THE VANILLA EXTRACT, AND BEAT IT IN TO INCORPORATE.

9 GO GRAB THE WHIPPED COCONUT CREAM FROM THE REFRIGERATOR. USING A RUBBER SPATULA, GENTLY STIR A DOLLOP OF IT INTO THE WHIPPED EGG WHITE MIXTURE.

10 THEN, GENTLY FOLD IN THE REST OF THE COCONUT CREAM, DICED STRAWBERRIES, AND TOASTED ALMONDS. DON'T OVERMIX!

11 POUR THE MIXTURE INTO THE LINED PAN, AND USE A SPATULA TO SPREAD IT EVENLY.

12 FOLD THE PLASTIC WRAP OVER THE TOP, AND FREEZE THE SEMIFREDDO FOR AT LEAST 8 HOURS OR UNTIL FIRM. (YOU CAN KEEP IT FROZEN FOR UP TO 2 WEEKS.)

13 AT LEAST 1 HOUR (AND UP TO 1 WEEK) BEFORE YOU'RE READY TO SERVE THE SEMIFREDDO, MAKE THE SAUCE. START BY HEATING THE BALSAMIC VINEGAR IN A SMALL SAUCEPAN OVER HIGH HEAT.

14 WHEN IT STARTS TO BUBBLE, TURN THE HEAT DOWN TO MEDIUM AND SIMMER THE VINEGAR FOR 3 TO 5 MINUTES OR UNTIL THE VOLUME IS REDUCED BY HALF.

15 THE VINEGAR SHOULD BE THICK AND SYRUPY WHEN YOU DRAW A SPATULA THROUGH IT.

16 ADD THE STRAWBERRIES, HONEY, LEMON JUICE, VANILLA, AND SALT.

17 SIMMER THE MIXTURE OVER MEDIUM HEAT FOR 5 TO 10 MINUTES OR UNTIL THE STRAWBERRIES BREAK DOWN.

18 REMOVE THE SAUCEPAN FROM THE HEAT, AND USE A HAND BLENDER TO PURÉE THE SAUCE. I LEAVE SOME OF THE BERRIES INTACT, BUT YOU CAN KEEP BLENDING AWAY IF YOU PREFER A SMOOTHER SAUCE.

19 TASTE AND ADJUST WITH MORE HONEY OR LEMON JUICE IF NEEDED. COOL THE SAUCE TO ROOM TEMPERATURE. THE SAUCE CAN BE REFRIGERATED FOR UP TO 1 WEEK.

20 TO SERVE THE SEMIFREDDO, UNMOLD THE FROZEN BLOCK AND CUT IT INTO SLICES. A KNIFE DIPPED IN HOT WATER WORKS BEST.

21 TOP WITH THE SAUCE, FRESH BERRIES, TOASTED NUTS, AND FRESH MINT LEAVES.

KINDA READY!

EASY MEALS 'CAUSE YOU GOT A HEAD START

WHAT CAN I DO IF I'M ONLY KINDA READY?

Did you finish the last section of this cookbook, only to mutter to yourself, "there's absolutely no way I'm going to cook like this every night of the week"?

Good, because you're not supposed to.

Don't get me wrong; when I actually have the time, energy, and motivation to leisurely peruse my shelves of cookbooks, select a new recipe, go shopping for special ingredients, and settle in for a few hours of inspired cooking, it tickles the creative side of my brain. It's fun and rewarding—especially if someone else does the dishes afterward.

Most nights, however, the name of the game is to cram a healthy and delicious dinner into my family's mouths—pronto. And after a hectic day of working and running errands, prepping a meal entirely from scratch is rarely in the cards. I'd much rather scrounge around my refrigerator, slop a bunch of leftovers into a bowl, stir it all together, and call it a day.

But that would be gross. And it's also why the recipes in this "Kinda Ready" section are life savers: They transform pantry staples and leftovers into impromptu meals that'll satisfy the most discriminating palates.

In many ways, these dishes best represent how I normally cook—especially on busy weeknights when I'm sprinting to get supper on the table. On days I have a little extra time in the kitchen, I try to whip up a double batch of whatever I'm cooking. That way, I'll always have leftovers to incorporate into subsequent meals. Homemade sauces, dressings, and broth also come in handy when I need to add an extra boost of flavor. With just a few building blocks, I can cobble together an infinite number of flavor combinations.

Best of all, this is just the starting point: Once you see how easily you can combine ready-made ingredients into new creations, you'll be more than ready to dazzle with your own leftover makeovers.

IT'S NOT OFTEN THAT I'M ABSOLUTELY READY TO COOK FROM SCRATCH.

BUT ON THE OTHER HAND, I'M USUALLY NOT TOTALLY UNPREPARED, EITHER.

MORE OFTEN THAN NOT, I HAVE A BUNCH OF PRE-MADE COMPONENTS LIKE SAUCES OR LEFTOVERS SQUIRRELED AWAY IN MY KITCHEN...

...YOU KNOW, STUFF LIKE LAST NIGHT'S KALUA PIG OR SUNDAY GRAVY, PLUS A BOTTLE OR TWO OF READY-MADE STIR-FRY SAUCE, SALAD DRESSING, OR HOT SAUCE.

IF I'M LUCKY, I MIGHT EVEN HAVE SOME EXTRA FRIED GREEN PLANTAINS OR CAULI RICE SITTING IN THE FREEZER.

THIS IS MY SWEET SPOT.

I LOVE IT WHEN I HAVE A BUNCH OF BUILDING BLOCKS IN MY KITCHEN, AND ALL I HAVE TO DO IS COMBINE 'EM IN NEW AND INTERESTING WAYS!

HANGRY SOUP

MAKES 6 SERVINGS
⏱ 45 MINUTES
(10 MINUTES HANDS-ON)

When you're so hungry that you're angry, you need to make this soup. It'll calm the beast within.

INGREDIENTS:

- 4 cups Sunday Gravy (page 152)
- 6 cups Bone Broth (page 76) or chicken stock
- 3 cups thinly sliced cabbage, chard, or kale leaves
- 2 medium carrots, thinly sliced
- ½ pound Yukon Gold potatoes, peeled and cubed (optional)
  Kosher salt
  Freshly ground black pepper
- 2 tablespoons minced basil
- 2 tablespoons minced Italian parsley
- 2 teaspoons sherry vinegar (optional)

I'M HANGRY!

FEED ME NOW!

INSTRUCTIONS:

1. IN A LARGE SAUCEPAN, COMBINE THE LEFTOVER SUNDAY GRAVY...

2. ...AND THE BROTH.

3. TOSS IN THE VEGETABLES, AND STIR TO MIX WELL.

4. BRING IT ALL TO A BOIL OVER HIGH HEAT.

5. COVER THE POT AND DECREASE THE HEAT TO MEDIUM-LOW (OR JUST ENOUGH TO MAINTAIN A SIMMER).

6. COOK FOR **20** TO **25** MINUTES OR UNTIL THE VEGGIES ARE TENDER. IF THE SOUP IS TOO THICK, ADD A BIT MORE BROTH.

(NEED TO SPEED THIS UP? USE A PRESSURE COOKER! COOK THE INGREDIENTS UNDER HIGH PRESSURE FOR 5 MINUTES.)

7 SEASON TO TASTE WITH SALT AND PEPPER. IF DESIRED, ADD A SPLASH OF SHERRY VINEGAR FOR A BIT OF ACIDITY AND BRIGHTNESS. LADLE INTO BOWLS, AND GARNISH WITH FRESH HERBS. YOU CAN REFRIGERATE THIS SOUP FOR UP TO 3 DAYS OR FREEZE IT FOR UP TO 3 MONTHS.

ROASTED CARROTS WITH GINGER SESAME SAUCE

MAKES 4 SERVINGS
⏱ **35 MINUTES**
(5 MINUTES HANDS-ON)

Sweet and tender oven-roasted carrots are pretty much the best thing ever. But shower this dish with fresh chives and my creamy, tangy Ginger Sesame Sauce, and the flavor dial of this dish gets turned all the way up to 11.

INGREDIENTS:

¼ **cup Ginger Sesame Sauce (page 66)**

1 **pound young carrots, scrubbed and patted dry**

2 **tablespoons olive oil**

Kosher salt

Freshly ground black pepper

¼ **cup chopped chives**

1 **tablespoon toasted sesame seeds (follow the toasting instructions on page 66)**

> YOU DON'T EVEN NEED TO PEEL THE CARROTS!

INSTRUCTIONS:

1 PREHEAT THE OVEN TO 425°F WITH THE RACK IN THE MIDDLE POSITION. GRAB YOUR GINGER SESAME SAUCE, AND PLACE THE CARROTS IN A SINGLE LAYER ON A PARCHMENT-LINED RIMMED BAKING SHEET.

2 DRIZZLE THE OLIVE OIL ON THE CARROTS, AND SPRINKLE SALT AND PEPPER ON THEM.

3 ROAST IN THE OVEN FOR **30** MINUTES OR UNTIL THE CARROTS ARE TENDER.

4 SPOON ON SOME GINGER SESAME SAUCE, AND TOP WITH CHIVES AND SESAME SEEDS.

5 THIS DISH TASTES GREAT AT ROOM TEMPERATURE AND STRAIGHT FROM THE FRIDGE, TOO.

BACON BRUSSELS SPROUTS WITH KIMCHI APPLESAUCE

MAKES 6 SERVINGS
⏱ **45 MINUTES**
(20 MINUTES HANDS-ON)

Believe it or not, one of my most popular recipes of all time is also one of my simplest: oven-roasted Brussels sprouts with smoky bacon. It's hard to improve upon a classic, but I think I've done it with this dish. Instead of cooking the bacon in the oven with the sprouts, I decided to crisp it separately, so that it stays wonderfully crunchy when this dish is served. And of course, the addition of spicy, tangy Kimchi Applesauce lends a whole new flavor dimension. Try it and see!

INGREDIENTS:

- **1** cup Kimchi Applesauce (page 64)
- **4** slices thick-cut bacon, cut crosswise into ¼-inch slices
- **2** pounds Brussels sprouts, trimmed and cut into halves (or quarters if your sprouts are really big)
- **½** teaspoon kosher salt
- **¼** teaspoon freshly ground black pepper

I LOVE B.S.!

INSTRUCTIONS:

1 Make or grab some Kimchi Applesauce. Preheat the oven to 425°F with the rack in the middle position. Cook the bacon in a large skillet over medium heat for 10 to 12 minutes until crisp.

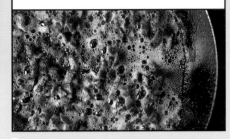

2 Use a slotted spoon to transfer the bacon to a paper towel–lined plate.

3 Toss the Brussels sprouts into the bacon drippings left in the skillet and sprinkle with salt and pepper.

4 Stir well to evenly coat all the B.S. (Brussels sprouts).

5 Transfer the Brussels sprouts to a rimmed baking sheet and roast in the oven for 25 minutes or until tender and browned. Toss the sprouts at the halfway point to ensure even cooking.

If you haven't already made your Kimchi Applesauce, stop procrastinating and do it. It takes just 5 minutes.

6 Transfer the sprouts to a large bowl. Toss with the Kimchi Applesauce, and top with the bacon bits.

CHILLED ASIAN ZOODLE SALAD WITH CHICKEN + AVOCADO

MAKES 4 SERVINGS
⏱ **25 MINUTES**

Spiralizing vegetables never gets old—especially when the result is a drop-dead-gorgeous green zoodle salad with shredded chicken.

Raw zucchini and carrot noodles are the perfect substitute for starchy, gummy strands of pasta in this salad. Slices of buttery avocado, toasted sesame seeds, and fragrant herbs lend extra texture and flavor to this dish, too. Best of all, with pre-made dressing and leftover chicken, this salad can be assembled in no time at all.

INGREDIENTS:

½   cup Ginger Sesame Sauce (page 66)

4   cups cooked and shredded Roast-Ahead Chicken Breasts (page 84)

4   medium zucchini, ends trimmed

2   medium carrots, peeled

    Kosher salt

2   tablespoons fresh cilantro

2   tablespoons minced fresh mint

2   scallions, thinly sliced

1   avocado, peeled, pitted, and thinly sliced

1   tablespoon black sesame seeds, toasted

INSTRUCTIONS:

1 MAKE SURE YOU HAVE GINGER SESAME SAUCE AND COOKED CHICKEN ON HAND. USE A SPIRALIZER, JULIENNE PEELER, MANDOLINE SLICER, OR A KNIFE TO TURN THE ZUCCHINI AND CARROTS INTO NOODLES.

2 IF THE ZUCCHINI AND CARROT NOODLES ARE TOO LONG, CUT THEM INTO SHORTER SEGMENTS. BLOT THE NOODLES WITH A PAPER TOWEL OR KITCHEN TOWEL. AFTER ALL, NO ONE LIKES SOGGY ZOODLES.

3 IN A LARGE BOWL, TOSS TOGETHER THE NOODLES, CHICKEN, AND GINGER SESAME SAUCE. SEASON WITH SALT TO TASTE.

4 ADD THE FRESH HERBS AND SCALLIONS.

5 TOP WITH SLICED AVOCADO AND SESAME SEEDS.

SRIRACHA SUNBUTTER ZOODLES + CHICKEN

MAKES 1 SERVING
⏱ **10 MINUTES**

Who says vegetables have to be bland? Spiralized zucchini is fun to make and eat—especially when it's paired with an irresistibly fiery, tangy, and easy-to-make sauce. Zoodles for the win!

INGREDIENTS:

- 3   tablespoons Spicy Thai No-Nut Sauce (page 58)
- 1   cup cooked and shredded Roast-Ahead Chicken Breasts (page 84)
- 1   medium zucchini, ends trimmed
- 1   small carrot, peeled
- ¼   avocado, peeled, pitted, and thinly sliced
- ½   cup ripe cherry tomatoes, halved
- 1   small scallion, thinly sliced
- 1   tablespoon fresh cilantro leaves
- 1   teaspoon toasted sesame seeds

INSTRUCTIONS:

1 YOU'LL NEED SPICY THAI NO-NUT SAUCE AND COOKED CHICKEN FOR THIS RECIPE. USE A SPIRALIZER, JULIENNE PEELER, OR MANDOLINE SLICER TO CUT THE ZUCCHINI AND CARROT INTO LONG NOODLES.

2 IN A BOWL, TOSS THE NOODLES WITH THE SPICY THAI NO-NUT SAUCE AND CHICKEN.

3 TRANSFER TO A SERVING BOWL, AND GARNISH WITH AVOCADO SLICES, CHERRY TOMATOES, HERBS, AND SESAME SEEDS.

4 EAT IT UP. BY THE WAY, THIS DISH IS ALSO TASTY WITH COOKED SHRIMP.

RED PESTO COODLES

MAKES 4 SERVINGS
⏱ **10 MINUTES**

Vegetable spiralizers work on more than just zucchini, you know. Case in point: cucumbers.

Raw, spiral-cut cucumber noodles (or "coodles") are a crisp, refreshing stand-in for pasta, capably soaking in the flavors of your favorite sauces and broths. Toss some freshly cut coodles with my no-cook Pesto Pomodori Secchi, and you won't even need to turn on the stove to get this vibrant vegetable side on the dinner table.

INGREDIENTS:

¼   **cup Pesto Pomodori Secchi (page 73)**

2   **English cucumbers, washed and ends trimmed**

¼   **cup fresh basil leaves, cut into ribbons**

2   **tablespoons toasted pine nuts**

#TEAM COODLES

INSTRUCTIONS:

1 Make or grab some Pesto Pomodori Secchi. Then, use a spiralizer, julienne peeler, or mandoline slicer to cut the cucumbers into long noodles. If your "coodles" are unmanageably long, cut 'em into shorter segments.

2 Blot the spiralized coodles between paper towels or clean kitchen towels.

3 In a large bowl, toss the coodles with pesto. Divide into serving bowls.

4 Top with basil and pine nuts.

5 Eat it up!

GRILLED ROMAINE + BROCCOLINI SALAD

MAKES 4 SERVINGS

⏱ **20 MINUTES**

If you think salads are delicate and boring, your vegetables probably haven't seen any live-fire action. Use a searing-hot grill to give your greens a quick char and some smokiness, and you'll marvel at the robust flavors of this salad.

INGREDIENTS:

¼ cup Green Beast Dressing (page 48)

Avocado oil or olive oil

2 heads romaine lettuce (about 1 pound), trimmed with core intact, and cut in half lengthwise

2 bunches broccolini (about 1 pound), ends trimmed, washed, and dried

2 bunches scallions (about ¼ pound), ends trimmed, washed, and dried

1 medium red onion, peeled and sliced into thick rings

2 mandarin oranges, sliced in half crosswise

Kosher salt

Freshly ground black pepper

2 tablespoons minced fresh chives

2 tablespoons fresh basil, cut into thin ribbons

2 tablespoons minced fresh Italian parsley or fresh dill

INSTRUCTIONS:

1 GRAB SOME GREEN BEAST DRESSING. DRIZZLE SOME OIL ON **2** BAKING SHEETS. RUB THE LETTUCE, BROCCOLINI, SCALLIONS, ONION, AND ORANGES IN THE OIL.

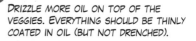

2 DRIZZLE MORE OIL ON TOP OF THE VEGGIES. EVERYTHING SHOULD BE THINLY COATED IN OIL (BUT NOT DRENCHED).

3 SEASON WITH SALT AND PEPPER.

4 GRILL THE VEGETABLES OVER A MEDIUM-HOT FIRE FOR **3** TO **5** MINUTES, TURNING ONCE, UNTIL NICELY CHARRED ON BOTH SIDES. (TIP: THE SCALLIONS WILL FINISH COOKING FIRST, AND THE ONIONS LAST.)

5 PLACE THE ORANGES CUT-SIDE DOWN AND COOK UNTIL DARK GRILL MARKS APPEAR.

6 TRANSFER THE VEGETABLES TO A PLATTER.

7 SQUEEZE THE ORANGES OVER THE SALAD (OR SERVE THEM AS A GARNISH, AND MAKE YOUR GUESTS SQUEEZE THEIR OWN).

8 SPOON THE DRESSING ON TOP.

GARNISH GENEROUSLY
WITH FRESH HERBS.

MEXICAN WATERMELON + CUCUMBER SALAD

MAKES 6 SERVINGS

⏱ **15 MINUTES**

On sweltering summer days, this Mexican Watermelon + Cucumber Salad is like a welcome splash of cool water. Refreshing and sweet, with a punch of spicy pepper and tangy lime, this dish will have you clamoring for more.

INGREDIENTS:

- ¼ cup Smoky Lime Pepitas (page 46)
- ¼ cup thinly sliced red onions
- 1 small seedless watermelon (about 5 pounds), cubed
- 1 English cucumber, cut into ½-inch slices
- ¼ cup extra-virgin olive oil
- 1 teaspoon ancho chili powder
- ½ teaspoon kosher salt
- ¼ teaspoon cayenne pepper
- 2 limes, finely grated zest and juice
- 2 tablespoons fresh mint leaves

INSTRUCTIONS:

1. HAVE YOU TOASTED UP SOME SMOKY LIME PEPITAS YET? IF NOT, GO DO IT ALREADY.

2. TAKE THE BITE OFF THE ONIONS BY SOAKING THEM IN A BOWL OF ICE WATER FOR ABOUT 10 MINUTES.

3. IN A LARGE BOWL, COMBINE THE WATERMELON, SLICED CUCUMBER, DRAINED ONIONS...

4. ...OLIVE OIL, CHILI POWDER, SALT...

5. ...CAYENNE PEPPER, LIME ZEST, AND LIME JUICE. TOSS TO MIX. TASTE FOR SEASONING, AND ADJUST AS NECESSARY.

6. GARNISH WITH FRESH MINT LEAVES AND TOASTED PEPITAS. SERVE IMMEDIATELY.

DID SOMEONE SAY WATERMELON?!?

HEY! YOU HAVE EYES!

WINTER DATE NIGHT SALAD

MAKES 4 SERVINGS
⏱ **30 MINUTES**

Just 'cause I'm calling this "Winter Date Night Salad" doesn't mean you need to make goo-goo eyes at your partner while feeding each other forkfuls of radicchio and chicken. It just means that this is a fantastically delicious winter salad that's hearty enough for dinner.

Also, it has dates in it.

INGREDIENTS:

- ½ **cup Nutty Dijon Vinaigrette (page 53)**
- 4 **cups cooked and shredded Roast-Ahead Chicken Breasts (page 84)**
- 1 **medium apple, cored and thinly sliced**

  Juice from ½ lime
- 4 **Belgian endives, ends trimmed and leaves separated**
- 1 **medium radicchio, cored and thinly sliced**
- 2 **large dried Medjool dates, pitted and thinly sliced**
- ¼ **cup minced fresh chives**
- ¼ **cup chopped fresh parsley**
- ¼ **cup toasted hazelnuts, roughly chopped**
- ¼ **cup dried cranberries (optional)**

> AND LIKE ALL GREAT RELATIONSHIPS, THIS SALAD IS COLORFUL, BITTER, SWEET, AND SUPER NUTTY!

190

INSTRUCTIONS:

1. GOT SOME NUTTY DIJON VINAIGRETTE AND COOKED CHICKEN? GOOD. START BY TOSSING THE APPLE SLICES IN LIME JUICE TO KEEP THEM FROM TURNING BROWN.

2. IN A LARGE BOWL, COMBINE THE APPLE, CHICKEN, ENDIVES, RADICCHIO, AND DATES.

3. ADD THE DRESSING AND FRESH HERBS.

4. TOSS WITH SALAD TONGS, OR WITH "NATURE'S TONGS": YOUR (CLEAN) HANDS.

5. TOP WITH HAZELNUTS AND DRIED CRANBERRIES, IF DESIRED.

THAI GREEN APPLE SLAW

MAKES 4 SERVINGS
⏱ **30 MINUTES**

Inspired by a remarkably crunchy and refreshing salad at Portland's PaaDee, this Southeast Asian slaw pairs beautifully with any number of grilled or roasted proteins. It reminds me of the fresh, colorful green papaya salads we ate on our travels through Thailand and Vietnam, but let's be realistic: Green papaya isn't as easy to track down as green apples. Besides, I have zero patience for peeling and shredding green papaya.

Hey—if I'm given the choice, I'll always pick the laziest option, as long as it's also a delicious one.

INGREDIENTS:

- ¼ **cup Thai Citrus Dressing (page 47)**
- 2 **Granny Smith apples, peeled, cored, and cut into thin matchsticks**
- 2 **medium carrots, peeled and cut into thin matchsticks**
- 1 **large red bell pepper, cored and cut into thin matchsticks**
- ¼ **small red onion, thinly sliced**
- 2 **scallions, sliced on the bias**
- 1 **tablespoon minced cilantro**
- 2 **tablespoons torn fresh basil leaves**
- ¼ **cup toasted cashews, roughly chopped or crushed**

INSTRUCTIONS:

1. MAKE SURE YOU HAVE THAI CITRUS DRESSING ON HAND. IF NOT, MAKE SOME NOW.

2. IN A LARGE BOWL, COMBINE THE APPLES, CARROTS, BELL PEPPER...

3. ...ONIONS, SCALLIONS, CILANTRO, AND BASIL.

4. ADD THE THAI CITRUS DRESSING TO TASTE, AND TOSS THE SALAD.

5. TOP WITH CASHEWS AND SERVE.

FLANK STEAK SUPER SALAD

MAKES 6 SERVINGS
⏱ 30 MINUTES

But what makes this a *super* salad, you ask? Is it the juicy and tender flank steak? The crisp, tartly-sweet slices of nectarine? Or the buttery avocado and bright bursts of cherry tomatoes? The answer, of course, is all of the above—plus the double-whammy of crunchy onion rings and onion dressing. When you shift into full-on feast mode, this is the salad you'll want to make—and eat.

INGREDIENTS:

- ¼ cup Creamy Onion Dressing (page 49)
- 1½ pounds flank steak, cut into 4 equal pieces
- Kosher salt
- 1 tablespoon ghee or fat of choice
- 10 lightly packed cups mixed lettuces (8 ounces)
- 1 nectarine, thinly sliced
- 1 Hass avocado, peeled and sliced
- 1 cup cherry tomatoes
- 1 serving Red Hot Onion Rings (page 262) (optional)

> SKIRT STEAK WILL ALSO WORK FOR THIS RECIPE, BUT BECAUSE IT'S THINNER, IT'LL COOK IN JUST 3 TO 5 MINUTES OVER MEDIUM–HIGH HEAT.

INSTRUCTIONS:

1. GOT SOME CREAMY ONION DRESSING ON HAND? YOU'LL NEED IT FOR THIS RECIPE.

2. PAT THE STEAKS DRY, AND SPRINKLE BOTH SIDES WITH SALT. WHEN YOU'RE READY TO COOK, MELT THE GHEE IN A LARGE SKILLET OR GRILL PAN OVER MEDIUM–HIGH HEAT.

3. ADD 2 STEAKS TO THE HOT PAN.

4. COOK FOR 6 TO 8 MINUTES, FLIPPING EVERY 2 MINUTES, UNTIL THE STEAKS ARE WELL-BROWNED AND THE INTERNAL TEMPERATURE REACHES 125°F.

5. TRANSFER TO A PLATTER, AND COOK THE REMAINING STEAKS. TENT THE MEAT WITH FOIL, AND REST IT FOR 10 MINUTES.

6. SLICE THE STEAKS AGAINST THE GRAIN INTO ¼-INCH STRIPS.

7. TOSS THE LETTUCE IN A LARGE BOWL, AND ADD THE STEAK, NECTARINE, AVOCADO, AND CHERRY TOMATOES. MAKE IT PRETTY.

8. TOP WITH ONION RINGS IF YOU HAVE 'EM.

9

SERVE WITH CREAMY ONION DRESSING.

SWITCH IT UP:
ASIAN FLANK STEAK SALAD

CRAVING A STEAK SALAD WITH MORE ASIAN FLAIR? USE LEAFY ASIAN SALAD GREENS LIKE TATSOI, MIZUNA, OR BABY MUSTARD GREENS, AND DRESS THE SALAD WITH GINGER SESAME SAUCE (PAGE 66), SPICY THAI NO-NUT SAUCE (PAGE 58), OR SRIRACHA RANCH DRESSING (PAGE 57). TOP WITH CHOPPED MACADAMIA NUTS.

WHOLE ROASTED CAULIFLOWER WITH NUTTY DIJON VINAIGRETTE

MAKES 4 SERVINGS
⏱ 2 HOURS
(10 MINUTES HANDS-ON)

Haven't yet spotted whole roasted cauliflower on a restaurant menu? Trust me: you will soon. Beautifully crusted on the outside, tender and silky on the inside, this visually striking preparation of cauliflower is popular among chefs for a host of reasons: It's budget-friendly, simple to prepare, and guaranteed to impress guests either as an eye-popping centerpiece or side.

Spoon some tangy Nutty Dijon Vinaigrette on a roasted head of cauliflower, shower it with fresh herbs, and carve it up tableside. It's perfect for when your vegetarian buddies drop by for dinner!

INGREDIENTS:

- ¼ cup Nutty Dijon Vinaigrette (page 53)
- 1 whole cauliflower head (about 2 pounds)
- ½ cup extra-virgin olive oil
   Kosher salt
- ¼ cup minced fresh Italian parsley

↻ **SWITCH IT UP:**
ROASTED CAULIFLOWER WITH WHATEVER YOU WANT

HAZELNUT GARLIC SAUCE ISN'T THE ONLY WAY TO DRESS UP A WHOLE ROASTED CAULIFLOWER. TRY IT WITH ROMESCO SAUCE (PAGE 65), SRIRACHA RANCH (57), TONNATO SAUCE (51), XO SAUCE (PAGE 54), OR WHATEVER ELSE FLOATS YOUR BOAT.

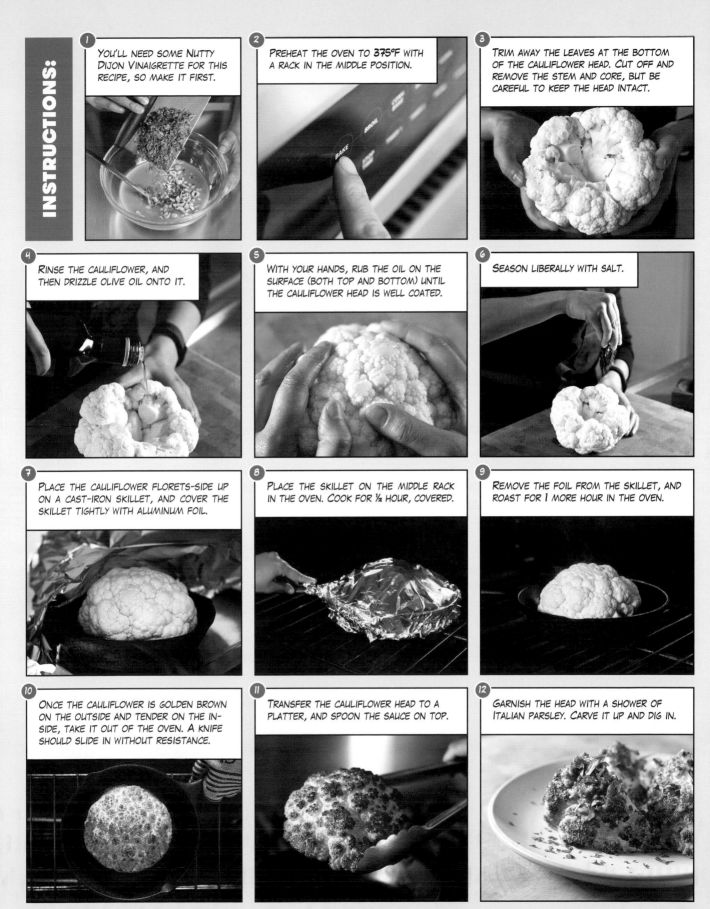

1. You'll need some Nutty Dijon Vinaigrette for this recipe, so make it first.

2. Preheat the oven to 375°F with a rack in the middle position.

3. Trim away the leaves at the bottom of the cauliflower head. Cut off and remove the stem and core, but be careful to keep the head intact.

4. Rinse the cauliflower, and then drizzle olive oil onto it.

5. With your hands, rub the oil on the surface (both top and bottom) until the cauliflower head is well coated.

6. Season liberally with salt.

7. Place the cauliflower florets-side up on a cast-iron skillet, and cover the skillet tightly with aluminum foil.

8. Place the skillet on the middle rack in the oven. Cook for ½ hour, covered.

9. Remove the foil from the skillet, and roast for 1 more hour in the oven.

10. Once the cauliflower is golden brown on the outside and tender on the inside, take it out of the oven. A knife should slide in without resistance.

11. Transfer the cauliflower head to a platter, and spoon the sauce on top.

12. Garnish the head with a shower of Italian parsley. Carve it up and dig in.

ROASTED CATALAN SHRIMP

MAKES 2 SERVINGS
⏱ 15 MINUTES

Paired with a fresh salad, roasted vegetables, or a generous scoop of Cauli Rice (page 80), roasted shrimp makes for an incredibly fast and easy dinner—especially when you have a jar of Romesco Sauce (page 65) at the ready. Catalan shrimp can also be enjoyed on its own; just close your eyes and pretend you're hanging out in a *pintxos* bar in San Sebastián after a day at the beach. After all, this is Spanish food at its best: unfussy, beautiful, and delicious.

INGREDIENTS:

1   cup Romesco Sauce (page 65)

1   pound fresh or frozen shrimp (21-25 count)

1½   tablespoons melted ghee, avocado oil, or olive oil, divided

1   teaspoon smoked paprika, divided

¼   teaspoon kosher salt

¼   teaspoon freshly ground black pepper

1   lemon, cut in half crosswise, and visible seeds removed

INSTRUCTIONS:

1 Don't have any Romesco Sauce? Go make some.

2 If using frozen shrimp, thaw it under running water for 5 to 7 minutes.

3 Meanwhile, preheat the oven to 400°F with a rack in the middle position.

4 Peel the shrimp, leaving the tails attached.

5 De-vein those suckers, too.

6 In a medium bowl, toss the shrimp with 1 tablespoon of ghee, ½ teaspoon of paprika, salt, and pepper.

7 Arrange the shrimp in a single layer on a parchment-lined baking sheet.

8 Roast in the oven for 6 to 8 minutes or until the shrimp is cooked through.

9 Heat a small skillet over medium-high heat. Once it's hot, add ½ tablespoon of ghee or oil, and place the lemon halves cut-side down in the skillet.

10 Cook for 1 to 2 minutes until browned.

11 Season the cooked shrimp with the remaining ½ teaspoon of paprika...

12 ...and the juice of the lemons.

13 Serve with Romesco Sauce.

197

MACADAMIA-CRUSTED SRIRACHA RANCH SALMON

MAKES 4 SERVINGS
⏱ 30 MINUTES
(10 MINUTES HANDS-ON)

Of all the ways to roast salmon, this is my favorite. On a pre-heated roasting pan coated with ghee, the salmon cooks perfectly, without drying out. The layers of spicy Sriracha Ranch and crunchy macadamia nuts also help keep the fish deliciously tender.

INGREDIENTS:

¼ cup Sriracha Ranch Dressing (page 57)

1 (1½-pound) skin-on salmon fillet

1 tablespoon ghee, avocado oil, or olive oil

1 teaspoon kosher salt
   Freshly ground black pepper

½ cup dry-roasted and salted macadamia nuts, roughly chopped

¼ cup minced fresh dill or Italian parsley (optional)

🔄 **SWITCH IT UP:**
NAKED SALMON ON A HOT PAN

NO SRIRACHA RANCH OR MAC NUTS ON HAND? JUST FOLLOW STEPS 2 THROUGH 9, AND YOU'LL HAVE A QUICK, TENDER FILLET OF SALMON THAT CAN BE SEASONED WITH LEMON, PEPPER, AND DILL, OR SERVED WITH ANY NUMBER OF SAUCES.

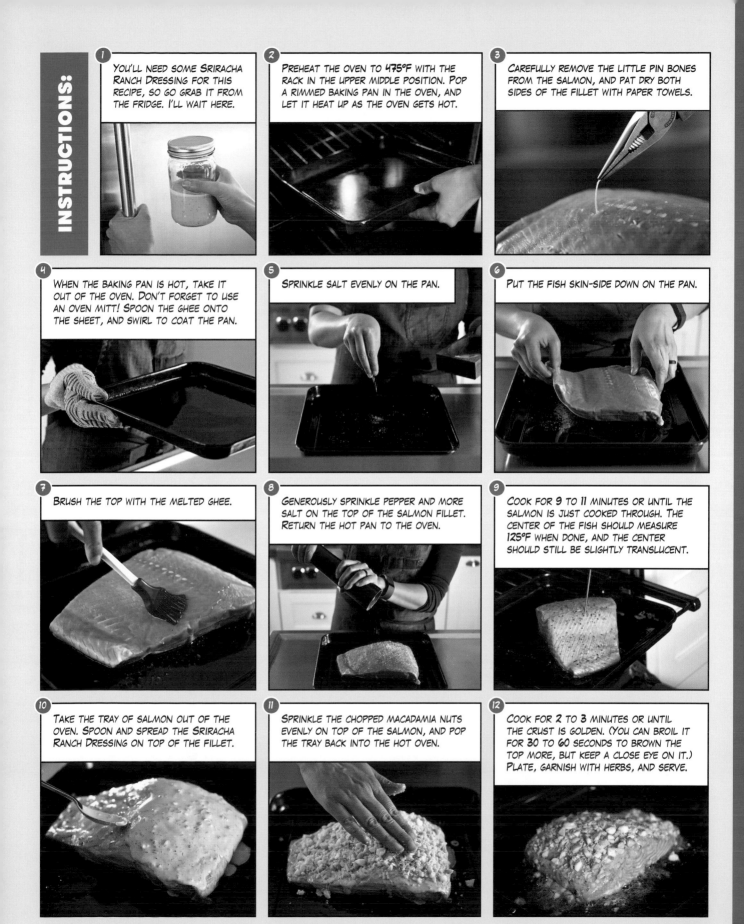

INSTRUCTIONS:

1. You'll need some Sriracha Ranch Dressing for this recipe, so go grab it from the fridge. I'll wait here.

2. Preheat the oven to 475°F with the rack in the upper middle position. Pop a rimmed baking pan in the oven, and let it heat up as the oven gets hot.

3. Carefully remove the little pin bones from the salmon, and pat dry both sides of the fillet with paper towels.

4. When the baking pan is hot, take it out of the oven. Don't forget to use an oven mitt! Spoon the ghee onto the sheet, and swirl to coat the pan.

5. Sprinkle salt evenly on the pan.

6. Put the fish skin-side down on the pan.

7. Brush the top with the melted ghee.

8. Generously sprinkle pepper and more salt on the top of the salmon fillet. Return the hot pan to the oven.

9. Cook for 9 to 11 minutes or until the salmon is just cooked through. The center of the fish should measure 125°F when done, and the center should still be slightly translucent.

10. Take the tray of salmon out of the oven. Spoon and spread the Sriracha Ranch Dressing on top of the fillet.

11. Sprinkle the chopped macadamia nuts evenly on top of the salmon, and pop the tray back into the hot oven.

12. Cook for 2 to 3 minutes or until the crust is golden. (You can broil it for 30 to 60 seconds to brown the top more, but keep a close eye on it.) Plate, garnish with herbs, and serve.

199

CHOOSE-YOUR-OWN-ADVENTURE EGG MUFFINS

MAKES 12 MUFFINS
⏱ 30 MINUTES
(10 MINUTES HANDS-ON)

Remember the old Choose Your Own Adventure books from the 1980s? The ones where you, the pre-teen reader, could determine your fate by flipping to the pages that correspond to your (usually poor) choices? These books were supposed to be fun, but more often than not, my decisions led to bizarrely grim endings: I'd get myself blown up by a mechanical dog, attacked by a swarm of bees, or abducted by aliens and split in half by a transdimensional portal.

Fortunately, my Choose-Your-Own-Adventure Egg Muffins don't call for any life-or-death decisions. Instead, you get to pick your favorite fillings for these deliciously portable mini-frittatas. I like to chop up and use whatever left-overs are languishing in the fridge, from meatballs to stir-fries. And no matter what you decide to use, a happy ending is guaranteed.

INGREDIENTS:

- **2** cups leftover cooked meat and/or vegetables like Pot Sticker Stir-Fry (page 304) or Easy Chicken Tinga (page 116) with chopped broccoli
- **8** large eggs
- **1½** tablespoons (10.5 grams) coconut flour
- **¾** teaspoon kosher salt

INSTRUCTIONS:

1 PREHEAT THE OVEN TO 375°F WITH THE RACK IN THE MIDDLE POSITION. LINE A 12-CUP MUFFIN TIN WITH PARCHMENT MUFFIN LINERS. (USE PARCHMENT LINERS OR THE MUFFINS WILL STICK.)

2 DIVIDE THE SEASONED, COOKED FILLING INTO EACH CUP IN THE MUFFIN TIN (ABOUT 2 HEAPING TABLESPOONS IN EACH CUP).

3 IN ANOTHER LARGE BOWL, WHISK TOGETHER THE EGGS, COCONUT FLOUR, AND SALT. TRY TO MAKE SURE THERE ARE NO LUMPS.

4 POUR THE MIXTURE INTO EACH CUP EVENLY, LEAVING ¼ INCH OF SPACE AT THE TOP.

5 BAKE THE EGG MUFFINS IN THE OVEN FOR 20 MINUTES, ROTATING THE MUFFIN TIN HALFWAY THROUGH THE COOKING PROCESS.

6 THE EGG MUFFINS ARE READY WHEN THE TOPS SPRING BACK WHEN YOU TOUCH THEM AND A TOOTHPICK INSERTED IN THE CENTER COMES OUT CLEANLY.

7 PLACE THE TIN ON A WIRE RACK TO COOL THE MUFFINS FOR 5 MINUTES. THEN, POP THEM OUT OF THE TIN AND PLACE THEM ON THE WIRE RACK TO FINISH COOLING.

8 EAT THEM NOW, OR PACK THE COOLED MUFFINS IN A SEALED CONTAINER IN THE REFRIGERATOR FOR UP TO 4 DAYS OR IN THE FREEZER FOR UP TO 6 MONTHS.

DUXELLES CHICKEN

MAKES 4 SERVINGS
⏱ **45 MINUTES**
(15 MINUTES HANDS-ON)

Remember when I told you that Duxelles would come in handy—but you didn't believe me? Well, you should have listened to me, because this easy weeknight recipe would have knocked your flippin' socks off. Too bad, so sad. No Duxelles Chicken for you.

Stop crying! I'm just kidding!

Duxelles is a cinch to make, so even if you find yourself in a less-than-prepared state, you have plenty of time to hop to it. And you'll be glad you did 'cause this chicken dinner is a winner. Bite through the golden crisp skin, and you'll sink your teeth into tender, flavorful chicken and mushrooms.

INGREDIENTS:

1   cup Duxelles (page 75)

8   bone-in, skin-on chicken thighs

2   teaspoons kosher salt

HEY! HOW DID THESE MUSHROOMS GET INSIDE MY CHICKEN?

INSTRUCTIONS:

1   MAKE SURE YOU HAVE DUXELLES ON HAND.

2   PREHEAT THE OVEN TO 425°F (OR 400°F ON CONVECTION SETTING) WITH THE RACK IN THE MIDDLE POSITION. SET A WIRE RACK ATOP A FOIL-LINED BAKING SHEET.

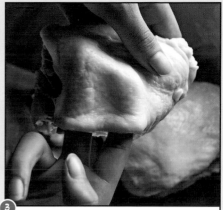

3   USE YOUR FINGERS TO GENTLY SEPARATE THE SKIN OF EACH CHICKEN THIGH AWAY FROM THE MEAT TO FORM A POCKET.

4   CAREFULLY STUFF 2 TABLESPOONS OF DUXELLES UNDER THE SKIN OF EACH THIGH. SEASON THE CHICKEN (TOP AND BOTTOM) WITH SALT, AND ARRANGE IN A SINGLE LAYER ON THE WIRE RACK, SKIN-SIDE DOWN.

5   COOK IN THE OVEN FOR 20 MINUTES. THEN, FLIP OVER EACH THIGH AND BAKE, SKIN-SIDE UP, FOR 20 MINUTES MORE...

6   ...UNTIL THE SKIN IS CRISP AND GOLDEN AND A THERMOMETER REGISTERS 165°F IN THE THICKEST PART OF EACH THIGH.

7   REST FOR 5 MINUTES, AND SERVE. LEFTOVERS CAN BE REFRIGERATED FOR UP TO 4 DAYS OR FROZEN FOR UP TO 3 MONTHS.

ORANGE SRIRACHA CHICKEN

MAKES 4 SERVINGS
⏱ **2 HOURS**
(30 MINUTES HANDS-ON)

Do I really have to explain why you should make this dish? I mean, you saw the name of this recipe, right?

INGREDIENTS:

2   teaspoons kosher salt

10 chicken drumsticks (about 3½ pounds)

• MARINADE •

1   medium yellow onion, roughly chopped

1   cup fresh basil leaves, packed

½   cup fresh orange juice

4   medium garlic cloves, roughly chopped

1   tablespoon fish sauce

1   tablespoon aged balsamic vinegar

1   teaspoon tomato paste

½   teaspoon freshly ground black pepper

• SAUCE •

½   cup fresh orange juice

2   tablespoons honey

1   tablespoon Nom Nom Sriracha (page 56) or store-bought sriracha

1   tablespoon ghee, avocado oil, or olive oil

1   teaspoon coconut aminos

1   teaspoon toasted sesame seeds (optional)

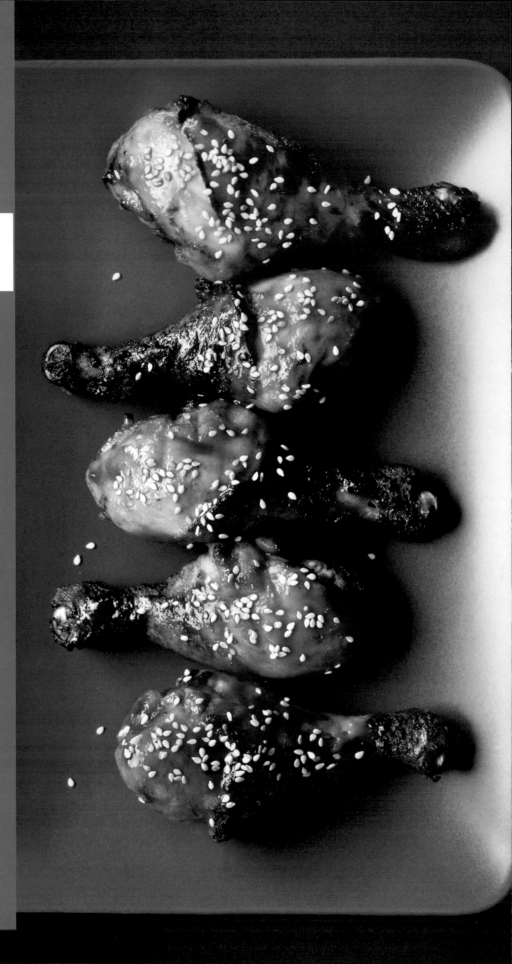

1 IN A LARGE BOWL, SPRINKLE THE SALT ON THE CHICKEN, AND THEN SET IT ASIDE.

2 TO MAKE THE MARINADE, TOSS THE ONION, BASIL, ORANGE JUICE, GARLIC, FISH SAUCE, VINEGAR, TOMATO PASTE, AND PEPPER IN A HIGH-POWERED BLENDER.

3 PURÉE UNTIL SMOOTH.

4 POUR THE MIXTURE OVER THE CHICKEN, COATING THE DRUMSTICKS WELL. COVER AND MARINATE IN THE REFRIGERATOR FOR AT LEAST AN HOUR AND UP TO 12 HOURS.

5 WHEN YOU'RE READY TO COOK, TAKE THE CHICKEN OUT OF THE FRIDGE AND PREHEAT THE OVEN TO 400°F. PLACE A WIRE RACK ON TOP OF A FOIL-LINED BAKING SHEET.

SET TEMP
400°F

6 TRANSFER THE DRUMSTICKS TO THE WIRE RACK. SPOON THE EXTRA MARINADE ONTO EACH PIECE OF CHICKEN.

7 BAKE FOR 40 MINUTES OR UNTIL COOKED THROUGH AND THE SKIN IS GOLDEN BROWN, FLIPPING EACH PIECE AND TURNING THE BAKING SHEET AT THE HALFWAY POINT.

8 WHILE THE CHICKEN'S IN THE OVEN, MAKE THE SAUCE. IN A SMALL SAUCEPAN, STIR TOGETHER THE ORANGE JUICE, HONEY, SRIRACHA, GHEE, AND COCONUT AMINOS.

9 COOK OVER HIGH HEAT. ONCE THE SAUCE IS AT A BOIL, TURN DOWN THE HEAT TO LOW, AND REDUCE THE SAUCE UNTIL THICKENED (ABOUT 3 TO 5 MINUTES). TASTE AND ADJUST THE SEASONING IF NEEDED.

10 AFTER THE CHICKEN'S BEEN IN THE OVEN FOR 40 MINUTES, BRUSH A THIN LAYER OF THE SAUCE ON EACH DRUMSTICK. ROAST THE CHICKEN FOR 5 MORE MINUTES.

11 TAKE THE TRAY OUT OF THE OVEN AND USE A BRUSH TO GLAZE THE DRUMSTICKS WITH THE REMAINING SAUCE. PLATE IT ALL UP.

12 IF DESIRED, ADD A SPRINKLE OF TOASTED SESAME SEEDS.

REFRIGERATE EXTRAS FOR UP TO 4 DAYS.

PAPER-WRAPPED CHICKEN

MAKES 4 SERVINGS
⏱ **30 MINUTES**
(10 MINUTES HANDS-ON)

In the '70s and '80s, Henry grew up in his parents' Chinese restaurant. There, he bussed tables, washed dishes, manned (boyed?) the deep fryer, and prepped food. (Henry must have overdosed on restaurant work; these days, I'm the only one puttering around our kitchen.)

One of the dishes on the menu was Paper-Wrapped Chicken. Working alongside his cousins, Henry would tuck marinated pieces of chicken into sheets of shiny foil, and then carefully fold them into three-sided pouches, origami-style. The packets would later be cooked to order.

My version doesn't much resemble my in-laws' restaurant dish, but it's just as packed with Asian flavors, and can be prepped up to 1 day in advance of cooking.

Now, if only I could coax Henry back into the kitchen to help me make these packets for dinner. . . .

INGREDIENTS:

- ½ cup All-Purpose Stir-Fry Sauce (page 67)
- 4 cups sliced bok choy

  Kosher salt

  Freshly ground black pepper
- 4 (6-ounce) boneless, skinless chicken breasts or thighs
- 8 shiitake mushrooms, thinly sliced
- 2 large shallots, thinly sliced

INSTRUCTIONS:

1. SET THE OVEN TO 450°F WITH THE RACK IN THE MIDDLE, AND MAKE ALL-PURPOSE STIR-FRY SAUCE IF YOU DON'T HAVE ANY. IT'LL TAKE LESS THAN 5 MINUTES.

2. GRAB 4 LARGE PARCHMENT SHEETS, AND FOLD EACH IN HALF. DRAW HALF A HEART ON EACH SHEET SO THAT WHEN YOU CUT THEM OUT, YOU GET FULL HEARTS.

3. UNFOLD THE PAPER HEARTS AND LAY THEM FLAT. PLACE A CUP OF SLICED BOK CHOY ON ONE SIDE OF EACH HEART. SPRINKLE SALT AND PEPPER ON THE BOK CHOY.

4. SALT AND PEPPER THE CHICKEN, TOO. THAN, PLACE A PIECE OF CHICKEN ATOP EACH PILE OF BOK CHOY.

5. TOP WITH MUSHROOMS AND SHALLOTS. SPOON 2 TABLESPOONS OF ALL-PURPOSE STIR-FRY SAUCE ONTO EACH MOUND.

6. FOLD THE OTHER HALF OF EACH HEART OVER THE TOP. TIGHTLY CRIMP THE EDGES TOGETHER, STARTING AT THE TOP-CENTER OF EACH HEART. AT THE POINTED BOTTOM END, TWIST THE PAPER TO SEAL WELL.

7. PLACE THE PARCHMENT PACKETS ON A RIMMED BAKING SHEET.

8. BAKE IN THE OVEN FOR 15 TO 20 MINUTES OR UNTIL THE CHICKEN IS FULLY COOKED. THE BREASTS SHOULD REGISTER 150°F ON AN INSTANT-READ THERMOMETER, AND THE THIGHS SHOULD REGISTER 165°F.

9 AS SOON AS THE PACKETS ARE OUT OF THE OVEN, CAREFULLY CUT THEM OPEN. SERVE IMMEDIATELY.

THANKSGIVING BITES

MAKES 30 (2-INCH) PATTIES
⏱ 45 MINUTES

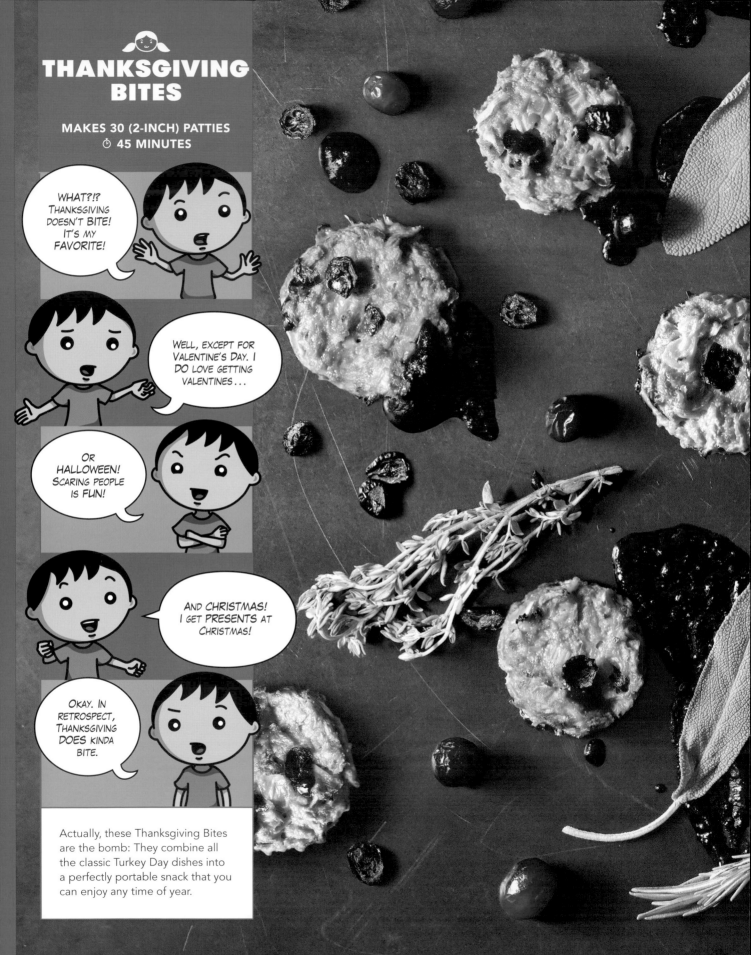

WHAT?!? THANKSGIVING DOESN'T BITE! IT'S MY FAVORITE!

WELL, EXCEPT FOR VALENTINE'S DAY. I DO LOVE GETTING VALENTINES . . .

OR HALLOWEEN! SCARING PEOPLE IS FUN!

AND CHRISTMAS! I GET PRESENTS AT CHRISTMAS!

OKAY. IN RETROSPECT, THANKSGIVING DOES KINDA BITE.

Actually, these Thanksgiving Bites are the bomb: They combine all the classic Turkey Day dishes into a perfectly portable snack that you can enjoy any time of year.

IS THIS SUPPOSED TO LOOK FESTIVE, OR DID WE ACCIDENTALLY DROP A BUNCH OF TWIGS AND FOOD ON THE TABLE?

INGREDIENTS:

- ½ cup Cran-Cherry Sauce (page 68)
- 1 tablespoon ghee, avocado oil, or olive oil
- 1 small onion, minced (about 100 grams)
- 1 medium carrot, minced (about 85 grams)
- 1 medium celery stalk, minced (about 40 grams)
- 1 cup finely chopped Brussels sprouts (about 100 grams)
- 2½ teaspoons kosher salt, divided
- 2 garlic cloves, minced
- 1 large sweet potato (about 230 grams), peeled
- 1 pound ground turkey thighs
- 1 large egg, beaten
- ¼ cup dried cranberries
- ½ teaspoon minced fresh rosemary
- 1 teaspoon minced fresh sage
- 1 teaspoon minced fresh thyme
- ¼ teaspoon freshly ground black pepper

INSTRUCTIONS:

1. IF YOU'RE PLANNING TO SERVE THESE NIBBLES WITH CRAN-CHERRY SAUCE, MAKE SURE YOU HAVE SOME AT THE READY. (OF COURSE, IF IT'S TOO MUCH TROUBLE, DON'T WORRY ABOUT IT. THESE BITES ARE REALLY GOOD JUST ON THEIR OWN.)

2. SET THE OVEN TO 400°F ON CONVECTION MODE (OR 425°F ON REGULAR MODE IF CONVECTION'S NOT AN OPTION) WITH A RACK PLACED IN THE MIDDLE POSITION.

3. LINE 2 RIMMED BAKING SHEETS WITH PARCHMENT PAPER, AND SET THEM ASIDE.

4. MELT THE GHEE IN A SKILLET OVER MEDIUM HEAT. ONCE IT'S SHIMMERING, ADD THE ONIONS, CARROTS, AND CELERY.

5. COOK, STIRRING, FOR 5 MINUTES OR UNTIL THE VEGETABLES HAVE SOFTENED.

6. ADD THE BRUSSELS SPROUTS, AND STIR IN ½ TEASPOON OF SALT.

7. COOK FOR ABOUT 2 MINUTES OR UNTIL THE LEAVES HAVE WILTED.

8. ADD THE GARLIC. STIR FOR 30 SECONDS OR UNTIL FRAGRANT.

9 TRANSFER THE COOKED VEGETABLES TO A PLATTER. SPREAD IT OUT IN A SINGLE LAYER AND COOL TO ROOM TEMPERATURE.

10 USE EITHER A GRATER OR THE SHREDDER ATTACHMENT OF A FOOD PROCESSOR TO SHRED THE SWEET POTATOES. YOU SHOULD END UP WITH APPROXIMATELY 2 CUPS.

11 IN A LARGE BOWL, COMBINE ALL THE INGREDIENTS (EXCEPT THE CRAN-CHERRY SAUCE), INCLUDING THE COOKED VEGGIES, SWEET POTATO, TURKEY, BEATEN EGG, DRIED CRANBERRIES, HERBS, PEPPER, AND THE 2 REMAINING TEASPOONS OF SALT.

12 USING YOUR HANDS, GENTLY MIX ALL THE INGREDIENTS TOGETHER UNTIL COMBINED, BUT DON'T OVERWORK THE MIXTURE.

13 PINCH OFF A BIT OF THE MIXTURE, FLATTEN IT INTO A PATTY, AND COOK IT WITH A BIT OF GHEE OR OIL IN A SKILLET OVER MEDIUM HEAT FOR 1 TO 2 MINUTES ON EACH SIDE UNTIL COOKED THROUGH. TASTE IT. IF IT NEEDS MORE SEASONING, ADD SOME MORE SALT TO THE MEAT MIXTURE.

14 USING A SPOON OR A #60 DISHER, SCOOP OUT HEAPING 1 TABLESPOON-SIZE BALLS...

15 ...AND ARRANGE THEM ABOUT 2 INCHES APART ON THE LINED BAKING SHEETS.

16 SMOOSH EACH BALL INTO ½-INCH PATTIES.

17 POP ONE TRAY INTO THE OVEN AND COOK FOR 15 MINUTES, ROTATING ONCE AT THE MIDWAY POINT, OR UNTIL THE PATTIES ARE COOKED THROUGH.

18 REPEAT WITH THE OTHER TRAY OF PATTIES.

19 SERVE THESE THANKSGIVING BITES WITH CRAN-CHERRY SAUCE. THEY CAN BE KEPT IN A SEALED CONTAINER IN THE FRIDGE FOR UP TO 1 WEEK OR IN THE FREEZER FOR UP TO 3 MONTHS. YOU CAN FRY THEM UP STRAIGHT OUT OF THE FREEZER IN A SKILLET OVER MEDIUM-HIGH HEAT.

JÍBARITOS (FRIED PLANTAIN SANDWICHES)

MAKES 4 SANDWICHES
⏱ 10 MINUTES

The *jíbarito*—a sandwich that uses flattened fried plantains in place of bread—has Puerto Rican DNA, but was actually invented in Chicago, at the late, great Borinquen Restaurant. The crispy sandwich's popularity has steadily spread from the Midwest to the coasts, and it's not hard to see why. From the first time I tried a *jíbarito* (at Sol Food in San Rafael, California), I was hooked on the crisp, twice-fried plantain patties and savory meat fillings. If you're lucky (or prepared) enough to have fried green plantains, salsa, and leftover meat on hand, you're in for a special treat.

INGREDIENTS:

- **8** pieces **Fried Green Plantains (page 98)**
- **½** cup **Roasted Garlic Mayonnaise (page 52) (optional)**
- **3** cups cooked meat like **Pressure Cooker Carne Mechada (page 144)**, **Pressure Cooker Kalua Pig (page 128)**, or **Easy Chicken Tinga (page 116)**
- **½** cup **Salsa Ahumada (page 72)**, **Fruit + Avocado Salsa (page 70)**, or sauce of choice
- **½** cup cherry tomatoes, halved (optional)
- **¼** cup fresh herbs (optional)

INSTRUCTIONS:

1 GRAB SOME FRIED GREEN PLANTAINS, ROASTED GARLIC MAYONNAISE, LEFTOVER MEAT, AND YOUR FAVORITE SALSA. HERE, I HAVE PRESSURE COOKER CARNE MECHADA AND FRUIT + AVOCADO SALSA (MADE USING RIPE MANGO AS MY FRUIT).

2 YOU KNOW HOW TO MAKE A SANDWICH, RIGHT? SLATHER A PIECE OF FRIED PLANTAIN WITH SOME ROASTED GARLIC MAYONNAISE (IF DESIRED), AND THEN SPOON ON SOME MEAT AND YOUR FAVORITE SALSA. PUT ANOTHER PLANTAIN ON TOP. CONGRATULATIONS: IT'S A SANDWICH!

3 MAKE SANDWICHES UNTIL YOU'RE OUT OF PLANTAINS, MEAT, OR BOTH. THEN, PICK UP YOUR JÍBARITOS AND SCARF 'EM DOWN.

4 PLAY AROUND WITH DIFFERENT FILLINGS. THIS ONE USES PRESSURE COOKER KALUA PIG, CHERRY TOMATOES, AND GUACAMOLE.

JÍBARITOS ARE THE PERFECT EXAMPLE OF A LEFTOVER MAKEOVER. ALWAYS MAKE EXTRA FOOD, AND TAKE A FEW MINUTES TO THINK CREATIVELY ABOUT HOW YOU CAN COMBINE DIFFERENT DISHES INTO SOMETHING NEW AND INCREDIBLE. (HENRY CALLS THIS THE VOLTRON PRINCIPLE, NAMED AFTER THE 80S CARTOON FEATURING FIVE MECHANICAL LIONS THAT COMBINE TO FORM A GIGANTIC HUMANOID ROBOT. YES, HENRY IS A BIG NERD.)

BITE ME.

LEFTACOS

Sick of eating leftovers? Give them a makeover by spooning them onto Nature's Tortillas (page 79), Grain-Free Tortillas (page 78), or Fried Green Plantains (page 98). Add some salsa or one of the other sauces from the "Get Set!" section of this book, and top everything with a garnish of fresh herbs, chopped onions, or even strips of crunchy bacon. These aren't leftovers anymore—or even mere tacos. They're LEFTACOS!

OLLIE'S CRACKLIN' CHICKEN (PAGE 278) AND SUNBUTTER HOISIN SAUCE (PAGE 59)

PRESSURE COOKER CARNE MECHADA (PAGE 144) AND SLICED AVOCADO

PRESSURE COOKER SALSA CHICKEN (PAGE 290) STUFFED IN A BELL PEPPER

PRESSURE COOKER CARNE MECHADA (PAGE 144) AND FRUIT + AVOCADO SALSA (PAGE 70)

POT STICKER STIR-FRY (PAGE 304) AND NOM NOM SRIRACHA (PAGE 56)

SCRAMBLED EGGS WITH SHRIMP + SCALLIONS (PAGE 266) AND SRIRACHA RANCH DRESSING (PAGE 57)

CRISPY BACON, SCRAMBLED EGGS, AND STORE-BOUGHT TOMATO SALSA

EASY CHICKEN TINGA (PAGE 116) WITH SLICED RADISH AND LIME

SCRAMBLED EGGS, PRESSURE COOKER KALUA PIG (PAGE 128), AND SALSA AHUMADA (PAGE 72)

ROAST-AHEAD CHICKEN BREASTS (PAGE 84) AND SALSA AHUMADA (PAGE 72)

SALT + PEPPER FRIED PORK CHOPS (PAGE 124)

PORK CHICHARRÓN NACHOS

MAKES 4 SERVINGS
⏱ **30 MINUTES**

Puffy, airy, crunchy, salty fried pork rinds are the perfect substitute for bland tortilla chips. To make a big plate of crowd-pleasing nachos, just top 'em with crisped pork, creamy guacamole, and a simple salsa—or whatever else gets you going. It's pork-on-pork action!

INGREDIENTS:

2   cups Pressure Cooker or Slow Cooker Kalua Pig (page 128), Pressure Cooker Bo Ssäm (page 132), or Slow Cooker Bo Ssäm (page 134)

4   ounces chicharrónes (fried pork rinds)

• GUACAMOLE •

1   small shallot, minced

   Juice from 1 lime

½   teaspoon kosher salt

2   medium Hass avocados, halved, pitted, and peeled

• JICAMA SALSA •

½   cup finely diced jicama

½   cup finely diced mango

¼   cup finely diced cucumber

   Juice from ½ lime

¼   teaspoon paprika

• GARNISH •

¼   cup fresh cilantro (optional)

3   fresh radishes, thinly sliced (optional)

I LIKE TO USE CHICHARRÓNES OR PORK RINDS FROM EPIC OR 4505 MEATS. BOTH ARE MADE USING PALEO-FRIENDLY INGREDIENTS, AND AVAILABLE IN STORES AND ONLINE.

1 PREPARE THE GUACAMOLE. IN A SMALL BOWL, SOAK THE SHALLOT IN LIME JUICE AND SALT FOR 10 MINUTES.

2 WHILE THE SHALLOT IS SOAKING, GRAB YOUR LEFTOVER PORK. SHRED IT AND TOSS IT INTO A SKILLET OVER MEDIUM HEAT.

3 COOK THE MEAT, STIRRING OCCASIONALLY, FOR 5 TO 8 MINUTES OR UNTIL CRISPED AND GOLDEN. TRANSFER IT TO A PLATE.

4 TO FINISH MAKING THE GUACAMOLE, MASH ONE OF THE AVOCADOS IN A BOWL WITH A FORK. ADD THE SHALLOT MIXTURE TO THE MASHED AVOCADO AND STIR TO COMBINE.

5 CUBE THE OTHER AVOCADO INTO ½-INCH PIECES, AND ADD IT TO THE MIXTURE IN THE BOWL. GENTLY COMBINE THE MASHED AVOCADO AND THE CUBED AVOCADO.

6 TASTE AND ADJUST WITH SALT AND/OR LIME JUICE.

7 NEXT, WHIP UP A SIMPLE JICAMA SALSA BY TOSSING TOGETHER THE JICAMA, MANGO, CUCUMBER, LIME JUICE, AND PAPRIKA IN A BOWL. SEASON TO TASTE WITH LIME JUICE.

8 SPREAD THE CHICHARRÓNES ON A PLATTER.

9 TOP WITH THE CRISPY PORK. DO YOUR BEST TO MAKE SURE EACH CHICHARRÓN IS STUFFED WITH A BIT OF PORKY GOODNESS.

10 TOP THE NACHOS WITH GUACAMOLE . . .

11 . . . AND SALSA.

12 IF YOU WANT, GARNISH WITH CILANTRO AND/OR RADISH SLICES BEFORE SERVING.

NOT EATING RIGHT AWAY? YOU CAN STUFF THESE PEPPERS AHEAD OF TIME, AND BAKE THEM WHEN YOU'RE READY TO CHOW DOWN.

STUFFED SUNDAY PEPPERS

MAKES 4 SERVINGS
⏱ **45 MINUTES**
(10 MINUTES HANDS-ON)

Just like your favorite superhero, Sunday Gravy comes to the rescue yet again! As you're probably beginning to suspect, Sunday Gravy is one of the most versatile make-ahead recipes in this book. Learn to repurpose it, and you can easily assemble a weeknight meal in just minutes—and no one will guess your dish's secret origin.

Of course, Sunday Gravy is pretty tasty, so I can't blame you if you already polished off your leftovers. In that case, just brown ¾ pound of ground beef with some salt and pepper in a skillet, and then simmer the meat in 1½ cups of marinara sauce. Then, use this meat sauce in place of the Sunday Gravy in this recipe. Problem solved.

INGREDIENTS:

- 2 **cups Sunday Gravy (page 152)**
- 4 **medium bell peppers**
- 2 **cups riced cauliflower (see instructions on page 80)**
- ¼ **cup tablespoons fresh basil, cut into thin ribbons and divided**
- ½ **teaspoon salt**
  Freshly ground black pepper
- ¼ **teaspoon red pepper flakes (optional)**
- ½ **cup Bone Broth (page 76), chicken stock, or water**

INSTRUCTIONS:

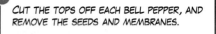

1 GO GRAB SOME SUNDAY GRAVY FROM THE FRIDGE, AND PREHEAT THE OVEN TO 350°F.

2 CUT THE TOPS OFF EACH BELL PEPPER, AND REMOVE THE SEEDS AND MEMBRANES.

3 IN A MEDIUM BOWL, MIX TOGETHER THE SUNDAY GRAVY, RICED CAULIFLOWER, HALF OF THE MINCED BASIL, SALT, PEPPER, AND RED PEPPER FLAKES, IF USING. TASTE THE SEASONING AND ADJUST IF NEEDED.

4 PLACE THE HOLLOWED-OUT PEPPERS IN AN 8 BY 8-INCH BAKING DISH. SPOON 1 CUP OF THE FILLING INTO EACH OF THE PEPPERS.

5 POUR BROTH, STOCK, OR WATER IN THE BOTTOM OF THE BAKING DISH.

6 BAKE FOR 25 TO 35 MINUTES OR UNTIL THE PEPPERS ARE TENDER AND THE FILLING IS PIPING HOT. TOP WITH THE REMAINING BASIL, AND SERVE IMMEDIATELY.

MONDAY FRITTATA

MAKES 2 SERVINGS
⏱ 30 MINUTES
(10 MINUTES HANDS-ON)

You can add just about anything to this simple one-skillet supper—even yesterday's Sunday Gravy.

INGREDIENTS:

- 1 **cup Sunday Gravy (page 152) or cooked meat of choice**
- 1 **tablespoon ghee**
- 1 **cup Swiss chard leaves, cut into ribbons**
- 4 **large eggs**
- 2 **tablespoons coconut milk**
- 1 **teaspoon kosher salt**
- ¼ **teaspoon freshly ground black pepper**
- 2 **tablespoons fresh basil, cut into thin ribbons**

INSTRUCTIONS:

1 MAKE SURE YOU HAVE SUNDAY GRAVY (OR YOUR COOKED MEAT OF CHOICE) AT THE READY. PREHEAT THE OVEN TO 350°F.

2 HEAT THE GHEE IN AN 8-INCH OVEN-PROOF SKILLET OVER MEDIUM HEAT. ADD THE SUNDAY GRAVY TO THE SKILLET. COOK, STIRRING, UNTIL HEATED THROUGH.

3 ADD THE JULIENNED SWISS CHARD TO THE SKILLET, AND MIX THOROUGHLY.

4 IN A MEDIUM BOWL, BEAT TOGETHER THE EGGS, COCONUT MILK, SALT, AND PEPPER.

5 POUR THE EGG MIXTURE INTO THE SKILLET, AND COOK UNDISTURBED ON THE STOVE FOR 3 TO 5 MINUTES OR UNTIL THE BOTTOM OF THE FRITTATA IS SET.

6 PUT THE SKILLET IN THE OVEN. COOK FOR 10 TO 15 MINUTES UNTIL THE TOP IS SET, AND THEN CRANK THE HEAT UP TO BROIL FOR ANOTHER 2 MINUTES OR UNTIL THE FRITTATA PUFFS UP AND IS COOKED ALL THE WAY THROUGH.

7 GARNISH THE FRITTATA WITH THE BASIL. SLICE AND SERVE. YOU CAN REFRIGERATE ANY LEFTOVERS FOR UP TO 4 DAYS.

XO PORK WITH BLISTERED GREEN BEANS

MAKES 4 SERVINGS
⏱ **30 MINUTES**

Got some XO Sauce (page 54) in the fridge? Good—because it pairs beautifully with ground pork. Add spring-picked green beans that have been quickly blistered in a sizzling-hot skillet, and you've got yourself a brand new addiction.

INGREDIENTS:

- ¼ cup XO Sauce (page 54)
- ¼ cup ghee, avocado oil, or olive oil
- 1 pound green beans, trimmed
- Kosher salt
- 1 large shallot, minced
- 1½ pounds ground pork
- Freshly ground black pepper

NOT A PORK LOVER? MAKE THIS WITH GROUND CHICKEN OR TURKEY INSTEAD!

INSTRUCTIONS:

1 XO SAUCE IS REQUIRED FOR THIS RECIPE, SO MAKE SURE YOU HAVE SOME. HEAT A LARGE SKILLET ON HIGH FOR 5 MINUTES. ONCE THE PAN IS CRAZY-HOT, ADD THE GHEE (OR OIL) AND THE GREEN BEANS. SPRINKLE A PINCH OF SALT ON THE BEANS.

2 COOK, STIRRING, FOR 3 TO 5 MINUTES OR UNTIL THE GREEN BEANS ARE BLISTERED AND TENDER. TRANSFER 'EM TO A PLATTER, LEAVING THE HOT OIL IN THE SKILLET.

3 TURN DOWN THE HEAT TO MEDIUM. TOSS IN THE SHALLOTS AND GROUND PORK, AND COOK UNTIL IT'S NO LONGER PINK.

4 STIR IN THE XO SAUCE, AND SEASON TO TASTE WITH SALT AND PEPPER.

5 MIX THE GREEN BEANS BACK IN, AND STIR TO COMBINE. PLATE AND SERVE.

SWITCH IT UP:
**SPICY PORK WITH
GREEN BEANS**

XO SAUCE IS LIKE NOTHING ELSE, BUT IF YOU DON'T HAVE ANY, GIVE THIS A TRY INSTEAD: MIX TOGETHER ½ CUP ALL-PURPOSE STIR-FRY SAUCE (PAGE 67), 1 TEASPOON ARROWROOT POWDER, AND ½ TEASPOON RED PEPPER FLAKES. USE THIS MIXTURE INSTEAD OF THE XO SAUCE IN STEP 4.

WEEKNIGHT MEATBALLS

MAKES 24 MEATBALLS
⏱ 40 MINUTES
(15 MINUTES HANDS-ON)

Weeknight Meatballs are another reason to always have Duxelles (page 75) prepped and ready to go. Mushrooms make the world go 'round, and they give these balls a boost of extra umami power.

My other super-secret ingredient? Gelatin. It's not just for jiggly desserts, people. As a matter of fact, gelatin is an amazing gluten-free meatball binder that adds texture as well as nutrients.

A quick tip: Before rolling out your meatballs, fry up a spoonful of the mixture in a skillet and taste it for seasoning. That way, you won't risk baking up a batch of bland balls.

And when you're all done with dinner, save the leftovers. You can plop these meatballs into soups (like the Simple Egg Drop Soup on page 244), add them to salads, or serve them with zucchini noodles. Me? I like to chop 'em up and make meatball egg scrambles.

INGREDIENTS:

- ½   cup Duxelles (page 75)
- 2   teaspoons powdered gelatin
- 1   pound ground beef
- 1   pound ground pork
- ½   cup finely diced yellow onion (about ½ an onion)
- ¼   cup minced fresh Italian parsley
- 6   garlic cloves, minced
- 2   teaspoons kosher salt

INSTRUCTIONS:

1. GOT DUXELLES? AWESOME. PREHEAT THE OVEN TO 400°F WITH A RACK IN THE MIDDLE. POUR ¼ CUP OF WATER IN A SHALLOW BOWL, AND SPRINKLE THE POWDERED GELATIN ON THE LIQUID.

2. LET IT STAND FOR 5 TO 10 MINUTES OR UNTIL THE GELATIN BLOOMS (WHICH IS JUST A FANCY WAY OF SAYING "UNTIL THE GELATIN POWDER ABSORBS THE WATER").

3. USING YOUR HANDS, GENTLY MIX TOGETHER THE BLOOMED GELATIN WITH ALL OF THE OTHER INGREDIENTS IN A LARGE BOWL. BE CAREFUL NOT TO OVERWORK THE MEAT.

4. FORM THE MEAT MIXTURE INTO 1½-INCH BALLS. I LIKE TO SCOOP 'EM OUT USING A #24 DISHER, WHICH HOLDS 3 TABLESPOONS AND MAKES PERFECTLY SIZED MEATBALLS.

5. ROLL THE BALLS BETWEEN YOUR HANDS TO MAKE SURE THEY'RE PRETTY AND ROUND.

6. ARRANGE ALL THE MEATBALLS ON A LARGE PARCHMENT-LINED BAKING SHEET.

7. BAKE FOR 15 TO 20 MINUTES OR UNTIL THE MEATBALLS ARE COOKED THROUGH.

8. SERVE. THESE MEATBALLS WILL KEEP IN THE REFRIGERATOR FOR UP TO 4 DAYS AND IN THE FREEZER FOR UP TO 6 MONTHS.

SWITCH IT UP:
MEATBALL SOUP

GOT LEFTOVER MEATBALLS? PLOP THEM INTO BOWLS OF SIMPLE EGG DROP SOUP (PAGE 244) FOR A PROTEIN-PACKED MEAL.

SWITCH IT UP:
MEATBALLS 'N' GRAVY

ONE MORE LEFTOVER MAKEOVER IDEA: SIMMER MEATBALLS IN UMAMI GRAVY (PAGE 69) FOR AN UMAMI EXPLOSION!

AFTER ALL, IN OTHER PARTS OF THE WORLD, PEOPLE EAT ALL SORTS OF STUFF FOR BREAKFAST EVERY DAY, FROM MEAT AND FISH TO VEGETABLES AND STEW!

REMEMBER THE STREET VENDORS WE SAW IN VIETNAM, SERVING UP STEAMING BOWLS OF SOUP TO MORNING COMMUTERS?

YOU DON'T EVEN HAVE TO GO THAT FAR OUTSIDE YOUR COMFORT ZONE. HAVE SOME SAUSAGES AND SAUERKRAUT FOR BREAKFAST!

(THESE SAUSAGES ARE FROM PORTLAND'S FEASTWORKS!)

AND YOU KNOW WHAT ELSE YOU COULD EAT IN THE MORNING BESIDES PANCAKES AND WAFFLES? EGGS!

REHEAT SOME LEFTOVER ASIAN CITRUS BRUSSELS SPROUTS SLAW (PAGE 258) IN A HOT SKILLET, AND COOK AN EGG IN IT.

FEELING AMBITIOUS? HARD-BOIL A BUNCH OF EGGS, CUT 'EM IN HALF, AND TOP THEM WITH WHATEVER'S IN YOUR REFRIGERATOR.

OR JUST SCRAMBLE SOME EGGS WITH DUXELLES (PAGE 75), A PINCH OF SALT, A FEW DROPS OF FISH SAUCE, AND CHIVES!

MAKE A BREAKFAST SALAD. TOSS SALAD GREENS WITH SLICED ROAST-AHEAD CHICKEN BREAST (PAGE 84), SMOKY LIME PEPITAS (PAGE 46), AND THAI CITRUS DRESSING (PAGE 47)!

START THE DAY WITH MEAT AND VEGGIES! JUST TOP A BOWL OF ZOODLES WITH LEFT-OVER POT STICKER STIR-FRY (PAGE 304).

OR TOSS LEFTOVER CHICKEN INTO A PAN WITH CHERRY TOMATOES AND SPINACH, AND SEASON WITH SALT AND PEPPER. IT'S EASY!

PRIME RIB HASH

MAKES 4 SERVINGS
⏱ **30 MINUTES**

People ask me all the time what I eat for breakfast. When I tell them I heat up leftovers, their eyes glaze over. But leftovers don't have to be boring, people. In fact, here's one easy way to turn last night's food scraps into a spicy, hearty breakfast that wouldn't be out of place on a high-end brunch menu.

You're welcome, by the way.

INGREDIENTS:

- **1** pound leftover Primetime Rib Roast (page 148)
- **2** tablespoons ghee
- **1** medium yellow onion, diced small

  Kosher salt
- **2** garlic cloves, minced
- **2** medium sweet potatoes, peeled and cut into ½-inch dice
- **1** red bell pepper, seeded and cut into ½-inch dice
- **¼** teaspoon cayenne pepper

  Freshly ground black pepper
- **¼** cup minced fresh Italian parsley
- **2** tablespoons chopped chives

INSTRUCTIONS:

1 DICE YOUR LEFTOVER PRIME RIB INTO ½-INCH CUBES. (ANY OTHER MEAT WILL WORK, TOO, BUT THEN DON'T CALL IT PRIME RIB HASH.)

2 HEAT THE GHEE IN A LARGE SKILLET OVER MEDIUM HEAT. WHEN THE FAT IS SHIMMERING, ADD THE ONIONS AND A SPRINKLE OF SALT. COOK FOR 3 TO 5 MINUTES OR UNTIL THE ONIONS HAVE SOFTENED.

3 ADD THE GARLIC. COOK FOR 30 SECONDS OR UNTIL FRAGRANT. ADD THE DICED SWEET POTATOES AND A BIT MORE SALT.

4 STIR WELL. COVER THE SKILLET AND STEAM FOR 5 MINUTES.

5 STIR, COVER AGAIN, AND COOK FOR ANOTHER 3 MINUTES OR UNTIL THE SPUDS ARE TENDER AND SLIGHTLY BROWNED.

6 TOSS IN THE RED BELL PEPPER AND PRIME RIB. SEASON WITH CAYENNE PEPPER, SALT, AND PEPPER. COOK, STIRRING GENTLY, UNTIL THE MEAT HAS HEATED THROUGH.

7 PLATE AND TOP WITH FRESH HERBS.

USE DIFFERENT VARIETIES OF SWEET POTATO TO MAKE YOUR HASH POP WITH COLOR AND TEXTURE!

WANNA KEEP YOUR BURGERS TENDER? DON'T SALT 'EM UNTIL RIGHT BEFORE GRILLING.

HOISIN-GLAZED BURGERS

MAKES 4 BURGERS
⏱ **15 MINUTES**

Are burger nights getting boring? I've got just the thing. Hoisin sauce is often called "Chinese barbecue sauce," so fire up the grill and glaze your meat patties with this sweet-and-savory sauce. And don't forget the spicy Asian pickles, too!

INGREDIENTS:

¼ **cup Sunbutter Hoisin Sauce (page 59)**

½ **cup Fridge-Pickled Cucumbers (page 74)**

1½ **pounds ground beef (80% beef, 20% fat)**

Ghee or avocado oil

2 **teaspoons kosher salt**

½ **teaspoon freshly ground black pepper**

1 **head butter lettuce**

2 **tomatoes, sliced**

1 **medium red onion, thinly sliced**

INSTRUCTIONS:

1. DO YOU HAVE SUNBUTTER HOISIN SAUCE AND FRIDGE-PICKLED CUCUMBERS? GOOD.

2. HEAT YOUR GRILL TO MEDIUM HOT, AND DIVIDE THE BEEF INTO 4 EQUAL PORTIONS. FORM THEM INTO BALLS.

3. FLATTEN EACH BALL BETWEEN YOUR PALMS INTO A ¾-INCH-THICK BURGER PATTY.

4. USE YOUR THUMB TO CREATE A SLIGHT DIMPLE IN THE CENTER OF EACH PATTY. THIS WAY, WHEN YOUR BURGERS PUFF UP IN THE MIDDLE DURING THE COOKING PROCESS, THEY'LL STILL END UP FLAT.

5. ONCE THE GRILL IS HOT, GREASE THE GRATES WITH A PAPER TOWEL DIPPED IN GHEE OR OIL. SPRINKLE SALT AND PEPPER ON ONE SIDE OF THE BURGER PATTIES.

6. PLACE THE BURGERS SEASONED-SIDE UP ON THE GRILL. COOK UNDISTURBED FOR ABOUT 3 MINUTES OR UNTIL GRILL MARKS APPEAR. (NO GRILL? JUST USE A GRILL PAN OR SKILLET OVER MEDIUM-HIGH HEAT.)

7. FLIP EACH BURGER PATTY, AND SEASON THE GRILLED SIDE WELL WITH SALT AND PEPPER. GRILL FOR 3 MINUTES MORE OR UNTIL THE DESIRED DONENESS IS REACHED.

8. BRUSH THE BURGER TOPS WITH SUNBUTTER HOISIN SAUCE.

9. AS SOON AS THE SAUCE WARMS THROUGH, TRANSFER THE BURGERS TO A PLATTER.

10. SERVE WITH LETTUCE LEAVES, TOMATOES, ONIONS, AND FRIDGE-PICKLED CUCUMBERS.

ASPARAGUS BEEF

MAKES 4 SERVINGS
⏱ **30 MINUTES**

Stir-fries are my go-to weeknight dish—and this one's a regular on the menu at our house. But don't sweat it if you prefer broccoli or snow peas to asparagus, or shrimp or chicken to beef. The beauty of this recipe is that it works with just about any combination of veggies and meat you can throw at it.

INGREDIENTS:

½   **cup All-Purpose Stir-Fry Sauce (page 67)**

1   **teaspoon arrowroot powder**

1½   **pounds flank steak, thinly sliced against the grain**

1   **tablespoon avocado oil**

1   **teaspoon fish sauce**

½   **teaspoon sesame oil**

½   **teaspoon kosher salt**

1   **tablespoon ghee or avocado oil**

1   **large shallot, thinly sliced**

2   **scallions, roots trimmed, cut into 2-inch segments**

¼   **pound fresh shiitake mushrooms, stemmed and sliced**

2   **garlic cloves, minced**

1   **pound thin asparagus stalks, tough ends trimmed, cut into 2-inch segments**

1   **large carrot, peeled and thinly sliced on the diagonal**

1. MAKE SOME ALL-PURPOSE STIR-FRY SAUCE. IT'LL TAKE LESS THAN 5 MINUTES!

2. IN A SMALL BOWL OR CUP, WHISK TOGETHER THE ALL-PURPOSE STIR-FRY SAUCE AND ARROWROOT POWDER.

3. IN A BOWL, COMBINE THE STEAK, AVOCADO OIL, FISH SAUCE, SESAME OIL, AND SALT. MARINATE FOR 5 TO 10 MINUTES.

4. ADD THE GHEE OR OIL TO A LARGE SKILLET OVER MEDIUM-HIGH HEAT. ONCE THE FAT IS SHIMMERING AND HOT, ADD THE STEAK.

5. STIR-FRY THE MEAT FOR 1 TO 2 MINUTES OR UNTIL MOSTLY COOKED. (DON'T FREAK OUT IF IT'S A LITTLE PINK.) YOU CAN DO THIS IN 2 BATCHES TO AVOID OVERCROWDING AND STEAMING THE MEAT IN THE PAN.

6. TRANSFER THE BEEF TO ANOTHER PLATTER, LEAVING ANY LIQUID IN THE SKILLET.

7. ADD THE SHALLOTS, SCALLIONS, AND SHIITAKE MUSHROOMS TO THE SKILLET.

8. COOK FOR 2 TO 3 MINUTES OR UNTIL THE SHALLOTS ARE TRANSLUCENT AND THE MUSHROOMS HAVE SOFTENED.

9. ADD THE GARLIC. STIR FOR 30 SECONDS OR UNTIL FRAGRANT. DON'T LET IT BURN!

10. TOSS IN THE ASPARAGUS AND CARROTS.

11. COOK, STIRRING, UNTIL THE CARROTS AND ASPARAGUS ARE TENDER-CRISP.

12. ADD THE BEEF AND SAUCE TO THE VEGETABLES, AND STIR TO COMBINE.

13. ONCE THE SAUCE THICKENS AND THE BEEF COOKS THROUGH, PLATE IT AND SERVE.

TRY IT WITH CAULI RICE (PAGE 80), OKAY?

SPICY BACON HONEY NUTS

&

HURRICANE PIG NUTS

MAKES 4 CUPS
⏱ **1 HOUR**
(30 MINUTES HANDS-ON)

I LIKE TO MUNCH ON THESE NUTS RIGHT OUT OF THE PANTRY, BUT THEY MAKE A TERRIFIC SALAD TOPPING, TOO.

Spicy sriracha? Check. Smoky, crisp bacon? Check. Crunchy, honey-roasted nuts? Check. With this killer combination of ingredients, can these Spicy Bacon Honey Nuts possibly get any better?

Actually, yes. They can indeed.

If you've ever tasted Hurricane Popcorn, the addictive snack from Hawaii, you know how furikake can transform an already tasty treat into a nuclear-powered flavor bomb. Add some to your porky nuts, and these Hurricane Pig Nuts will make your head explode (in a good way, of course).

INGREDIENTS:

- 8   **ounces bacon**
- 1   **large egg white**
- 3   **tablespoons Nom Nom Sriracha (page 56) or store-bought sriracha**
- 2   **tablespoons honey**
- 1   **teaspoon kosher salt**
- ½   **pound raw, unsalted almonds**
- ½   **pound raw, unsalted cashews**
- 2   **tablespoons furikake (if you're making Hurricane Pig Nuts)**

INSTRUCTIONS:

1 Stick the bacon in the freezer for 20 minutes to make it easier to slice. Once it has firmed up, cut the bacon crosswise into ¼-inch pieces.

2 Preheat the oven to 300°F with the rack in the middle position. In a large bowl, whisk together the egg white, sriracha, honey, and salt.

3 Toss in the nuts, making sure they're well coated in the spicy mixture.

4 Line a large rimmed baking sheet with parchment or a silicone baking mat.

5 Transfer the nuts to the lined sheet with a slotted spoon. Make sure the nuts are in a single layer.

6 Bake the nuts for 20 to 30 minutes or until golden brown and crunchy, turning the tray halfway through. Be careful not to burn your nuts!

7 While the nuts are roasting, toss the bacon into a large cast-iron skillet, and place it on a burner set to medium heat. By heating the skillet and bacon together, you'll lower the chances of scorching the bacon.

8 Cook the bacon for about 15 minutes or until the drippings are released and the bacon gets crunchy and crisp.

9 Using a slotted spoon, transfer the bacon to a paper towel–lined plate. Set aside until the nuts are ready.

10 Toss the nuts with the warm bacon bits, and cool to room temperature.

11 If you're making Hurricane Pig Nuts, toss in the furikake, too.

(Furikake, by the way, is a classic Japanese seasoning made of toasted sesame seeds, seaweed, and bonito.)

12 Serve now or keep refrigerated in a covered container for up to 1 week.

CHIA MUESLI PARFAIT

MAKES 6 SERVINGS
🕐 **8 HOURS**
(15 MINUTES HANDS-ON)

Whenever I'm facing an insanely busy week ahead, I make a big batch of these fiber-packed grab-and-go Chia Muesli Parfaits. Inspired by the fruity, nutty muesli bowls we ate every morning while traipsing through Europe, these mildly sweet breakfast pots are a cinch to make. Instead of oats, I use Paleo-friendly chia pudding, which gives my muesli a texture that closely resembles the original.

INGREDIENTS:

½   cup chia seeds

2   cups Vanilla Almond Milk (page 160) or 2 cups almond milk mixed with 1 teaspoon vanilla extract

¾   cup fresh orange juice

1   cup sliced almonds

½   teaspoon ground cinnamon

1   large Braeburn or Fuji apple, peeled and cored

2   cups finely minced fresh fruit, such as peaches, nectarines, pears, or fresh berries

> IF YOU WANT, YOU CAN ADD SOME HONEY, BUT WITH THE FRUIT AND JUICE, YOU PROBABLY WON'T EVEN MISS IT!

INSTRUCTIONS:

1 IN A MEDIUM JAR OR BOWL, COMBINE THE CHIA SEEDS AND VANILLA ALMOND MILK.

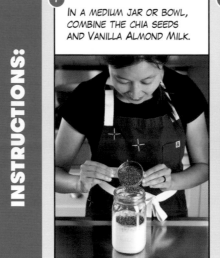

2 STIR, COVER, AND REFRIGERATE THE CHIA MIXTURE OVERNIGHT OR UNTIL IT THICKENS INTO A PUDDING-LIKE CONSISTENCY.

3 IN A LARGE BOWL, COMBINE THE ORANGE JUICE, SLICED ALMONDS, AND CINNAMON.

4 GRATE THE APPLE AND IMMEDIATELY STIR IT INTO THE NUT AND JUICE MIXTURE.

5 ADD THE THICKENED CHIA PUDDING TO THE FRUIT AND NUTS, AND STIR TO COMBINE THE INGREDIENTS.

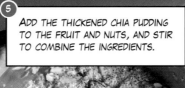

6 IN SMALL BOWLS OR 12-OUNCE JARS, ALTERNATE LAYERS OF THE CHIA MUESLI AND FRESH FRUIT. THESE PARFAITS WILL KEEP IN THE FRIDGE FOR UP TO 4 DAYS.

BUT... WHAT CAN I DO IF I'M NOT READY?

Some people profess to love cooking regardless of the circumstances. Busy day at work? Hungry family? No problem. For these culinary zen masters, cooking is a form of stress relief. Languidly and lovingly hand-crafting meals from scratch, they expertly layer flavors and slowly bubble braises and stews to perfection. As they dance in the blissful glow of their ovens, they release the pent-up pressures of the day.

BUT ME? NOT SO MUCH.

BESIDES, I'M A TERRIBLE DANCER.

That's just not my style. Most nights, I'm fending off cranky kids demanding dinner. They don't care that I was slammed with work all day, or that my growling stomach makes it hard to concentrate on cooking. I'm also messy and unmotivated. Mentally, there are times when I'm just not ready at all to cook.

BUT THAT DOESN'T MEAN I GET A PASS ON COOKING.

AND NEITHER DO YOU!

Trust me: I know what it's like to be utterly exhausted, frazzled, and hangry. For a dozen years, I frantically juggled working graveyard shifts at the hospital and raising two rambunctious boys—not to mention blogging and running the business of Nom Nom Paleo. Most nights, cooking healthy meals was the last thing in the world I wanted to do.

ESPECIALLY WHEN THERE'S SOMETHING GOOD AND TRASHY TO WATCH ON TV!

But dwelling on the negative is self-defeating, and I know that cooking's the only way to guarantee my family eats a nutritious home-cooked meal, so I just buck up and do it. And you know what? Without fail, as soon as I get in the kitchen and start cooking, the task ahead is never as daunting as it initially seemed.

Armed with a few pantry items and a head full of recipe ideas, I found that I could quickly and easily crank out deliciously nourishing suppers that satisfied my family *and* yielded enough leftovers to freeze for a busy evening down the road.

That's why I put together this "Not Ready" section, and crammed its pages with quick meals that don't require pre-made components or a lot of effort. Busy people have no patience for fussy recipes, so I made sure these simple, flavor-packed dishes can be ready in 45 minutes or less.

THESE RECIPES CAN GO FROM STOVE TO MOUTH IN NO TIME FLAT!

In fact, most of these dishes require very little hands-on time, so don't you dare pick up the telephone and order takeout; instead, tie on an apron and hustle into the kitchen. As Sam Sifton wrote, "Cooking is a practice, same as Buddhism, CrossFit, and sobriety. You just have to do it until that's what you do. Don't start tomorrow. Start tonight."

GARAM MASALA VEGETABLE SOUP

MAKES 6 SERVINGS
⏱ 45 MINUTES
(15 MINUTES HANDS-ON)

Spices like those in Indian garam masala aren't just flavor boosters—they're some of the most nutrient-dense and antioxidant-rich foods you can find on grocery shelves. They're a win-win, boosting both flavor and health.

INGREDIENTS:

½   **cup raw cashews**

1   **tablespoon ghee or extra-virgin olive oil**

1   **small yellow onion, diced**

1   **large carrot, peeled and diced**

    Kosher salt

4   **garlic cloves, minced**

1   **tablespoon minced ginger**

1   **tablespoon garam masala or Indian curry powder**

1   **small head cauliflower (about 800 grams), core removed and cut into florets**

1   **medium sweet potato (about 300 grams), peeled and diced**

6   **cups Bone Broth (page 76) or chicken stock**

    Freshly ground black pepper

    Juice from 1 lime or lemon

    Fresh cilantro leaves

CAN'T FIND GARAM MASALA AT THE STORE? JUST USE YOUR FAVORITE CURRY POWDER.

INSTRUCTIONS:

1 TOAST THE CASHEWS IN A PREHEATED 300°F OVEN FOR 8 TO 10 MINUTES UNTIL GOLDEN, TOSSING AT THE HALFWAY POINT. SET ASIDE.

2 HEAT THE GHEE IN A LARGE SAUCEPAN OVER MEDIUM HEAT. WHEN THE OIL IS SHIMMERING, ADD THE ONIONS, CARROTS, AND A GENEROUS SPRINKLE OF SALT.

3 COOK, STIRRING, FOR ABOUT 5 MINUTES OR UNTIL SLIGHTLY SOFTENED.

4 TOSS IN THE GARLIC, GINGER, AND GARAM MASALA.

5 SAUTÉ FOR 30 SECONDS OR UNTIL FRAGRANT.

6 ADD THE CAULIFLOWER, SWEET POTATO, AND BROTH.

7 BRING TO A BOIL.

8 COVER THE POT AND LOWER THE HEAT TO MAINTAIN A SIMMER.

9 COOK THE SOUP FOR 15 MINUTES OR UNTIL THE VEGETABLES ARE FORK-TENDER.

10 REMOVE THE POT FROM THE HEAT. USING AN IMMERSION BLENDER, PURÉE THE CONTENTS UNTIL SMOOTH. TASTE AND ADJUST WITH SALT AND PEPPER AS NEEDED.

11 SQUEEZE AND STIR IN THE LIME OR LEMON JUICE, AND LADLE THE SOUP INTO BOWLS.

12 TOP WITH TOASTED NUTS AND CILANTRO. REFRIGERATE EXTRAS FOR UP TO 4 DAYS, OR FREEZE FOR UP TO 2 MONTHS.

ANCHO TOMATO CHICKEN SOUP

MAKES 4 SERVINGS
⏱ **30 MINUTES**

When I made this rich and smoky soup, both of my kids demanded seconds. I think that says it all.

TO CRANK UP THE HEAT, ADD RED PEPPER FLAKES OR A SLICED JALAPEÑO PEPPER OR TWO.

INGREDIENTS:

- 2 tablespoons ghee or extra-virgin olive oil
- 1 medium yellow onion, diced

  Kosher salt
- 4 garlic cloves, peeled and smashed
- 2 teaspoons ancho chile powder
- 1 (15-ounce) can diced fire-roasted tomatoes, drained (or 2 medium tomatoes that you have charred yourself)
- 4 cups Bone Broth (page 76) or chicken stock
- 6 skinless, boneless chicken thighs or breasts, sliced into ½-inch-thick strips
- 2 bunches Swiss chard, stemmed and leaves thinly sliced

  Freshly ground black pepper
- 2 limes, 1 juiced and the other cut into wedges
- 1 Hass avocado, thinly sliced or cubed
- ½ cup fresh cilantro leaves

  Plantain chips (optional)

1 In a large saucepan, melt the ghee over medium heat. Add the onions and a generous sprinkle of salt. Sauté for 5 minutes or until softened.

2 Toss in the garlic and cook for 1 minute or until fragrant.

3 Stir in the ancho chile powder.

4 Add the drained tomatoes and cook for 10 minutes, stirring frequently, until they break down and darken.

5 Remove the saucepan from the heat, and use a hand blender to blitz the contents until a rough paste forms.

6 Pour in the broth.

7 Blend until smooth. (Want to stop here? Just bring to a simmer and season with salt and pepper. You'll end up with a smoky tomato soup!)

8 Return the saucepan to high heat. Add the chicken and chard to the soup.

(Swiss chard isn't normally found in Mexican-inspired dishes, but I like to add extra vegetables whenever I can.)

9 Bring the soup to a boil, stirring occasionally.

10 Lower the heat and simmer until the chicken is cooked through, about 6 to 8 minutes.

11 Remove the soup from the heat, and add the juice from 1 lime. Taste again for seasoning, and adjust as needed.

12 Ladle the soup into bowls and garnish with avocado, cilantro, and if desired, plantain chips. Serve with lime wedges. Refrigerate any leftover soup for up to 4 days or freeze up to 2 months.

SIMPLE EGG DROP SOUP

MAKES 1 SERVING
⏱ **5 MINUTES**

You can make this hearty, single-serving egg drop soup in a flash—provided you have some broth and eggs on hand. Serving more than one? Just multiply the ingredients by the number of soup-slurpers.

(Math is a critical life skill, kids.)

INGREDIENTS:

1½ cups Bone Broth (page 76) or chicken stock

Fish sauce (optional)

Kosher salt

1 large egg

1 hot chile pepper, thinly sliced (optional)

1 scallion, thinly sliced (optional)

1 tablespoon cilantro leaves (optional)

> WANNA TURN THIS INTO A MORE SUBSTANTIAL SUPPER? ADD SOME LEFTOVER MEAT OR POULTRY TO THE SOUP, OR BULK IT UP WITH VEGGIES. JUST TOSS IN THESE EXTRAS AS SOON AS YOUR BROTH IS BOILING, AND BEFORE YOU ADD THE EGG.

INSTRUCTIONS:

1 IN A SAUCEPAN, BRING THE BROTH TO A BOIL OVER MEDIUM-HIGH HEAT. SEASON TO TASTE WITH FISH SAUCE AND/OR SALT.

2 CRACK THE EGG IN A SMALL BOWL AND SEASON WITH A FEW ADDITIONAL DROPS OF FISH SAUCE AND A PINCH OF SALT.

3 WHISK WELL WITH A FORK.

4 REMOVE THE BROTH FROM THE HEAT. STIR THE SOUP AS YOU SLOWLY POUR IN THE EGG FROM HIGH ABOVE THE POT.

5 THE EGG, WHICH COOKS AS IT HITS THE HOT LIQUID, SHOULD BE SOFT AND WISPY (AND NOT OVERCOOKED OR CHUNKY).

6 TRANSFER THE SOUP TO A BOWL.

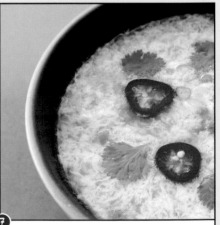

7 FANCY IT UP WITH YOUR FAVORITE ADD-INS. EASY GARNISHES INCLUDE SLICED SPICY PEPPERS (LIKE RED JALAPEÑOS), MINCED SCALLIONS, AND CILANTRO LEAVES . . .

⑧ BUT I ESPECIALLY LOVE ADDING CRISPED-UP SLOW COOKER OR PRESSURE COOKER KALUA PIG (PAGE 128) TO MY EGG DROP SOUP!

SÚP MĂNG TÂY CUA (CRAB + ASPARAGUS SOUP)

MAKES 4 SERVINGS
⏱ 15 MINUTES

Egg drop soup can be dressed up any number of ways, but one of my favorites is this Vietnamese version. Served on special occasions, Súp Măng Tây Cua features crab meat and asparagus (a.k.a. *măng tây*, or "Western bamboo")—a vegetable first introduced to Vietnam by the French during the colonial era.

Traditionally, white asparagus is used in this recipe, but I prefer the more widely available green stuff. Still, if you happen to spot some fresh white asparagus at the market, give it a shot.

INGREDIENTS:

6   cups Bone Broth (page 76) or chicken stock, divided

2   teaspoons fish sauce

½   teaspoon ground white pepper

    Kosher salt

1   pound asparagus, ends trimmed, cut into ½-inch coins

½   pound lump crab meat

1½ tablespoons arrowroot powder

4   large eggs, barely beaten together in a medium-sized bowl

½   cup cilantro, chopped

2   scallions, thinly sliced

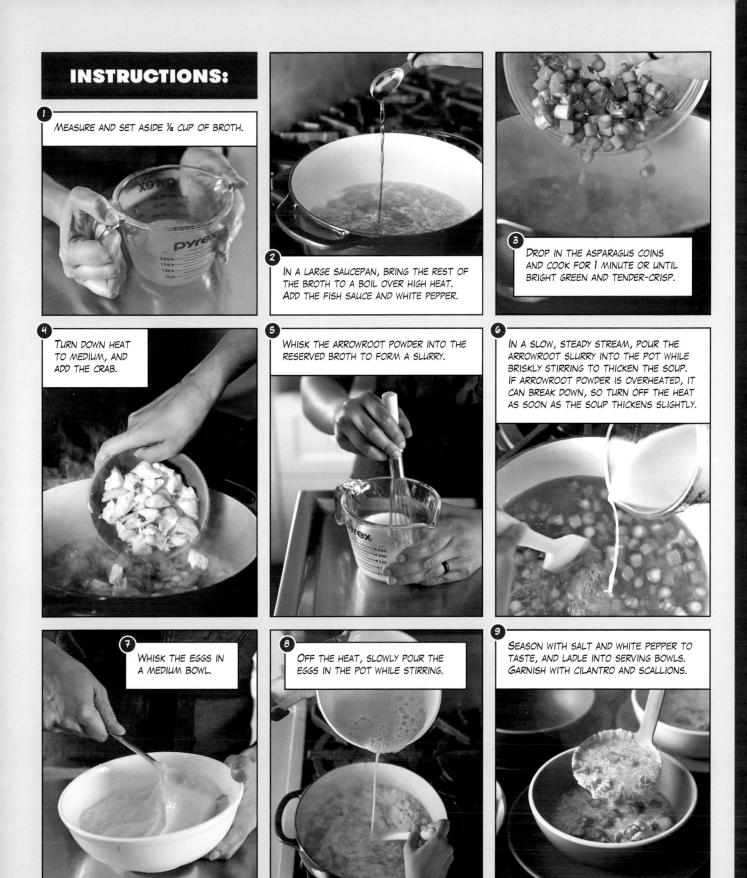

INSTRUCTIONS:

1 MEASURE AND SET ASIDE ½ CUP OF BROTH.

2 IN A LARGE SAUCEPAN, BRING THE REST OF THE BROTH TO A BOIL OVER HIGH HEAT. ADD THE FISH SAUCE AND WHITE PEPPER.

3 DROP IN THE ASPARAGUS COINS AND COOK FOR 1 MINUTE OR UNTIL BRIGHT GREEN AND TENDER-CRISP.

4 TURN DOWN HEAT TO MEDIUM, AND ADD THE CRAB.

5 WHISK THE ARROWROOT POWDER INTO THE RESERVED BROTH TO FORM A SLURRY.

6 IN A SLOW, STEADY STREAM, POUR THE ARROWROOT SLURRY INTO THE POT WHILE BRISKLY STIRRING TO THICKEN THE SOUP. IF ARROWROOT POWDER IS OVERHEATED, IT CAN BREAK DOWN, SO TURN OFF THE HEAT AS SOON AS THE SOUP THICKENS SLIGHTLY.

7 WHISK THE EGGS IN A MEDIUM BOWL.

8 OFF THE HEAT, SLOWLY POUR THE EGGS IN THE POT WHILE STIRRING.

9 SEASON WITH SALT AND WHITE PEPPER TO TASTE, AND LADLE INTO SERVING BOWLS. GARNISH WITH CILANTRO AND SCALLIONS.

IT KEEPS IN THE FRIDGE FOR UP TO 4 DAYS.

HOT + SOUR SOUP

MAKES 6 SERVINGS
⏱ 40 MINUTES

This spicy-sour soup has long been a mainstay of Chinese restaurant menus, but you can make it in less time than it takes for the delivery person to drive over. It'll taste better, too—and it won't contain any mystery ingredients.

INGREDIENTS:

1	tablespoon ghee or fat of choice
1	large leek julienned, white and light green parts only
¼	pound fresh shiitake mushrooms, thinly sliced
1	pound pork shoulder, sirloin roast, or tenderloin, cut into thin matchsticks
2	tablespoons coconut aminos
2	garlic cloves, minced
1	tablespoon minced ginger
1	can (8 ounces) sliced bamboo shoots, rinsed and drained
6	cups Bone Broth (page 76) or chicken stock, divided
1½	tablespoons arrowroot powder
2	large eggs, beaten
¼	cup rice vinegar
1	teaspoon sesame oil
½	teaspoon ground white pepper
	Kosher salt
2	scallions, sliced on the bias

AS YOU CAN SEE, MY MOM REALLY LIKES EGG DROP SOUP VARIATIONS!

1 MELT THE GHEE IN A LARGE SAUCEPAN OVER MEDIUM-HIGH HEAT. WHEN THE FAT IS SHIMMERING, ADD THE LEEKS AND SHIITAKE MUSHROOMS.

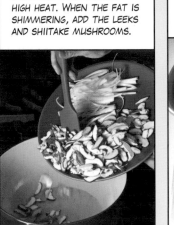

2 COOK, STIRRING, FOR **2** MINUTES OR UNTIL THE LEEKS AND MUSHROOMS HAVE COOKED DOWN. ADD THE PORK AND STIR-FRY UNTIL NO LONGER PINK.

3 ADD THE COCONUT AMINOS, GARLIC, AND GINGER. STIR FOR **30** SECONDS OR UNTIL FRAGRANT. TOSS IN THE BAMBOO SHOOTS.

4 MEASURE OUT AND SET ASIDE ABOUT ½ CUP OF THE BROTH. POUR THE REST OF THE STOCK INTO THE SAUCEPAN AND BRING TO A BOIL OVER HIGH HEAT. THEN, TURN DOWN THE HEAT TO MEDIUM AND MAINTAIN A SIMMER.

5 WHISK THE ARROWROOT POWDER INTO THE RESERVED BROTH TO MAKE A SLURRY.

6 IN A SLOW, STEADY STREAM, POUR THE ARROWROOT SLURRY INTO THE POT WHILE BRISKLY STIRRING TO THICKEN THE SOUP. IF ARROWROOT POWDER IS OVERHEATED, IT CAN BREAK DOWN, SO TURN OFF THE HEAT AS SOON AS THE SOUP THICKENS SLIGHTLY.

7 REMOVE THE POT FROM THE HEAT. SLOWLY POUR IN THE BEATEN EGGS WHILE STIRRING.

8 STIR IN THE RICE VINEGAR, SESAME OIL, AND WHITE PEPPER. SEASON TO TASTE WITH SALT, AND ADJUST WITH A BIT MORE VINEGAR AND WHITE PEPPER IF DESIRED.

9 LADLE THE SOUP INTO SERVING BOWLS AND GARNISH WITH SCALLIONS. LEFTOVERS CAN BE KEPT REFRIGERATED FOR UP TO **4** DAYS.

HOBO STEW

MAKES 6 SERVINGS
⏱ **45 MINUTES**

Also known as "Mulligan Stew," this soup originated in the early 1900s as a community meal prepared in American hobo camps. The only consistent ingredients were a pot and a campfire, but most versions included meat and any vegetables that were on hand.

My take on this stew is just as inexpensive, satisfying, tasty, and versatile—and it doesn't have to be made outdoors. Just brown some meat, add broth, and toss in whatever veggies you have in your crisper. Hobo Stew freezes beautifully, too. Go make some!

INGREDIENTS:

2	pounds ground beef
½	teaspoon kosher salt, plus extra to taste
1	small yellow onion, diced
3	garlic cloves, minced
¼	cup tomato paste
3	carrots, cut into ¼-inch-thick coins
½	pound green beans, trimmed and cut into 1½-inch pieces
1	pound potatoes, cut into ¾-inch cubes
4	cups Bone Broth (page 76) or chicken stock
	Freshly ground black pepper
5	ounces fresh baby kale or frozen kale
1	tablespoon sherry vinegar
¼	cup minced fresh Italian parsley

IS THIS MADE OUT OF ORGANIC HOBOS?

1 IN A LARGE STOCKPOT OVER MEDIUM HEAT, COOK THE BEEF, BREAKING IT INTO PIECES WITH A SPATULA OR SPOON. SEASON THE BEEF WITH ½ TEASPOON OF SALT.

2 ONCE THE BEEF'S NO LONGER PINK (ABOUT 10 MINUTES), USE A SLOTTED SPOON TO TRANSFER THE MEAT TO A SEPARATE PLATE. REMOVE ALL BUT ABOUT 1 TABLESPOON OF BEEF FAT IN THE POT.

3 ADD THE ONIONS TO THE RESERVED BEEF FAT IN THE POT. SAUTÉ THE ONIONS FOR 5 TO 7 MINUTES OR UNTIL TRANSLUCENT.

4 ADD THE GARLIC AND STIR FOR 15 SECONDS OR UNTIL FRAGRANT.

5 MIX IN THE TOMATO PASTE AND COOK UNTIL THE BOTTOM OF THE POT DEVELOPS A COPPER-COLORED COATING. POUR IN THE BROTH TO DEGLAZE, SCRAPING OFF THE YUMMINESS THAT'S STUCK TO THE POT.

6 ADD THE BROWNED BEEF, CARROTS, GREEN BEANS, AND POTATOES. INCREASE THE HEAT TO HIGH AND BRING THE STEW TO A BOIL. THEN, DECREASE THE HEAT TO LOW TO MAINTAIN A SIMMER.

7 COVER AND COOK FOR 20 TO 30 MINUTES OR UNTIL THE VEGETABLES ARE TENDER. SEASON WITH SALT AND PEPPER TO TASTE.

(ALTERNATIVELY, YOU CAN USE A PRESSURE COOKER TO COOK THE CONTENTS UNDER HIGH PRESSURE FOR 5 MINUTES.)

8 ADD THE KALE, AND STIR UNTIL WILTED.

9 STIR IN THE VINEGAR. LADLE UP THE STEW, TOP WITH ITALIAN PARSLEY, AND SERVE. EXTRAS CAN BE REFRIGERATED FOR UP TO 4 DAYS OR FROZEN FOR UP TO 2 MONTHS.

HARICOT VERTS + HEIRLOOM CHERRY TOMATO SALAD

MAKES 4 SERVINGS
⏱ **10 MINUTES**

Nothing says summer like a plate of vibrant green beans, juicy tomatoes…and spending as little time as possible in a hot kitchen.

There's nothing complicated about this 10-minute vegetable side; a quick blanch-and-shock and a toss with olive oil and balsamic vinegar are all it takes to prepare this delectably gorgeous picnic salad.

INGREDIENTS:

1	large shallot, thinly sliced
¼	cup aged balsamic vinegar
	Kosher salt
1	pound green beans, trimmed
¼	cup ripe cherry tomatoes, halved
¼	cup fresh basil, cut into thin ribbons
	Extra-virgin olive oil
	Freshly ground black pepper

DON'T GET HUNG UP ON THE WORD "BEANS." GREEN BEANS ARE MORE POD THAN BEAN ANYWAY, AND THEY'RE TASTY AND GOOD FOR YOU!

INSTRUCTIONS:

1 SOAK THE SLICED SHALLOT IN THE BALSAMIC VINEGAR.

2 FILL A LARGE STOCKPOT WITH WATER, AND TOSS IN A BIG PINCH OF SALT. BRING THE WATER TO A BOIL OVER HIGH HEAT, AND THEN ADD THE GREEN BEANS TO THE POT.

3 COOK FOR 2 TO 4 MINUTES OR UNTIL BRIGHT GREEN AND TENDER-CRISP.

4 TRANSFER THE GREEN BEANS TO A LARGE BOWL OF ICE WATER TO HALT THE COOKING PROCESS. WAIT 5 MINUTES. THEN, TOSS THE DRAINED BEANS INTO AN EMPTY BOWL.

5 FISH THE SHALLOT SLICES OUT OF THE BALSAMIC VINEGAR, AND ADD THEM TO THE GREEN BEANS ALONG WITH THE CHERRY TOMATOES AND BASIL. DRIZZLE WITH OLIVE OIL AND SOME OF THE RESERVED VINEGAR.

6 SEASON WITH SALT AND PEPPER, AND TOSS BEFORE SERVING.

MANGO CABBAGE SLAW

MAKES 4 SERVINGS
⏱ **30 MINUTES**

Cabbage slaw may sound boring to you, but once you taste this combination of sweet mango, tongue-tingling jalapeño, tangy lime, and fresh mint, you'll never look at cabbage slaws the same way ever again.

INGREDIENTS:

¼ **cup thinly sliced shallot or red onion**

Juice from 2 limes

2 **mangoes, peeled, pitted, and thinly sliced**

½ **small cabbage, cored and thinly sliced**

¼ **cup fresh mint leaves, thinly sliced**

1 **jalapeño pepper, thinly sliced (optional)**

Kosher salt

Freshly ground black pepper

≠WHOO!≠ SPICY!

INSTRUCTIONS:

1 IN A SMALL BOWL, SOAK THE THINLY SLICED SHALLOTS IN THE LIME JUICE WITH A CUBE OF ICE FOR AT LEAST 10 MINUTES.

2 WHEN YOU'RE READY TO ASSEMBLE THE SALAD, TOSS THE MANGO AND SLICED CABBAGE INTO A LARGE BOWL. ADD THE SOAKED SHALLOTS AND LIME JUICE.

3 ADD THE MINT AND JALAPEÑO PEPPER (IF YOU WANT YOUR SLAW TO PACK HEAT).

4 SEASON WITH SALT AND PEPPER TO TASTE, AND TOSS WELL.

5 PLATE IT UP AND SERVE IT WITH SOMETHING MEATY.

SUNNYSIDE SALAD

MAKES 1 SERVING
⏱ 10 MINUTES

You know it's true: Eggs are the ultimate protein. After all, they're inexpensive, packed with nutrients, easy to make, and delicious. Plus, when you add an egg to a plate of greens, you magically turn it into a complete meal—and that's precisely what I aim to do here. This is not a traditional egg salad, but there are times when you just want to make a super-fast salad— one that can be whipped up at a moment's notice for breakfast, lunch, or dinner.

Yeah, I know some folks swear that the perfect sunny–side up egg features a runny yolk and whites that are cooked through—but with no brown edges at all. Me? I say the "right" way to cook eggs is whichever way you like them made. And my favorite preparation features crispy, frizzled whites and silky, gooey yolks.

INGREDIENTS:

2   **cups spring salad mix**

1   **large carrot, thinly sliced into ribbons with a vegetable peeler**

1   **tablespoon ghee or avocado oil**

2   **large eggs**

Flake sea salt

Freshly ground black pepper

Aged balsamic vinegar

1 PLACE A SMALL CAST-IRON SKILLET OVER HIGH HEAT.

2 IN THE MEANTIME, PILE THE SALAD GREENS AND CARROT RIBBONS IN A SERVING BOWL.

3 ONCE THE SKILLET IS SCREAMING HOT, ADD A BIG DOLLOP OF GHEE OR OIL.

4 CRACK **2** EGGS INTO A SMALL BOWL, AND GENTLY POUR THEM INTO THE SKILLET.

5 THE WHITES THAT TOUCH THE SKILLET WILL BLISTER AND COOK RIGHT AWAY, BUT THE RAISED WHITES NEAR THE YOLK WILL NEED SOME EXTRA HELP TO COOK THROUGH...

...SO TILT THE SKILLET AWAY FROM YOU TO AVOID GETTING SPLATTERED, AND USE AN OFFSET SPOON TO BASTE THE WHITES WITH THE HOT GHEE (OR AVOCADO OIL).

6 ONCE THE WHITES OF THE EGGS ARE SET, TURN OFF THE HEAT. WHEN YOU PEEK UNDERNEATH, THE EGGS SHOULD BE CRISPY AND GOLDEN BROWN.

7 USING A SPATULA, CAREFULLY TRANSFER THE CRISPY FRIED EGGS ONTO THE GREENS.

8 SEASON TO TASTE WITH SALT AND PEPPER, AND DRIZZLE BALSAMIC VINEGAR ON TOP.

9 THE SWEET TANG OF VINEGAR TIES THE DISH TOGETHER, AND WHEN MIXED WITH THE SOFT YOLK, IT'LL FORM AN INSTANT SALAD DRESSING. (ACID + FAT = DRESSING!)

10 REALLY: THERE'S NO BETTER FAST FOOD.

THAI MUSHROOM STIR-FRY

MAKES 4 SERVINGS
⏱ 30 MINUTES

This recipe was inspired not by our trips to Southeast Asia, but by a dish dreamed up by our good friend Chef Gregory Gourdet at Departure Restaurant + Lounge in Portland, Oregon. I'm only half-joking when I say that we made Portland our second home so that we can savor GG's Asian-inspired food all the time. Whenever I taste his umami-packed creations, my brain shifts into overdrive, coming up with ways to reverse-engineer GG's recipes for busy home cooks. Luckily, I think I managed to hack this one. This spicy mushroom dish will make you want to pick up and move to Portland, too.

INGREDIENTS:

- **2** tablespoons ghee, avocado oil, or olive oil
- **1** large leek, white and light green parts only, thinly sliced crosswise
- **1** large shallot, minced
- **4** garlic cloves, thinly sliced
- **2** teaspoons minced ginger
- **1** Thai chile pepper or serrano pepper, minced
- **2** pounds mixed mushrooms, sliced into uniform pieces
- **2** tablespoons fish sauce
  Juice from 1 lime
- **2** tablespoons roughly chopped fresh cilantro
- **2** tablespoons roughly chopped fresh mint

INSTRUCTIONS:

1 THIS RECIPE IS ALL ABOUT THE PREP, SO GET TO IT. MINCING AND SLICING ALL THE INGREDIENTS TAKES A BIT OF WORK, BUT ONCE IT'S DONE, THE COOKING TAKES JUST MINUTES.

(I USE CREMINI AND SHIMEJI MUSHROOMS, AND THINLY SLICED KING TRUMPET, OYSTER, AND SHIITAKE MUSHROOMS.)

2 HEAT THE GHEE IN A LARGE SKILLET OVER MEDIUM-HIGH. ADD THE LEEK, SHALLOT, GARLIC, GINGER, AND CHILE PEPPER.

3 COOK, STIRRING, FOR 2 TO 3 MINUTES OR UNTIL THE VEGETABLES ARE SOFTENED.

4 ADD THE MUSHROOMS TO THE SKILLET.

5 SAUTÉ FOR 8 TO 10 MINUTES OR UNTIL THE MUSHROOMS ARE TENDER AND LIGHTLY BROWNED.

6 ADD THE FISH SAUCE. STIR TO COMBINE.

8 REMOVE THE SKILLET FROM THE HEAT, AND SQUEEZE IN THE LIME JUICE. SHOWER WITH HERBS, AND SERVE IMMEDIATELY.

7 TASTE AND ADJUST WITH A BIT MORE FISH SAUCE IF NEEDED. TRUST YOUR PALATE!

THIS IS MY SUPER TALENTED, UMAMI-OBSESSED FRIEND, CHEF GREGORY GOURDET. HE'S ONE OF MY BIGGEST INSPIRATIONS IN THE KITCHEN!

ASIAN CITRUS BRUSSELS SPROUTS SLAW

MAKES 8 SERVINGS
⏱ **30 MINUTES**

A tangy orange-ginger dressing gives this warm slaw a zesty zing that'll brighten your plate. Plus, it keeps well in the fridge, and can be eaten cold, hot, or at any temperature in between.

INGREDIENTS:

- 2¼ pounds Brussels sprouts
- 3 tablespoons melted ghee, coconut oil, lard, or tallow
- ½ teaspoon kosher salt

• SAUCE •

- 1 tablespoon ghee, coconut oil, lard, or tallow
- 1 tablespoon grated ginger
- 1 small shallot, minced
- 2 garlic cloves, minced
- ¼ cup fresh orange juice
- 3 tablespoons coconut aminos
- 1½ tablespoons rice vinegar
- ½ teaspoon fish sauce
- 1 teaspoon sesame oil

• GARNISH •

- 2 scallions, thinly sliced
- ¼ cup minced fresh cilantro
- 1½ tablespoons toasted sesame seeds (follow the toasting instructions on page 66)

INSTRUCTIONS:

1 PREHEAT THE OVEN TO 450°F WITH THE RACK IN THE MIDDLE. WHILE THE OVEN'S HEATING UP, TRIM AWAY THE STEMS OF YOUR SPROUTS.

2 REMOVE ANY OUTER LEAVES THAT EASILY COME OFF OF THE SPROUTS.

3 SLICE THE SPROUTS THINLY WITH A KNIFE (OR JUST PASS 'EM THROUGH THE SLICING BLADE OF A FOOD PROCESSOR).

4 IN A LARGE BOWL, TOSS THE SHREDDED SPROUTS, MELTED GHEE, AND SALT.

5 MIX WELL WITH YOUR HANDS, AND THEN SPREAD THE SHREDDED SPROUTS EVENLY ON A FOIL-LINED RIMMED BAKING SHEET.

6 BAKE FOR 15 TO 20 MINUTES, FLIPPING AND TOSSING EVERY 5 MINUTES, OR UNTIL THE SPROUTS ARE BROWNED AND TENDER.

7 IN THE MEANTIME, PREPARE THE SAUCE. MELT THE GHEE OVER MEDIUM HEAT IN A SAUCEPAN. ONCE IT'S SHIMMERING, ADD THE GINGER, SHALLOT, AND GARLIC AND SAUTÉ UNTIL FRAGRANT, ABOUT 1 MINUTE.

8 NEXT, ADD THE ORANGE JUICE, COCONUT AMINOS, RICE VINEGAR, AND FISH SAUCE TO THE SAUCEPAN. BRING IT TO A BOIL.

9 LOWER THE HEAT, AND SIMMER FOR 5 TO 8 MINUTES OR UNTIL THE SAUCE SLIGHTLY THICKENS. REMOVE THE PAN FROM THE HEAT, AND STIR IN THE SESAME OIL.

10 ONCE THE SPROUTS ARE READY, TAKE THEM OUT OF THE OVEN, AND POUR THE SAUCE OVER THE ROASTED SPROUTS.

11 GARNISH WITH THE SCALLIONS, CILANTRO, AND SESAME SEEDS.

12 TOSS WELL, PLATE IT UP, AND EAT.

GRILLED BALSAMIC BOK CHOY WITH GOLDEN RAISINS

MAKES 4 SERVINGS
🕐 **15 MINUTES**

This dish will high-five your mouth.

INGREDIENTS:

6	bunches baby bok choy
¼	cup avocado oil or olive oil, plus extra for the grill
½	teaspoon kosher salt
	Freshly ground black pepper
	Aged balsamic vinegar
¼	cup golden raisins, soaked in hot water for 5 minutes or until plump
¼	cup toasted almond slices
	Fresh mint leaves

INSTRUCTIONS:

1 HEAT YOUR BACKYARD GRILL OR GRILL PAN TO MEDIUM. TRIM OFF THE WOODY ENDS OF EACH BUNCH OF BABY BOK CHOY, KEEPING THE BUNCHES INTACT. THEN, CUT EACH BUNCH IN HALF, LENGTHWISE THROUGH THE CENTER.

2 WASH THE BOK CHOY TO REMOVE ANY DIRT TRAPPED AT THE BASE OF THE LEAVES. SHAKE OFF THE WATER. PLACE THE BOK CHOY ON A PLATTER OR BAKING SHEET.

3 EVENLY DRIZZLE ¼ CUP AVOCADO OIL AND SPRINKLE SALT OVER THE BOK CHOY. USE YOUR HANDS TO COAT WELL.

4 WHEN THE GRILL (OR GRILL PAN) IS HOT, GREASE THE GRATES WITH A PAPER TOWEL DIPPED IN OIL.

(NO GRILL OR GRILL PAN? ROAST THE BOK CHOY CUT-SIDE UP ON A LINED BAKING SHEET IN A 400°F OVEN FOR 20 MINUTES. THEN, SKIP AHEAD TO STEP **7**.)

5 PLACE THE BOK CHOY CUT-SIDE DOWN ON THE GRILL. COOK FOR **3** MINUTES OR UNTIL NICELY CHARRED ON THE UNDERSIDE.

6 FLIP AND COOK FOR ANOTHER **3** MINUTES OR UNTIL THE BOK CHOY IS TENDER-CRISP.

7 TRANSFER TO A PLATE, AND SEASON WITH PEPPER TO TASTE. DRIZZLE BALSAMIC VINEGAR ON THE BOK CHOY, AND GARNISH WITH THE DRAINED RAISINS, ALMONDS, AND MINT LEAVES.

SWITCH IT UP:
GRILLED
UMAMI BOK CHOY

READY TO SWITCH UP THE FLAVORS OF THIS DISH? FOLLOW THE RECIPE ON THE PREVIOUS PAGE, BUT IN STEP 7, LEAVE OUT THE VINEGAR, RAISINS, AND ALMONDS. INSTEAD, DRIZZLE ON 1 TEASPOON OF FISH SAUCE AND THE JUICE FROM 1 LIME. GARNISH WITH A SPRINKLE OF TOASTED SESAME SEEDS BEFORE SERVING.

RED HOT ONION RINGS

MAKES 4 SERVINGS
⏱ **30 MINUTES**

When I was little, my mom would occasionally treat my sister and me to lunch at a local fast food joint, but I was never too thrilled about the onion rings that came with my burger. I hated sinking my teeth into an onion ring, only to come away with a long, slimy tendril of onion hanging from my mouth and an empty tube of greasy fried batter between my fingers.

Yuck.

As an adult, I've come to appreciate that: (1) onion rings, when cooked properly, can be insanely delicious, and (2) onion rings are better off without a thick coat of batter. My recipe for fiery onion rings requires just a quick dip in an egg wash before applying a thin layer of grain-free flour and spicy cayenne. Instead of having to guess whether your next bite will consist of mushy onions or a mouthful of batter, you'll be treated to a perfectly crispy morsel of sweet fried onions.

INGREDIENTS:

2   large egg whites

1   large yellow onion, thinly sliced into rings

1   cup arrowroot powder or tapioca flour

1   teaspoon cayenne pepper or shichimi togarashi (Japanese seven-spice chili pepper)

2   teaspoons kosher salt

1½   cups lard, ghee, or frying fat of choice

> NOT A FAN OF HOT AND SPICY ONION RINGS? YOU CAN LEAVE OUT THE PEPPER, AND SUBSTITUTE 1 TEASPOON OF GARLIC POWDER FOR AN EXTRA PUNCH OF FLAVOR!

1 In a large bowl, whisk the egg whites until frothy.

2 Coat the onion rings in the egg whites.

3 In a shallow plate, mix together the arrowroot powder, cayenne, and salt.

4 Heat the cooking fat in a large skillet over medium-high heat until the temperature of the oil reaches 360°F.

5 Take some rings out of the bowl, shaking off any excess egg white.

6 Place the rings in the seasoned "flour."

7 Coat the rings in the flour, dusting off any excess.

8 Gently drop a few rings into the oil.

9 Fry the rings for 3 to 5 minutes, flipping once, until crisp and golden.

10 Transfer the onion rings to a wire rack to drain off any excess oil.

11 Repeat with the remaining onion rings until done.

(You don't have to arrange the rings like this. Henry did it 'cause he's weird.)

12 Use these rings to top salads, soups, steaks, or burgers. Or just eat 'em.

PERSIAN CAULIFLOWER RICE

MAKES 6 SERVINGS
⏱ **30 MINUTES**

Golden, glistening Persian rice is fragrant with spices, and bejeweled with gem-colored dried fruits and crunchy nuts. It's become one of my favorite accompaniments to meaty kababs or roast chicken, but tracking down all of the traditional ingredients can be challenging—especially when you're short on time or funds. That's why I've kept my version as straightforward and wallet-friendly as possible, using turmeric and paprika instead of pricey saffron. Take note: Properly browning the onions is the key to this recipe. It takes a little longer, but it's well worth the wait.

INGREDIENTS:

- ½ cup currants or raisins
- 3 tablespoons olive oil or fat of choice, divided
- 1 small yellow or white onion, thinly sliced
- 3 garlic cloves, minced
- 1 medium cauliflower head, riced (or 20 ounces fresh or frozen riced cauliflower)
- 1½ teaspoon kosher salt
- ½ teaspoon ground turmeric
- 1 teaspoon sweet paprika
- ½ cup toasted almond slivers
- Freshly ground black pepper
- Fresh mint leaves (optional)

INSTRUCTIONS:

1. In a small bowl, soak the currants in ½ cup boiling water. Set them aside for 10 minutes to plump up.

2. Meanwhile, heat 2 tablespoons of olive oil in a large skillet over medium heat. Once it's shimmering, add the sliced onions.

3. Cook for 15 to 20 minutes, stirring often, until browned and softened.

(If you haven't riced your cauliflower yet, do it now. Cut it into small pieces, and pulse 'em in a food processor until they're the size of rice grains.)

4. Stir in the minced garlic, and cook for 30 seconds or until fragrant. Transfer to a dish and set aside.

5. Heat the remaining tablespoon of oil in the now-empty pan, and toss in the riced cauliflower.

6. Add the salt, turmeric, and paprika, and stir well to incorporate. Cover and cook for 5 to 10 minutes or until the rice is tender (but not mushy).

7. Turn off the stove. Add the onions, toasted almond slices, and drained currants, and mix well. Taste and adjust with salt and pepper as needed.

8. Garnish with mint if desired, and eat.

SCRAMBLED EGGS WITH SHRIMP + SCALLIONS

MAKES 4 SERVINGS
⏱ 10 MINUTES

Henry's parents still recall with amazement how he once inhaled four plates of soft-scrambled eggs with shrimp while on a train from southern China to Hong Kong. He was a teenager at the time, so his wolf-like hunger could be chalked up to surging adolescent hormones. But an equally likely explanation is that this classic Cantonese dish simply tastes amazing.

Seasoned with white pepper and sesame oil, these fluffy eggs are perfect for an end-of-day meal paired with a bowl of Cauli Rice (page 80)—though it's just as delicious for breakfast.

If you're feeling adventurous, feel free to substitute fresh crab meat or roast pork for the shrimp—you'll love every variation you try.

INGREDIENTS:

10 **large eggs**

¼ **cup Bone Broth (page 76) or chicken stock**

1 **teaspoon sesame oil**

1 **teaspoon kosher salt**

½ **teaspoon fish sauce**

Ground white pepper

2 **scallions, thinly sliced on the diagonal, plus extra for garnish**

¼ **cup ghee or avocado oil**

½ **pound shrimp (21-25 count per pound), shelled and deveined**

1 IN A LARGE BOWL, COMBINE THE EGGS, BROTH, SESAME OIL, SALT, FISH SAUCE, AND A PINCH OF WHITE PEPPER. BEAT UNTIL THE INGREDIENTS ARE WELL MIXED.

2 TOSS IN THE SCALLIONS.

3 ADD THE GHEE TO A LARGE CAST-IRON SKILLET OVER MEDIUM HEAT. ONCE THE FAT'S SHIMMERING, ADD THE SHRIMP.

4 COOK FOR **30** SECONDS PER SIDE OR UNTIL PEARLY-PINK AND COMPLETELY OPAQUE.

5 POUR IN THE EGG MIXTURE.

6 COOK, STIRRING, FOR **2** TO **3** MINUTES OR UNTIL A SOFT SCRAMBLE FORMS.

7 THE EGGS SHOULD BE SOFT-SCRAMBLED, NOT HARD AND DENSE. IF THE PAN'S TOO HOT, REMOVE IT FROM THE HEAT. THE RESIDUAL HEAT WILL FINISH OFF THE EGGS.

8 PLATE AND TOP WITH EXTRA SCALLIONS. SERVE IMMEDIATELY.

BORETA'S BREAKFAST

MAKES 1 SERVING
⏱ **5 MINUTES**

Over breakfast one sunny day in Los Angeles, our pal Justin Boreta (a.k.a. one-third of The Glitch Mob—my favorite electronic music group) told me all about his no-cook morning meal of choice: a bowl of canned sardines, avocado, pickles, and fresh dill—all mashed together. "I got the idea from Tim Ferriss, who said he'd been eating a can of sardines for breakfast," Justin said. "I love getting tons more protein and omega-3s with less meat. And sardines are also completely sustainable!"

They're surprisingly delicious, too—especially when combined with Justin's choice of flavor boosters. In fact, I've come to love this egg-free breakfast as much as I love The Glitch Mob's music!

INGREDIENTS:

1   **(4.375-ounce) can sardines in olive oil, drained**

2   **teaspoons stone-ground or Dijon-style mustard**

1   **small Hass avocado, cubed**

¼   **cup finely diced dill pickles**

     Kosher salt

     Freshly ground black pepper

     Juice from ½ lime

¼   **teaspoon gochugaru (Korean chili flakes) or red pepper flakes (optional)**

1   **tablespoon fresh dill, coarsely chopped**

1   **head endive, separated into spears (optional)**

INSTRUCTIONS:

1. IN A MEDIUM BOWL, COMBINE THE SARDINES AND MUSTARD.

2. THEN, MASH 'EM TOGETHER WITH A FORK.

3. TOSS IN THE CUBED AVOCADO...

4. ...AND DICED PICKLES.

5. ADD A PINCH OF SALT, A FEW CRANKS OF THE PEPPER MILL...

6. ...AND FRESH LIME JUICE.

7. MIX EVERYTHING TOGETHER, USING A FORK TO SMUSH SOME OF THE AVOCADO.

8. TOP WITH CHILI FLAKES, IF DESIRED, AND FRESH DILL. SERVE WITH ENDIVE SPEARS.

BORETA

SEARED SCALLOPS WITH ORANGE-SHALLOT SAUCE

MAKES 4 SERVINGS
⏱ 30 MINUTES

Who says you can't make a high-falutin' seafood dinner at home in less time than it takes to dry a load of laundry? Okay—I doubt anyone has ever actually said that, but if someone *did*, they'd be wrong. Prepared the right way, restaurant-style seared scallops are crisp-crusted on the outside, delicate on the inside, and a breeze to make.

For this recipe, use dry-packed scallops, not the cheaper wet-packed stuff. Wet-packed scallops may appear more plump, but they're often chemically preserved, bloated with water, tougher, and bland. Dry-packed scallops cost a little more, but they're also fresher and more concentrated in flavor.

INGREDIENTS:

1½   **pounds (about 20-30) dry-packed sea scallops**

     Kosher salt

     Freshly ground black pepper

¼   **cup ghee or avocado oil, divided**

1   **small shallot, minced**

4   **fresh thyme sprigs**

½   **cup fresh orange juice**

2   **tablespoons chilled ghee**

¼   **cup minced fresh chives**

1 USE YOUR FINGERS TO REMOVE THE SIDE MUSCLE ATTACHED TO EACH SCALLOP.

2 GENTLY BLOT THE SCALLOPS COMPLETELY DRY WITH PAPER TOWELS. UNLESS THEY'RE TOTALLY DRY, YOUR EXPENSIVE MORSELS FROM THE SEA WON'T SEAR PROPERLY.

3 SEASON BOTH SIDES WITH SALT AND PEPPER.

4 HEAT 2 TABLESPOONS OF GHEE IN A LARGE (12-INCH) HEAVY-BOTTOMED SKILLET OVER MEDIUM-HIGH HEAT UNTIL JUST SMOKING. PLACE HALF OF THE SCALLOPS FLAT-SIDE DOWN IN THE SKILLET IN A SINGLE LAYER.

5 COOK UNDISTURBED (I.E., DON'T MOVE THE SCALLOPS) FOR 1½ TO 2 MINUTES OR UNTIL THEY DEVELOP A GOLDEN BROWN SEAR. THEN, CAREFULLY FLIP THEM OVER.

6 USE A LARGE SPOON TO BASTE THEM WITH GHEE. COOK UNDISTURBED FOR 1 MINUTE OR UNTIL THE CENTER OF EACH SCALLOP IS OPAQUE AND THE SIDES ARE FIRM.

7 TRANSFER THE SCALLOPS TO A PLATE AND LOOSELY COVER WITH FOIL. ADD THE REMAINING 2 TABLESPOONS OF GHEE TO THE PAN AND REPEAT STEPS 4 THROUGH 6 TO COOK THE REMAINING SCALLOPS.

8 TURN OFF THE BURNER. ADD THE SHALLOTS AND THYME SPRIGS TO THE SKILLET. THERE SHOULD BE ENOUGH RESIDUAL HEAT IN THE PAN TO CONTINUE COOKING.

9 SAUTÉ FOR 2 MINUTES OR UNTIL THE SHALLOTS ARE TRANSLUCENT.

10 TURN THE HEAT TO MEDIUM-LOW, AND POUR IN THE ORANGE JUICE. SCRAPE THE BROWNED BITS FROM THE BOTTOM OF THE PAN, AND BRING THE SAUCE TO A SIMMER.

11 REMOVE THE PAN FROM THE HEAT. WHISK IN THE CHILLED GHEE A LITTLE BIT AT A TIME UNTIL THE SAUCE EMULSIFIES.

12 SEASON WITH SALT AND PEPPER TO TASTE.

13 REMOVE THE THYME. SERVE THE SCALLOPS WITH THE SAUCE AND A GARNISH OF CHIVES.

271

HONEY HARISSA SALMON

MAKES 4 SERVINGS
⏱ 30 MINUTES
(15 MINUTES HANDS-ON)

By cooking salmon in parchment, you can make perfectly delicate fish with tender vegetables, but that's only the half of it. These bold, umami-rich packets cover the entire flavor spectrum—from sweet and savory to spicy and tart.

Harissa, a Tunisian hot chile pepper paste, adds a lovely warmth to this dish, but if you can't find it at the store, sub in sriracha instead.

INGREDIENTS:

- **2** tablespoons harissa
- **2** tablespoons honey
- **1** tablespoon finely grated lemon zest (from 1 lemon)
- **2** medium carrots, peeled and cut into thin matchsticks
- **2** medium zucchini, cut into thin matchsticks
- **¼** cup pitted green olives, roughly chopped
- **2** garlic cloves, minced
- **2** tablespoons extra-virgin olive oil
- Juice from 1 lemon
- Kosher salt
- Freshly ground black pepper
- **4** (6-ounce) 1½-inch-thick salmon fillets, pinbones removed
- **1** tablespoon toasted sesame seeds

AVOIDING HONEY? USE ¼ CUP OF ORANGE JUICE IN ITS PLACE.

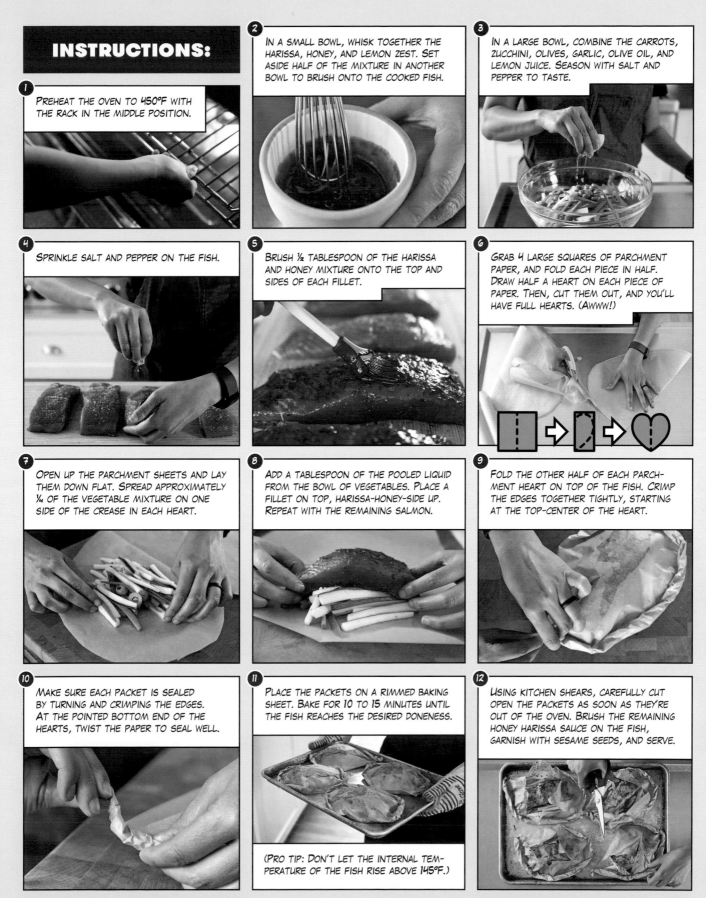

INSTRUCTIONS:

1 PREHEAT THE OVEN TO 450°F WITH THE RACK IN THE MIDDLE POSITION.

2 IN A SMALL BOWL, WHISK TOGETHER THE HARISSA, HONEY, AND LEMON ZEST. SET ASIDE HALF OF THE MIXTURE IN ANOTHER BOWL TO BRUSH ONTO THE COOKED FISH.

3 IN A LARGE BOWL, COMBINE THE CARROTS, ZUCCHINI, OLIVES, GARLIC, OLIVE OIL, AND LEMON JUICE. SEASON WITH SALT AND PEPPER TO TASTE.

4 SPRINKLE SALT AND PEPPER ON THE FISH.

5 BRUSH ½ TABLESPOON OF THE HARISSA AND HONEY MIXTURE ONTO THE TOP AND SIDES OF EACH FILLET.

6 GRAB 4 LARGE SQUARES OF PARCHMENT PAPER, AND FOLD EACH PIECE IN HALF. DRAW HALF A HEART ON EACH PIECE OF PAPER. THEN, CUT THEM OUT, AND YOU'LL HAVE FULL HEARTS. (AWWW!)

7 OPEN UP THE PARCHMENT SHEETS AND LAY THEM DOWN FLAT. SPREAD APPROXIMATELY ¼ OF THE VEGETABLE MIXTURE ON ONE SIDE OF THE CREASE IN EACH HEART.

8 ADD A TABLESPOON OF THE POOLED LIQUID FROM THE BOWL OF VEGETABLES. PLACE A FILLET ON TOP, HARISSA-HONEY-SIDE UP. REPEAT WITH THE REMAINING SALMON.

9 FOLD THE OTHER HALF OF EACH PARCHMENT HEART ON TOP OF THE FISH. CRIMP THE EDGES TOGETHER TIGHTLY, STARTING AT THE TOP-CENTER OF THE HEART.

10 MAKE SURE EACH PACKET IS SEALED BY TURNING AND CRIMPING THE EDGES. AT THE POINTED BOTTOM END OF THE HEARTS, TWIST THE PAPER TO SEAL WELL.

11 PLACE THE PACKETS ON A RIMMED BAKING SHEET. BAKE FOR 10 TO 15 MINUTES UNTIL THE FISH REACHES THE DESIRED DONENESS.

(PRO TIP: DON'T LET THE INTERNAL TEMPERATURE OF THE FISH RISE ABOVE 145°F.)

12 USING KITCHEN SHEARS, CAREFULLY CUT OPEN THE PACKETS AS SOON AS THEY'RE OUT OF THE OVEN. BRUSH THE REMAINING HONEY HARISSA SAUCE ON THE FISH, GARNISH WITH SESAME SEEDS, AND SERVE.

WANNA KNOW HOW I COME UP WITH MY RECIPE IDEAS? I OFTEN GET INSPIRATION FROM MY FOOD-RELATED TRAVELS.

THAT'S WHY I'M ALL ABOUT GASTROTOURISM!

MICHELLE: Ask anyone who knows me: I've worked hard to build up my savings, but I don't spend money on things like clothing, cars, or jewelry. For years, I wore the same wardrobe of threadbare T-shirts that I bought in college, and my handbag of choice is a canvas grocery sack that I got for free at the farmers' market. My wedding ring is just a stretchy band of silicone that I bought for under twenty bucks.

HENRY: But that doesn't mean you're a tightwad. You're not exactly shy about spending on ingredients and kitchen gadgets, right?

MICHELLE: And culinary experiences, too! When it comes to food-related fun, all bets are off. Sure, an incredible meal may disappear as soon as it slides down my gullet, but the memories will remain. And looking back at the most cherished moments in my life, virtually all of them involve meals shared with my favorite people. I won't skimp on food experiences.

HENRY: Yeah—you even plan our family vacations around where and what you want to eat. Then, once we arrive at our destination, we hunt for local culinary treasures while you obsessively jot notes into your phone about recipe ideas and flavor combinations.

MICHELLE: I guess I'm just *wai sek*—Cantonese for someone who "lives to eat." For me, life's all about the pleasures of food. As a family, we're lucky to have had opportunities to travel extensively, and when I'm far from home, I'd much rather search out new hole-in-the-wall eateries and skip the sights altogether.

HENRY: It's true: You're a textbook gastrotourist. I remember the first time we were in Florence, I took us to the Galleria dell'Accademia to see Michelangelo's David, but before we could get inside, you dragged me to search out some sort of beef dish instead.

MICHELLE: But we got to try the best *bollito misto* in the whole world! That Tuscan boiled beef was incredible! We got *bollito misto* sandwiches at Da Nerbone's market stand in the Piazza del Mercato, and dipped them in this amazing, life-changing meat broth, remember?

HENRY: I'll admit it—that beef was pretty great, and I'm glad you took us off the beaten path to find it. But I still think it's funny that of all the different types of experiences you could have while traveling, you tend to focus on just one aspect: eating.

MICHELLE: Well, here's how I look at it: If traveling is all about cultural immersion, what's more core to culture than food? I mean, with just one bite, we can experience something that's uniquely rooted in the place we're visiting. Besides, food is something you can't experience from afar, and traveling has given us the chance to have culinary experiences that we simply can't get here at home. And I'm not talking about shelling out big bucks for five-star restaurants in New York or Paris or Tokyo. It doesn't have to be expensive at all. Sometimes, it just means pausing to take a closer look at how the rest of the world eats.

HENRY: Like when we were at the farm in Thailand.

MICHELLE: Exactly! One of my all-time favorite culinary experiences took place on a small organic farm in a hillside community about an hour's drive from Chiang Mai. Our friend Mark Ritchie arranged for us to visit a family farm in rural Mae Tha, where the farmer, Bwosai Gantada, proudly showed us around her fields. There, we snipped and plucked ingredients from her lush garden. We squatted on the floor of the outdoor kitchen, and prepped the vegetables on towels spread on the ground. Then, we all helped Bwosai prepare a hearty, multi-course lunch cooked over a simple wood-burning pit. It was incredibly fresh and delicious.

HENRY: You were brimming with recipe ideas after that lunch on the farm, too.

MICHELLE: Totally—that one afternoon had a huge impact on the way I think about fresh ingredients and flavors. In fact, the curry and stir-fries we had at lunch that day inspired a bunch of the recipes in this book.

HENRY: We feasted on stir-fries and curries with vegetables, meat, and rice that were all grown right there on the farm. And after we polished it all off, we finished our meal with crisp rose apples and slices of ripe papaya. It was a memorable meal, and one that taught us a lot about food and sustainability.

MICHELLE: I remember being amazed at the fact that every single plant on the farm was hand-planted and hand-harvested—and irrigated with water pumped using an ingeniously rigged stationary bicycle. It made me want to never again waste a single piece of food—especially after seeing what it takes for small family farms to grow what we eat.

HENRY: Our trip to northern Thailand really opened my eyes to the subtleties of regional cuisines. I had always assumed that Thai food was limited to the powerfully sweet and spicy flavors of the south, and hadn't realized how the dishes of Chiang Mai are more heavily influenced by Lao, Burmese, and Chinese flavors. This went way beyond the stuff we were used to eating at Thai restaurants in the United States.

MICHELLE: I also took a bunch of cooking classes when we were there, and came away with a better understanding of how to use Thai spices and herbs. Looking back, I can see how much that one trip influenced the way I combine flavors in my cooking. Before, my recipes were primarily inspired by classic Californian fare, as well as the Chinese dishes from my childhood. But now, my cooking has more of a Southeast Asian bent. Have you noticed that?

HENRY: Definitely. It happens every time we come home from traveling abroad. When we got back from Vietnam, for example, you were obsessed with lemongrass, lime, and ginger. And when you came back from Central America—

MICHELLE: I know—I couldn't stop making fried green plantains! It's one of the reasons the recipe's in this book. I craved *patacones* for months afterward.

HENRY: But getting back to Thailand, one of the best examples of how you derive inspiration from our travels is your recipe for Cracklin' Chicken. It was originally inspired by our favorite dish at Cherng Doi Roast Chicken—an unassuming little grilled chicken joint off of Nimmanhaemin Road in Chiang Mai.

MICHELLE: Our pal Mark had recommended the place to us, and Cherng Doi Roast Chicken ended up being my favorite restaurant in the city—we went three times in one week! Its specialty is *gai yang nong krob*—marinated boneless chicken with crisp, golden skin, cooked directly on the grill. The heat of the grill melts the flavorful fat under the skin, seasoning the tender chicken as it cooks, and producing a perfectly crisp, amber exterior. There are nights when I still dream about that chicken.

HENRY: Best of all, it was super cheap!

MICHELLE: For me, the best thing was actually the inspiration it provided. When I got home, I just *had* to figure out a way to replicate the flavors of that

amazing chicken dish. I experimented with skin-on chicken thighs—de-boning them, pounding them flat, and frying them on hot cast-iron skillets while jumping to avoid the oil spatters. This was simpler than making *gai yang nong krob*—it was fried instead of grilled—but the flavor-to-effort ratio was off the charts. And that's how Cracklin' Chicken was born. I posted the recipe on our website soon after we got back from our trip, and it quickly became one of my most popular and enduring recipes.

HENRY: I think we can all agree that food travel gives us a unique look at different cultures, and can spur us to experiment with new and different flavors in the kitchen. But aren't there other travel experiences you've enjoyed that *aren't* food-related?

MICHELLE: Yes, but do you remember how I freaked out when an Asian elephant took our then-five-year-old on a solo ride under the surface of a murky river?

HENRY: I remember Ollie loving it!

MICHELLE: All I'm saying is that dining experiences can be just as memorable as crazy adventures—but without the risk of ending up in the hospital. After all, hospital food is pretty terrible.

HENRY: I love that you have such a one-track mind.

Ollie's
CRACKLIN' CHICKEN

MAKES 4 SERVINGS
⏱ **30 MINUTES**

My famous Cracklin' Chicken is the ultimate go-to dish for lazy but discriminating eaters like me. As anyone who's tried Cracklin' Chicken will tell you, these crispy-on-the-outside, tender-and-juicy-on-the-inside chicken thighs are tastier (and better for you) than any other fried chicken you've ever stuck inside your face-hole.

Just remember: Bone-in, skin-on thighs are a must for this recipe. If you use breasts, the chicken will turn out dry. And don't go skin-less—after all, this dish is all about the crispy, cracklin' skin!

INGREDIENTS:

8　bone-in, skin-on chicken thighs (about 4 pounds)

1　tablespoon kosher salt, divided

2　teaspoons ghee or avocado oil

IN A RUSH? ASK YOUR BUTCHER TO DE-BONE THE THIGHS FOR YOU SO YOU CAN SKIP SOME OF THE PREP. OH, AND SAVE THE BONES TO MAKE BONE BROTH (PAGE 76)!

MOM NAMED THIS RECIPE AFTER ME 'CAUSE I KEPT PESTERING HER TO DO IT!

SHE SAYS I'M REALLY GOOD AT BEING "ANNOYINGLY PERSISTENT."

1 BLOT THE CHICKEN DRY, AND STARTING AT ONE END OF EACH THIGH, CAREFULLY CUT OUT THE BONE WITH A PAIR OF SHARP KITCHEN SHEARS.

2 KEEP AS CLOSE TO THE BONE AS YOU CAN. WHEN YOU GET TO THE OTHER END, TRIM AROUND THE JOINT. REMOVE THE BONE.

3 IF EXTRA SKIN IS FLAPPING AROUND AND HANGING OFF THE THIGHS, TRIM IT. BUT DON'T CUT TOO MUCH AWAY, BECAUSE THE SKIN WILL SHRINK WHEN IT COOKS.

4 FLATTEN EACH THIGH WITH A MEAT POUNDER (OR CUT A GASH IN THE THICKEST PART SO EACH THIGH WILL LIE TOTALLY FLAT).

5 FLIP THE THIGHS SKIN-SIDE UP. SPRINKLE ½ TABLESPOON OF SALT ON THEM.

6 HEAT THE GHEE IN A LARGE CAST-IRON SKILLET OVER MEDIUM-HIGH HEAT. ONCE IT'S HOT, PLACE **3** TO **4** THIGHS SKIN-SIDE DOWN IN THE PAN IN A SINGLE LAYER. DON'T OVERCROWD THE SKILLET, FOLKS.

7 SEASON THE MEAT SIDE OF THE CHICKEN WITH A PINCH OF THE REMAINING SALT.

8 WHILE COOKING, COVER THE SKILLET WITH A STAINLESS STEEL SPLATTER SCREEN, OR LINE THE FLOOR IN FRONT OF YOUR STOVE WITH TOWELS. OTHERWISE, YOUR KITCHEN WILL PAY A SLICK, OIL-SPLATTERED PRICE.

ANOTHER OPTION: COOK THE CHICKEN IN A SKILLET PLACED ON AN OUTDOOR GRILL.

9 FRY THE CHICKEN FOR **7** TO **10** MINUTES OR UNTIL THE SKIN IS CRISPY AND GOLDEN, ROTATING THE PAN 90 DEGREES HALFWAY THROUGH TO MAKE SURE THE HEAT FROM THE BURNER IS UNIFORMLY DISTRIBUTED.

10 FLIP THE THIGHS AND COOK FOR **3** MORE MINUTES OR UNTIL COOKED THROUGH.

11 TRANSFER THE CRISPY THIGHS TO A WIRE RACK AND REST THEM FOR **5** MINUTES.

12 REPEAT STEPS **6** THROUGH **11** WITH THE REMAINING THIGHS. SLICE AND SERVE!

CANTONESE CRISPY CHICKEN THIGHS

MAKES 4 SERVINGS
⏱ 45 MINUTES

Inspired by both the Cantonese dishes of my childhood and a fantastic recipe by my pal Simone Miller, I came up with this deliriously tasty one-pan supper, featuring juicy chicken and crispy skin. It's a fast and easy dish—as long as you remember to soak your dried mushrooms in advance. Otherwise, you can use fresh shiitake mushrooms, but dried shiitakes give this dish an exponential boost of umami power that can't be beat.

INGREDIENTS:

- **6** **dried shiitake mushrooms, reconstituted in a bowl of water for at least 1 hour**
- **1** **tablespoon ghee, avocado oil, or olive oil**
- **1** **cup thinly sliced shallots**
  Kosher salt
- **6** **bone-in, skin-on chicken thighs**
- **1** **(2-inch) piece fresh ginger, peeled and cut into ¼-inch coins**
- **6** **garlic cloves, peeled and smashed**
- **¼** **teaspoon freshly ground black pepper**
- **1** **teaspoon fish sauce**
- **1** **cup Bone Broth (page 76) or chicken stock**
- **¼** **cup sliced scallions**
- **¼** **cup fresh cilantro**

INSTRUCTIONS:

1 RINSE THE DRIED MUSHROOMS. THEN, SOAK THEM IN A MEDIUM BOWL OF WATER AT LEAST 1 HOUR IN ADVANCE OF COOKING.

(IF PRESSED FOR TIME, USE FRESH MUSHROOMS INSTEAD.)

2 WHEN YOU'RE READY TO COOK, PREHEAT THE OVEN TO 450°F WITH THE RACK IN THE MIDDLE POSITION, AND HEAT A 12-INCH OVEN-SAFE SKILLET OVER MEDIUM HEAT.

3 HEAT THE GHEE OR OIL IN THE PAN. ADD THE SHALLOTS AND A SPRINKLE OF SALT.

4 COOK, STIRRING OCCASIONALLY, FOR 5 TO 10 MINUTES OR UNTIL THE SHALLOTS ARE SOFTENED.

5 WHILE THE SHALLOTS ARE COOKING, SPRINKLE KOSHER SALT LIBERALLY (ABOUT 2 TEASPOONS IN TOTAL) ON BOTH SIDES OF THE THIGHS.

6 SQUEEZE OUT THE EXCESS LIQUID FROM THE RECONSTITUTED MUSHROOMS, SLICE OFF THE WOODY STEMS (WHICH CAN BE RESERVED FOR MAKING BONE BROTH)...

7

...AND THINLY SLICE THE CAPS.

8

ONCE THE SHALLOTS HAVE WILTED, ADD THE MUSHROOMS, GINGER, AND GARLIC.

9 STIR FOR 1 MINUTE OR UNTIL AROMATIC. THEN, TRANSFER THE VEGGIES TO A PLATE. WIPE OUT ANY REMNANTS FROM THE PAN, AND RETURN IT TO THE STOVETOP.

10 CRANK UP THE HEAT TO MEDIUM-HIGH. THEN, SEAR THE CHICKEN SKIN-SIDE DOWN IN THE HOT PAN UNTIL NICELY BROWNED AND CRISPY, ABOUT 4 TO 5 MINUTES.

11 WHILE THE SKIN IS CRISPING, ADD FRESHLY GROUND PEPPER TO THE MEATY SIDE.

12 WHEN THE SKIN TURNS GOLDEN BROWN ...

13 ...FLIP THE PIECES OVER AND COOK FOR 2 MINUTES MORE.

14 STIR THE FISH SAUCE INTO THE BROTH. POUR IT INTO THE PAN, MAKING SURE TO AVOID GETTING LIQUID ON THE CRISPY SKIN.

15 ADD THE SHALLOTS, MUSHROOMS, AND GARLIC BACK TO THE PAN, TUCKING THEM BETWEEN THE CHICKEN PIECES. AGAIN, BE CAREFUL NOT TO COVER THE CRISPY SKIN.

16 TRANSFER THE PAN TO THE HOT OVEN AND ROAST FOR 15 TO 20 MINUTES OR UNTIL THE THIGHS REGISTER 165°F ON AN INSTANT-READ MEAT THERMOMETER.

17 TASTE THE SAUCE FOR SEASONING, AND ADJUST WITH MORE SALT AS NEEDED. GARNISH THE CHICKEN THIGHS WITH A SHOWER OF SLICED SCALLIONS AND FRESH CILANTRO, AND DIG IN!

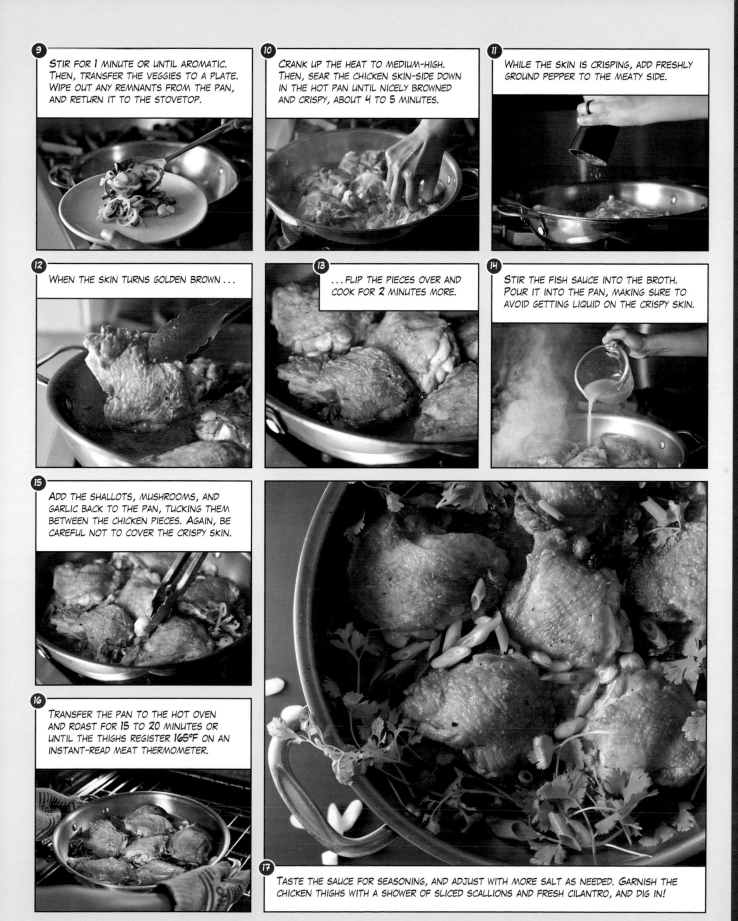

SWITCH IT UP:
ITALIAN CRISPY CHICKEN THIGHS

CRISPY CHICKEN THIGHS DON'T HAVE TO BE CANTONESE. IF YOU'RE IN THE MOOD FOR ITALIAN FLAVORS (OR YOU JUST DON'T HAVE DRIED SHIITAKES ON HAND), MAKE THIS INSTEAD. FOLLOW THE RECIPE ON THE PREVIOUS PAGE, BUT SUBSTITUTE THINLY SLICED FRESH CREMINI MUSHROOMS FOR DRIED SHIITAKES, AND LEAVE OUT THE GINGER COINS IN STEP 8. THEN, IN STEP 15, ADD A HANDFUL OF CHERRY TOMATOES TO THE PAN ALONG WITH THE SHALLOTS, MUSHROOMS, AND GARLIC. ONCE THE CHICKEN'S OUT OF THE OVEN, GARNISH IT WITH ROUGHLY CHOPPED ITALIAN PARSLEY AND BASIL.

284

UMAMI HELPS ENSURE HUMAN SURVIVAL, TOO, BECAUSE IT ALLOWS US TO RECOGNIZE PROTEIN-RICH FOODS.
HERE ARE JUST A FEW PALEO-FRIENDLY INGREDIENTS THAT ARE HIGH IN UMAMI.
Meat!
Eggs!
Seafood!
Seaweed!
Tomato Paste!
Mushrooms!
Garlic!
Fish Sauce!
Coconut Aminos!
Kimchi!
THE BEST PART? UMAMI SYNERGY!
COMBINING UMAMI-PACKED INGREDIENTS CAN CREATE AMPLIFIED AND LINGERING TASTE SENSATIONS!
WHEN IT COMES TO UMAMI, 1 + 1 = 8, MEANING WHEN YOU COMBINE TWO OR MORE UMAMI-RICH INGREDIENTS, YOU CAN BOOST THE FLAVORS OF YOUR DISHES EXPONENTIALLY!
THE MORAL OF THE STORY: TO MAKE YOUR DISHES POP WITH FLAVOR, REGULARLY COOK WITH INGREDIENTS THAT ARE NATURALLY HIGH IN UMAMI.
DO YOU EVER TAKE OFF YOUR SHADES?
NEVER.

CHICKEN CURRY IN A HURRY

MAKES 4 SERVINGS
⏱ 30 MINUTES

It's true: You can enjoy a satisfying Thai chicken curry on a weeknight without leaving home. I've pared down the classic recipe to the bare essentials, which means you can get this one-pot stew from stove to craw in less than 30 minutes. You'll love the complex spices, fresh herbs, and creamy coconut milk base. Ladle this curry over a steaming bowl of Cauli Rice, and your supper will be Thai-riffic!

INGREDIENTS:

- 1½ pounds boneless, skinless chicken thighs, trimmed of excess fat and sliced thin
- ½ teaspoon kosher salt
- 1 tablespoon coconut oil or ghee
- 1 small yellow onion, thinly sliced
- 2 tablespoons Thai green, yellow, or red curry paste
- 2 (14-ounce) cans full-fat coconut milk
- 2 tablespoons fish sauce
- 2 tablespoons apple juice
- 4 cups broccoli florets
- 1 medium red bell pepper, stemmed, seeded, and cut into thin strips
- Juice from 1 lime
- ½ cup fresh basil leaves
- ¼ cup fresh cilantro leaves

> UNLIKE DRY-SPICED INDIAN CURRIES, QUICK-COOKING THAI CURRIES ARE USUALLY MADE WITH CURRY PASTE, FRESH HERBS, AND COCONUT MILK. AND IF YOU'RE COOKING FOR KIDS, REMEMBER THAT GREEN AND YELLOW CURRIES ARE MILDER THAN RED.

INSTRUCTIONS:

1 IN A LARGE BOWL, TOSS THE CHICKEN THIGHS WITH SALT. SET THE CHICKEN ASIDE.

2 IN A LARGE SAUCEPAN OR DUTCH OVEN, HEAT THE OIL OVER MEDIUM HEAT UNTIL THE FAT SHIMMERS. ADD THE ONIONS.

3 COOK FOR 3 TO 5 MINUTES OR UNTIL SOFTENED.

4 STIR IN THE CURRY PASTE AND COOK FOR 30 SECONDS OR UNTIL IT'S FRAGRANT.

5 POUR IN THE COCONUT MILK, FISH SAUCE, AND APPLE JUICE.

6 CRANK THE STOVE UP TO HIGH, AND COOK FOR 2 MINUTES OR UNTIL THE SAUCE COMES TO A BOIL.

7 ADD THE CHICKEN AND BROCCOLI.

8 LOWER THE HEAT TO MEDIUM. COOK, MAINTAINING A SIMMER, FOR 5 MINUTES.

9 TOSS THE BELL PEPPER INTO THE POT. COOK FOR 1 TO 2 MINUTES MORE OR UNTIL THE VEGETABLES ARE TENDER-CRISP (MEANING THEY'RE COOKED ALL THE WAY THROUGH, BUT STILL HAVE SOME SNAP).

10 MAKE SURE THE CHICKEN IS COOKED THROUGH. REMOVE THE SAUCEPAN FROM THE HEAT, AND ADD THE LIME JUICE.

11 STIR IN THE BASIL AND CILANTRO.

12 PLATE AND SERVE IMMEDIATELY. PAIR THE CURRY WITH CAULI RICE (PAGE 80).

THAI ROAST CHICKEN

MAKES 4 SERVINGS
⏱ 45 MINUTES
(10 MINUTES HANDS-ON)

If you made the chicken curry recipe on the previous page, I bet you're wondering what to do with all the extra Thai curry paste. Well, wonder no more. This shockingly easy weeknight recipe calls for just five ingredients, and one of them is the lip-smackingly delicious curry paste that's sitting in your fridge.

Just don't mistake this recipe for an afterthought. Thai Roast Chicken is on the regular rotation at our house, and I love it for its simplicity and flavor. I usually make a double batch so I'll have plenty of leftovers to pack in the boys' school lunches or to shred for salads and soups.

Thai Roast Chicken is a gift that keeps giving—like *The Giving Tree*, only less stumpy and sad, and way more yummy.

INGREDIENTS:

1   cup full-fat coconut milk

2   tablespoons Thai green, yellow, or red curry paste

2   teaspoons fish sauce

1   teaspoon kosher salt

   Zest and juice from 1 lime, plus extra zest for garnish

8   bone-in, skin-on chicken thighs (about 4 pounds)

🔄 **SWITCH IT UP:**
OVEN-ROASTED PAPRIKA CHICKEN

No curry paste on hand? Make Oven-Roasted Paprika Chicken instead. In place of the curry paste, use 1 tablespoon paprika, 1 teaspoon garlic powder, and ½ teaspoon freshly ground black pepper in Step 1. Then, continue with the rest of the recipe.

INSTRUCTIONS:

1 IN A LARGE MEASURING CUP, COMBINE THE COCONUT MILK, CURRY PASTE, FISH SAUCE, KOSHER SALT, LIME ZEST, AND LIME JUICE.

2 WHISK WELL. TASTE AND ADJUST WITH MORE SALT IF NEEDED. THE MARINADE SHOULD BE SALTY, RICH, AND FLAVORFUL.

3 TOSS THE CHICKEN IN A LARGE BOWL OR FOOD STORAGE BAG, AND POUR THE MARINADE ON TOP OF THE THIGHS.

4 USING YOUR HANDS, MASSAGE THE MARINADE ALL OVER THE THIGHS. COVER AND REFRIGERATE FOR UP TO A DAY. (BUT IF YOU DON'T HAVE TIME TO MARINATE, DON'T WORRY. JUST KEEP GOING.)

5 WHEN YOU'RE READY TO COOK, SET THE OVEN TO 400°F ON CONVECTION MODE OR 425°F ON REGULAR MODE WITH THE RACK IN THE MIDDLE. (FOR CRISPIER SKIN, USE CONVECTION MODE IF YOU HAVE IT.)

6 PLACE A WIRE RACK ON TOP OF A RIMMED BAKING SHEET. WIPE OFF ANY EXCESS MARINADE FROM THE THIGHS, AND ARRANGE THEM IN A SINGLE LAYER, SKIN-SIDE DOWN, ON THE WIRE RACK.

7 ROAST THE CHICKEN FOR 20 MINUTES. THEN, FLIP THE PIECES SKIN-SIDE UP, AND ROTATE THE TRAY 180 DEGREES.

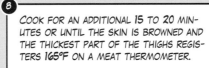

8 COOK FOR AN ADDITIONAL 15 TO 20 MINUTES OR UNTIL THE SKIN IS BROWNED AND THE THICKEST PART OF THE THIGHS REGISTERS 165°F ON A MEAT THERMOMETER.

9 I LIKE TO ADD FINELY GRATED LIME ZEST JUST BEFORE SERVING. LEFTOVERS CAN BE REHEATED, EATEN COLD, OR SHREDDED FOR SALADS OR SOUPS.

PRESSURE COOKER SALSA CHICKEN

MAKES 6 SERVINGS
⏱ 20 MINUTES
(5 MINUTES HANDS-ON)

SWITCH IT UP:
SLOW COOKER SALSA CHICKEN

NO PRESSURE COOKER? DON'T DESPAIR. YOU CAN MAKE SALSA CHICKEN IN A SLOW COOKER SET ON LOW FOR 4 TO 6 HOURS.

I've said it before: My favorite meal is one that someone else cooks for me. Sadly, that doesn't happen as often as I'd like, which is why I've had to resort to inventing recipes that are as easy as possible for my kitchen-challenged family to make for me. This one's a prime example: a ridiculously easy Mexican-inspired toss-it-in-the-pressure-cooker-and-forget-about-it recipe. This recipe doesn't even require the use of a knife, so your butterfingered kids have no excuse for avoiding kitchen duty.

By the way, I normally make Pressure Cooker Salsa Chicken with thighs (see my note below), but I know many of you prefer breasts, so I made sure this recipe works with chicken boobies. See how much I love you chicken breast lovers out there?

INGREDIENTS:

- 1   **teaspoon chili powder**
- ½   **teaspoon kosher salt**
- 2   **pounds boneless, skinless chicken breasts**
- 1   **cup store-bought roasted tomato salsa or Salsa Ahumada (page 72)**
- 12 **lettuce leaves or Grain-Free Tortillas (page 78)**

IF YOU PREFER TO USE BONELESS, SKINLESS THIGHS INSTEAD OF BREASTS, COOK 'EM UNDER HIGH PRESSURE FOR 10 MINUTES IN AN ELECTRIC PRESSURE COOKER, OR 9 MINUTES IN A STOVETOP PRESSURE COOKER.

INSTRUCTIONS:

1 IN A SMALL BOWL, COMBINE THE CHILI POWDER AND SALT.

2 ARRANGE THE CHICKEN BREASTS IN THE BOTTOM OF YOUR PRESSURE COOKER.

3 SPRINKLE THE SEASONING ON BOTH SIDES OF THE CHICKEN.

4 POUR THE SALSA EVENLY ON THE CHICKEN.

5 IF YOU'RE USING AN ELECTRIC PRESSURE COOKER, SET IT TO COOK UNDER HIGH PRESSURE FOR 7 MINUTES. IF YOU'RE USING A STOVETOP COOKER INSTEAD, COOK UNDER HIGH PRESSURE FOR 6 MINUTES.

6 WHEN THE CHICKEN'S DONE, IMMEDIATELY RELEASE THE PRESSURE MANUALLY, AND TRANSFER THE CHICKEN TO A BIG BOWL TO PREVENT OVERCOOKING.

7 SHRED THE CHICKEN. TASTE THE COOKING LIQUID AND ADJUST WITH SALT AND PEPPER IF NECESSARY.

8 POUR THE COOKING LIQUID ON TOP OF THE SHREDDED MEAT, AND TOSS WELL TO COAT.

9 SERVE THE CHICKEN WITH GRAIN-FREE TORTILLAS OR LETTUCE LEAVES. GARNISH WITH YOUR FAVORITE TACO TOPPINGS.

BÒ LÁ LỐT (BETEL LEAF BEEF ROLLS)

MAKES 30 ROLLS
⏱ 30 MINUTES

While traveling in Vietnam, I fell hard for these killer minced beef rolls. *Lá lốt* (a.k.a. betel leaves) are key; when cooked, they impart a spicy-sweet fragrance to the meaty filling. Make 'em and see.

INGREDIENTS:

• ROLLS •

1	pound ground beef
3	slices bacon, finely chopped
2	teaspoons minced garlic
1	tablespoon minced shallots
2	tablespoons grated fresh lemongrass
2	teaspoons Madras curry powder
2	teaspoons fish sauce
1	teaspoon freshly ground black pepper
½	teaspoon kosher salt
½	teaspoon arrowroot powder
30	fresh betel leaves
1	tablespoon avocado oil or melted ghee

• GARNISH •

¼	cup avocado oil
2	finely chopped scallions
2	tablespoons toasted cashews, roughly chopped
	Juice from 1 lime

MANY ASIAN MARKETS SELL FRESH BETEL LEAVES, BUT IN A PINCH, YOU CAN SUBSTITUTE SWISS CHARD LEAVES OR GRAPE LEAVES. OR FLIP TO PAGE 296 FOR ANOTHER WAY TO USE THE FILLING!

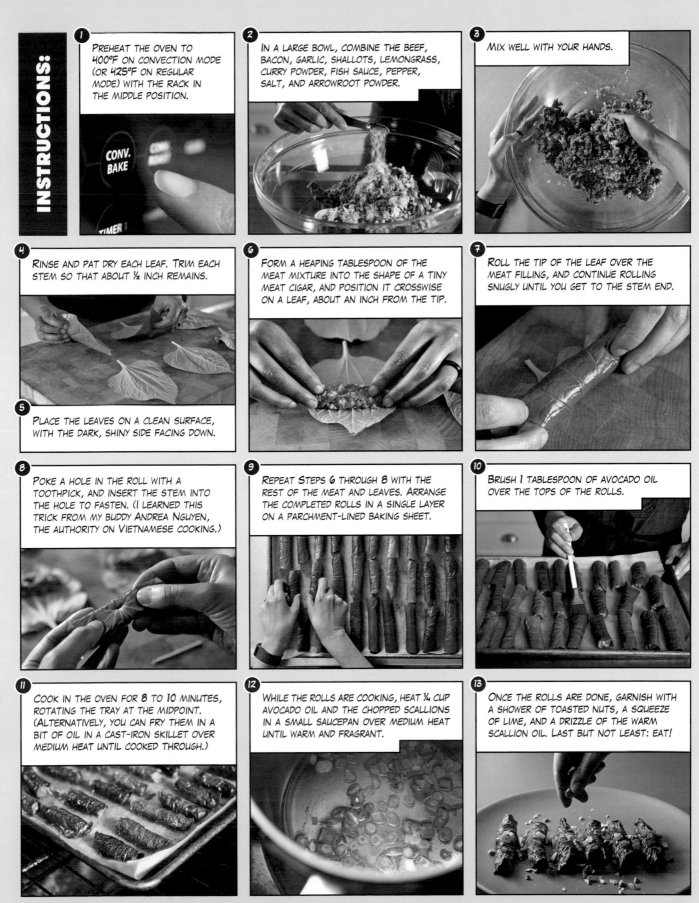

INSTRUCTIONS:

1 PREHEAT THE OVEN TO 400°F ON CONVECTION MODE (OR 425°F ON REGULAR MODE) WITH THE RACK IN THE MIDDLE POSITION.

2 IN A LARGE BOWL, COMBINE THE BEEF, BACON, GARLIC, SHALLOTS, LEMONGRASS, CURRY POWDER, FISH SAUCE, PEPPER, SALT, AND ARROWROOT POWDER.

3 MIX WELL WITH YOUR HANDS.

4 RINSE AND PAT DRY EACH LEAF. TRIM EACH STEM SO THAT ABOUT ½ INCH REMAINS.

5 PLACE THE LEAVES ON A CLEAN SURFACE, WITH THE DARK, SHINY SIDE FACING DOWN.

6 FORM A HEAPING TABLESPOON OF THE MEAT MIXTURE INTO THE SHAPE OF A TINY MEAT CIGAR, AND POSITION IT CROSSWISE ON A LEAF, ABOUT AN INCH FROM THE TIP.

7 ROLL THE TIP OF THE LEAF OVER THE MEAT FILLING, AND CONTINUE ROLLING SNUGLY UNTIL YOU GET TO THE STEM END.

8 POKE A HOLE IN THE ROLL WITH A TOOTHPICK, AND INSERT THE STEM INTO THE HOLE TO FASTEN. (I LEARNED THIS TRICK FROM MY BUDDY ANDREA NGUYEN, THE AUTHORITY ON VIETNAMESE COOKING.)

9 REPEAT STEPS 6 THROUGH 8 WITH THE REST OF THE MEAT AND LEAVES. ARRANGE THE COMPLETED ROLLS IN A SINGLE LAYER ON A PARCHMENT-LINED BAKING SHEET.

10 BRUSH 1 TABLESPOON OF AVOCADO OIL OVER THE TOPS OF THE ROLLS.

11 COOK IN THE OVEN FOR 8 TO 10 MINUTES, ROTATING THE TRAY AT THE MIDPOINT. (ALTERNATIVELY, YOU CAN FRY THEM IN A BIT OF OIL IN A CAST-IRON SKILLET OVER MEDIUM HEAT UNTIL COOKED THROUGH.)

12 WHILE THE ROLLS ARE COOKING, HEAT ¼ CUP AVOCADO OIL AND THE CHOPPED SCALLIONS IN A SMALL SAUCEPAN OVER MEDIUM HEAT UNTIL WARM AND FRAGRANT.

13 ONCE THE ROLLS ARE DONE, GARNISH WITH A SHOWER OF TOASTED NUTS, A SQUEEZE OF LIME, AND A DRIZZLE OF THE WARM SCALLION OIL. LAST BUT NOT LEAST: EAT!

YOU CAN MAKE THESE BEEF ROLLS ON YOUR BACKYARD GRILL, TOO. HEAT YOUR GRILL TO MEDIUM, AND COOK THE ROLLS WITH THE TOP DOWN, ROTATING THEM EVERY MINUTE OR SO UNTIL THE MEAT IS COOKED THROUGH AND THE BETEL LEAVES ARE WRINKLY AND FRAGRANT. I LIKE TO SKEWER MY ROLLS TO KEEP THEM FROM GETTING CAUGHT IN MY GRILL GRATES. KEEP A CLOSE EYE ON THE ROLLS AND MAKE SURE THEY DON'T BURN!

NO LÁ LỐT MEATBALLS

MAKES 24 MEATBALLS
⏱ **30 MINUTES**
(15 MINUTES HANDS-ON)

On the previous couple of pages, I extolled the virtues of using fragrant betel leaves, or *lá lốt*, to roll up seasoned, minced beef. But let's face it: On a busy weeknight, you probably won't have the time or energy to make a special trip to the Asian market. So what can you do if you've got no *lá lốt*?

Answer: Make these meatballs. It'd be a shame to deprive yourself of the rich flavors of these lemongrass and curry infused meatballs just because you don't have one specialty ingredient on hand. If you're cooking ahead, these meatballs can be frozen prior to cooking—just remember to thaw them overnight in the fridge before you pop them in the oven.

INGREDIENTS:

- **1 pound ground beef**
- **3 slices bacon, finely chopped**
- **2 teaspoons minced garlic**
- **1 tablespoon minced shallots**
- **2 tablespoons grated or finely minced fresh lemongrass**
- **2 teaspoons Madras curry powder**
- **2 teaspoons fish sauce**
- **1 teaspoon freshly ground black pepper**
- **½ teaspoon kosher salt**
- **½ teaspoon arrowroot powder**

INSTRUCTIONS:

1. PREHEAT THE OVEN TO 400°F ON CONVECTION MODE (OR 425°F ON REGULAR MODE) WITH A RACK IN THE MIDDLE. LINE A RIMMED BAKING SHEET WITH PARCHMENT.

2. IN A LARGE BOWL, COMBINE ALL THE INGREDIENTS.

3. MIX EVERYTHING WELL WITH YOUR HANDS, BUT DON'T OVERWORK THE MEAT. NO ONE LIKES TOUGH, RUBBERY MEATBALLS, RIGHT?

4. SCOOP A HEAPING TABLESPOON OF THE MIXTURE INTO YOUR HANDS, AND ROLL IT INTO A BALL. REPEAT UNTIL ALL THE MEAT'S BEEN TURNED INTO MEATBALLS.

5. ARRANGE THE MEATBALLS IN A SINGLE LAYER ON THE BAKING SHEET. MAKE SURE THEY'RE THE SAME SIZE SO THEY'LL COOK EVENLY, AND DON'T OVERCROWD THEM.

6. COOK IN THE OVEN FOR 10 TO 15 MINUTES, TURNING THE TRAY 180 DEGREES HALFWAY THROUGH THE COOKING TIME.

7. THE MEATBALLS ARE DONE WHEN THEY'RE BROWNED AND COOKED THROUGH. TRANSFER TO A PLATTER AND SERVE.

8. YOU CAN ENJOY THESE MEATBALLS AS-IS, OR SERVE 'EM ON ZOODLES, CAULI RICE (PAGE 80), OR A BED OF SALAD GREENS.

PERSONALLY, I LIKE THESE MEATBALLS ON A SUPER-SIMPLE GREEN SALAD TOSSED WITH THAI CITRUS DRESSING (PAGE 47).

ONCE THEY'RE COOKED, YOU CAN REFRIGERATE THESE MEATBALLS FOR UP TO 4 DAYS, OR FREEZE THEM FOR UP TO 3 MONTHS.

NO OFFENSE, OWEN, BUT I DON'T TAKE COOKING ADVICE FROM PEOPLE WHO HAVE NO IDEA HOW TO COOK.

SHEET PAN SAUSAGE SUPPER

MAKES 4 SERVINGS
⏱ 20 MINUTES
(5 MINUTES HANDS-ON)

I love sheet pan suppers 'cause fab, fuss-free dinners are my holy grail. Nothing beats tossing a bunch of stuff in the oven all at once. Plus, when I force my family to stab at the food straight from the sheet pan, I don't have any extra dishes to wash, either!

Sadly, one-pan suppers don't always turn out well. Not everything you want to toss onto a pan will cook at exactly the same time and temperature. Luckily, I've got the perfect combination of ingredients that cook *and* taste great together. Just make sure to slice the cabbage steaks to the specified width, and you'll be golden.

INGREDIENTS:

- ¼ cup avocado oil or extra-virgin olive oil, divided
- 1 small cabbage (2-3 pounds)
- 1 small red onion, cut into ½-inch rings
- Kosher salt
- Freshly ground black pepper
- 4 Italian sausages (about 2 pounds total)
- 2 medium Braeburn or Fuji apples, cored and sliced into wedges
- 2 tablespoons aged balsamic vinegar
- 2 tablespoons chopped fresh Italian parsley

INSTRUCTIONS:

1 PREHEAT THE OVEN TO 425°F. POUR AND SPREAD 2 TABLESPOONS OF OIL ONTO THE SURFACE OF A RIMMED BAKING SHEET.

3 SEPARATE THE ONION SLICES INTO RINGS OF 2 TO 3 LAYERS THICK.

5 NESTLE THE SAUSAGE AND APPLES INTO ANY EMPTY SPOTS ON THE PAN'S SURFACE.

7 COOK IN THE OVEN FOR 25 TO 30 MINUTES OR UNTIL THE CABBAGE IS TENDER AND THE SAUSAGES ARE COOKED THROUGH.

2 CUT THE BOTTOM OFF THE CABBAGE, AND SET THE FLAT END ON A CUTTING BOARD. CUT THE CABBAGE INTO ¾-INCH SLICES.

4 ARRANGE THE CABBAGE AND ONION IN A SINGLE LAYER ON THE BAKING SHEET. LIBERALLY SALT AND PEPPER EVERYTHING.

6 DRIZZLE THE REMAINING 2 TABLESPOONS OF OIL ONTO THE PAN.

8 DRIZZLE THE BALSAMIC VINEGAR ON TOP. GARNISH WITH ITALIAN PARSLEY, AND EAT.

NOMSTER BURGERS

MAKES 4 SERVINGS
⏱ **30 MINUTES**

Many Californians have a cult-like obsession with a certain fast food chain—in large part because of its so-called "Secret Menu." Among the most popular hidden burger options is one with grilled onions and mustard fried directly onto each patty—but I've taken my interpretation of this beast of a burger even further. My version features a mustard-fried, shallot-stuffed patty—with spicy sriracha and a crispy fried egg on top.

Seriously, folks: This fully loaded beef burger is monstrously (nom-strously?) delicious.

INGREDIENTS:

- **3** tablespoons ghee, avocado oil, olive oil, or fat of choice, divided
- **1** large shallot or ¼ large red onion, minced
- **1** pound ground beef
  Kosher salt
  Freshly ground black pepper
- **4** teaspoons Dijon-style mustard
- **1** head butter lettuce
- **2** tomatoes, sliced
- **4** large eggs, cooked according to the instructions on page 255 (optional)
- **1** tablespoon Nom Nom Sriracha (page 56) or store-bought sriracha (optional)

INSTRUCTIONS:

1. MELT 1 TABLESPOON OF GHEE IN A LARGE SKILLET OVER MEDIUM-LOW HEAT.

2. ADD THE SHALLOT. SAUTÉ FOR 3 TO 5 MINUTES UNTIL GOLDEN AND TRANSLUCENT.

3. TRANSFER THE SAUTÉED SHALLOT TO A BOWL TO COOL TO ROOM TEMPERATURE.

4. DIVIDE THE BEEF EVENLY INTO 4 EQUAL PORTIONS. USING YOUR FINGERS, SCULPT EACH PORTION INTO A CONCAVE BOWL.

5. TUCK ABOUT A TEASPOON OF COOKED SHALLOT INTO EACH BEEF BOWL.

6. THEN, SEAL UP THE HOLE TO FORM A BALL.

7. FLATTEN THE BALLS WITH YOUR HANDS TO MAKE SHALLOT-STUFFED BURGER PATTIES.

8. LIBERALLY SALT AND PEPPER ONE SIDE OF THE PATTIES.

9. HEAT 1 TABLESPOON OF GHEE IN A LARGE SKILLET OVER MEDIUM-HIGH HEAT.

10. PLACE 2 PATTIES SEASONED-SIDE DOWN IN THE HOT FAT.

11. SPRINKLE SALT AND PEPPER ON THE OTHER SIDE, TOO.

12. COOK UNDISTURBED FOR 3 MINUTES UNTIL A NICE CRUST FORMS ON THE BOTTOM.

13. NEXT, SPREAD A TEASPOON OF MUSTARD ON THE TOP OF EACH BURGER PATTY.

14. FLIP THE PATTIES OVER, AND COOK FOR ANOTHER 2 MINUTES OR UNTIL THE DESIRED DONENESS IS REACHED. REPEAT STEPS 9 THROUGH 14 TO COOK THE OTHER PATTIES.

15. SERVE EACH BURGER PATTY WITH LETTUCE AND TOMATOES. IF YOU'RE FEELING TRULY NOMSTROUS, ADD A CRISPY FRIED EGG AND A GENEROUS SQUIRT OF SRIRACHA. ENJOY!

CHICKEN + SHRIMP LAAP

MAKES 4 SERVINGS
⏱ **30 MINUTES**

One of our family's favorite dishes from Chiang Mai is *laap*, a Laotian minced meat salad featuring hot chili paste, toasted rice powder, bits of offal, and a shower of fresh herbs. Back at home, I wanted to replicate these flavors and textures, but quickly discovered how challenging it can be to re-create *laap* with Paleo-friendly supermarket ingredients. But after replacing the rice powder with coconut flour and the *naam phrik laap* paste with spices from my pantry, I now have a family-friendly *laap* recipe I can make on a moment's notice.

INGREDIENTS:

- 1 teaspoon coconut flour
- 1 tablespoon ghee or fat of choice
- 1 small shallot, thinly sliced
- 1 pound ground chicken thighs
- ½ pound large shrimp, peeled and chopped coarsely
- ½ Bone Broth (page 76) or chicken stock
- 2 tablespoons fish sauce
- 2 tablespoons fresh lime juice
- ½ teaspoon cayenne pepper
- 2 scallions, thinly sliced
- ¼ cup chopped cilantro
- ¼ cup minced fresh mint leaves
- 1 head butter lettuce, washed and spun dry, and separated into leaves

INSTRUCTIONS:

1. ON A PARCHMENT-LINED BAKING TRAY, TOAST THE COCONUT FLOUR IN A 300°F OVEN FOR 5 TO 7 MINUTES OR UNTIL THE FLOUR TURNS GOLDEN BROWN. (YOU CAN ALSO TOAST THE COCONUT FLOUR IN A DRY PAN OVER LOW HEAT INSTEAD.) SET ASIDE.

2. IN THE MEANTIME, HEAT THE GHEE IN A LARGE SKILLET OVER MEDIUM-HIGH HEAT. ADD THE SLICED SHALLOT AND SAUTÉ FOR 2 TO 3 MINUTES OR UNTIL SOFTENED.

3. ADD THE GROUND CHICKEN, AND BREAK IT UP WITH A SPATULA. COOK, STIRRING, FOR 3 TO 5 MINUTES UNTIL NO LONGER PINK.

4. ADD THE SHRIMP AND THE BROTH. STIR-FRY FOR ANOTHER 2 TO 3 MINUTES OR UNTIL THE SHRIMP IS COOKED THROUGH.

5. REMOVE THE PAN FROM THE HEAT AND ADD THE FISH SAUCE, LIME JUICE, TOASTED COCONUT FLOUR, AND CAYENNE PEPPER. ADJUST THE SEASONING TO TASTE.

6. SPRINKLE THE CHOPPED HERBS ON TOP. TO EAT, WRAP A HEAPING SPOONFUL OF LAAP IN A LETTUCE LEAF AND DEVOUR.

SOMETIMES, YOU'LL SEE LAAP SPELLED "LARB," BUT THAT'S BECAUSE "LARB" IS A BRITISH TRANSLITERATION. WHEN BRITS SAY "LARB," IT SOUNDS LIKE "LAAB" OR "LAAP," WHICH CLOSELY RESEMBLES THE THAI PRONUNCIATION. JUST REMEMBER: IT DOESN'T RHYME WITH "CARB"!

POT STICKER STIR-FRY

MAKES 6 SERVINGS
⏱ 40 MINUTES

The thing I love most about pot stickers is the umami-rich filling of pork, cabbage, and mushrooms. In fact, when I was a kid, there were times when I felt the urge to just empty the dumpling skins of their stuffing and tuck into a big bowl of pot sticker filling. Sadly, this sort of…*creativity* wasn't exactly encouraged at the dinner table.

But now that I'm an old bag, I do whatever I want—which explains the existence of this recipe.

INGREDIENTS:

1	tablespoon ghee
2	medium carrots, peeled and finely diced
2	shallots, minced
¼	pound shiitake mushrooms, stemmed and thinly sliced
	Kosher salt
4	garlic cloves, minced
1	tablespoon finely grated ginger
2	pounds ground pork
1	small Napa cabbage, cut in half and thinly sliced crosswise
2	tablespoons coconut aminos
2	teaspoons rice vinegar
1	teaspoon fish sauce
2	teaspoons toasted sesame oil
3	scallions, thinly sliced

1 In a 12-inch (or larger) skillet over medium heat, melt the ghee. Once it's hot, toss in the carrots, shallots, and mushrooms.

2 Add a sprinkle of salt, and sauté for 3 to 5 minutes or until the shallots are soft and the 'shrooms are pliable.

3 Toss in the garlic and ginger, and stir for 30 seconds or until fragrant.

4 Add the pork along with another sprinkle of salt, and break up the meat with a spatula or wooden spoon.

5 Crank up the heat to medium-high, and cook for about 5 minutes or until the pork is no longer pink.

6 Transfer the cooked pork with a slotted spoon to another platter. Leave the cooking liquid in the pan.

7 Throw the cabbage into the pan with another sprinkle of salt, and sauté for 3 to 5 minutes or until wilted.

8 Lower the heat to medium, and add the ground pork back into the skillet.

9 Stir to combine.

10 Season with coconut aminos, rice vinegar, and fish sauce. Taste and adjust with more seasoning if needed.

11 Remove the skillet from the heat. Finish with a drizzle of sesame oil and a generous sprinkle of scallions.

12 Serve and eat, but don't forget to save some to make Pot Sticker Tacos (page 212) or Choose Your Own Adventure Egg Muffins (page 200)!

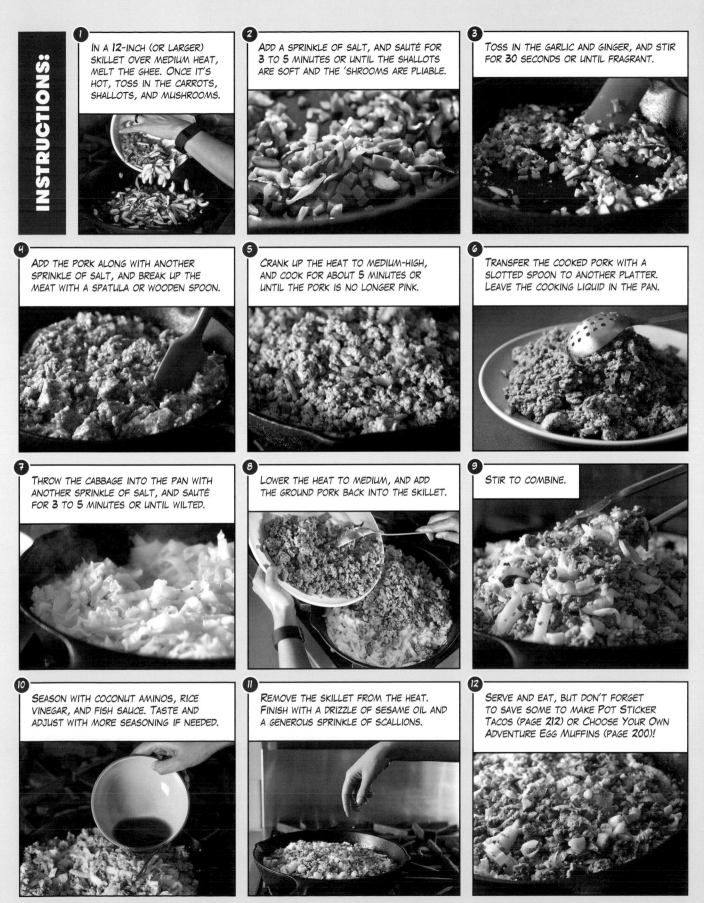

GOLDEN MILK

MAKES 3½ CUPS
⏱ 20 MINUTES
(5 MINUTES HANDS-ON)

If you're sore, achy, or under the weather—or even if you're feeling right as rain—treat yourself to this warm, healing, and delicious elixir.

Turmeric's been used in traditional Ayurvedic medicine for thousands of years to treat a wide range of conditions, and modern research suggests that it may help reduce inflammation, fight infections, and treat digestive problems. But to be properly absorbed into our bodies, turmeric needs to be consumed with a bit of fat, which is why it's often combined with coconut milk.

For countless generations, Golden Milk has been revered for its medicinal properties, and used in religious ceremonies throughout Southeast Asia. Aren't you lucky you can whip some up with just a few items from the grocery store?

INGREDIENTS:

- 1 **(14-ounce) can full-fat coconut milk**
- 1 **(3-inch) dried cinnamon stick**
- 2 **(1-inch) pieces fresh turmeric, peeled and thinly sliced (or 1 teaspoon dried turmeric)**
- 1 **(1-inch) piece fresh ginger, peeled and thinly sliced**
- ¼ **teaspoon freshly ground black pepper**
- 1 **tablespoon honey (optional)**
- **Ground cinnamon (for serving)**

INSTRUCTIONS:

1 COMBINE THE COCONUT MILK, CINNAMON, DRIED OR FRESH TURMERIC, GINGER, PEPPER, AND HONEY IN A SMALL SAUCEPAN.

2 STIR IN 2 CUPS OF WATER.

3 BRING THE CONTENTS OF THE POT TO A LOW BOIL OVER HIGH HEAT. THEN, LOWER THE HEAT TO MAINTAIN A SIMMER, STIRRING OCCASIONALLY FOR 10 MINUTES.

4 POUR THE MILK THROUGH A STRAINER OR CHEESECLOTH TO REMOVE THE CHUNKS.

5 IF DESIRED, STIR IN SOME HONEY.

6 POUR INTO MUGS, TOP WITH A DASH OF CINNAMON, AND SLURP AWAY. OR...

(7) . . . YOU CAN KEEP GOLDEN MILK IN A SEALED CONTAINER FOR UP TO 4 DAYS IN THE FRIDGE. BEFORE YOU DRINK IT, WARM THE MILK ON THE STOVE OVER MEDIUM HEAT, STIRRING WELL. AND DON'T FORGET TO ADD A SPRINKLE OF CINNAMON!

MANGO TURMERIC TONIC

MAKES 2 SERVINGS
⏱ 5 MINUTES

Turmeric-based beverages don't have to be served warm. With a blast of mango and a peppery kick, this frosty treat goes down easy.

INGREDIENTS:

2   cups frozen mango

2   (2-inch) pieces fresh turmeric root, peeled and coarsely chopped

1   (2-inch) piece fresh ginger, peeled and coarsely chopped

½   teaspoon freshly ground black pepper

12   ounces coconut water (or coconut milk if you prefer a creamier texture)

2   teaspoons honey (optional)

Juice from ½ lemon

INSTRUCTIONS:

USE A HIGH-SPEED BLENDER TO BLITZ TOGETHER ALL THE INGREDIENTS TO A SMOOTHIE-LIKE CONSISTENCY. POUR INTO GLASSES AND SERVE IMMEDIATELY.

WATERMELON COCONUT COOLER

MAKES 8 SERVINGS
⏱ **10 MINUTES**

Cold-pressed juice concoctions at the local smoothie joint are pretty darned refreshing, but they'll easily blow a watermelon-sized hole in your wallet. Thankfully, for just a few bucks, you can re-create this summertime cooler for all your sweaty pals. (This recipe assumes you have no more than 8 friends.)

You can blend this up ahead of time, and refrigerate it for up to 2 days. When it's time to serve, shake well and pour over ice.

INGREDIENTS:

3   **pounds seedless watermelon flesh**

1   **cup coconut water**

    Juice from 1 lime

    Sea salt

INSTRUCTIONS:

1   CUT UP THE WATERMELON...

2   ...AND ROUGHLY CHOP IT UP INTO CUBES.

3   THROW THE CUBES INTO A BLENDER AND POUR IN THE COCONUT WATER. (IF YOUR BLENDER HAS LESS THAN 64 OUNCES OF CAPACITY, BLEND IN SMALLER BATCHES.)

4   ADD THE JUICE AND A PINCH OF SEA SALT.

5   BLITZ UNTIL LIQUEFIED. IF YOUR BLENDER ISN'T SUFFICIENTLY POWERFUL AND LEFT SOME CHUNKY PULP IN THE LIQUID, FEEL FREE TO STRAIN IT OUT.

6   CHILL THE WATERMELON COOLER IN THE FRIDGE, OR SERVE IMMEDIATELY OVER ICE.

7   EASY BREEZY.

BERRY MACAROON TRAIL MIX

MAKES 4 CUPS
⏱ **30 MINUTES**
(10 MINUTES HANDS-ON)

Dense, coconutty macaroons (a.k.a. *congolais*) are often confused with airy, meringue-based *macarons*, but why choose between the two? This quick and easy trail mix mashes together the toasty coconut essence of macaroons and the sweet berry flavors of my favorite *macarons*. Best of all, this mix is free of added sugar!

INGREDIENTS:

2   **cups raw almonds**

    Zest from 1 lemon

1   **cup unsweetened coconut flakes**

½   **cup freeze-dried strawberries**

½   **cup freeze-dried blueberries**

INSTRUCTIONS:

1 PREHEAT THE OVEN TO 300°F. SPREAD THE ALMONDS IN A SINGLE LAYER ON A PARCHMENT-LINED RIMMED BAKING SHEET.

2 TOAST THE ALMONDS FOR 10 TO 15 MINUTES, SHAKING THE TRAY AT THE MIDPOINT TO TOSS THE NUTS. THE ALMONDS ARE READY WHEN THEY'RE TOASTY AND GOLDEN.

3 USING A RASP GRATER, FINELY ZEST THE LEMON ON TOP OF THE WARM NUTS. LET THE NUTS COOL TO ROOM TEMPERATURE.

4 SPREAD THE COCONUT FLAKES ON A PARCHMENT-LINED RIMMED BAKING SHEET, AND TOAST FOR 5 TO 10 MINUTES OR UNTIL GOLDEN. KEEP A CLOSE EYE ON THE COCONUT TO KEEP IT FROM BURNING!

5 REMOVE THE COCONUT FLAKES FROM THE OVEN, AND COOL TO ROOM TEMPERATURE.

6 IN A LARGE BOWL, COMBINE THE COOLED NUTS, COCONUT, AND FREEZE-DRIED FRUIT.

7 TOSS IT ALL TOGETHER AND SERVE. THIS TRAIL MIX CAN BE KEPT IN AN AIRTIGHT CONTAINER FOR UP TO 2 WEEKS.

WANT TO MAKE THIS TRAIL MIX EVEN FASTER?
START WITH DRY-ROASTED ALMONDS AND
PRE-TOASTED COCONUT FLAKES. THIS MAKES A
GREAT LAST-MINUTE HOSTESS GIFT, TOO.

WHEN LIFE GIVES US LEMONS, WE GRATE THEIR SKINS OFF!

"PB&J" ENERGY BALLS

MAKES 15 BALLS
⏱ **20 MINUTES**

Nope—there's no peanut butter or jelly in these bite-size energy balls, but their nutty crunch and sweet strawberry flavor never fail to bring back fond memories of munching on my favorite after-school snack. Unlike the PB&J sandwiches I used to make for myself, these home-made treats are made with just nuts and fruit (and a pinch of salt). So when you need a pick-me-up after a long run, a hard workout, or an afternoon of gardening like a maniac, just pop a ball or two in your mouth, and I guarantee you'll feel like a kid again.

INGREDIENTS:

½ **cup (10 grams) freeze-dried strawberries**

½ **cup (60 grams) dry-roasted unsalted almonds**

1 **cup (150 grams) pitted and chopped dried Medjool dates**

   Kosher salt

¼ **cup unsweetened shredded coconut, toasted in a 300°F oven until golden, about 3 minutes**

I HAD A JOKE ABOUT THESE BALLS ALL READY TO GO, BUT MOM SAYS IT'S NOT APPROPRIATE FOR A FAMILY COOKBOOK.

INSTRUCTIONS:

1. PULSE THE FREEZE-DRIED STRAWBERRIES IN A FOOD PROCESSOR UNTIL THEY FORM A POWDER. LET THE PINK DUST SETTLE.

2. TOSS IN THE ALMONDS.

3. PULSE TO ROUGHLY CHOP THE ALMONDS. TRANSFER THE CHOPPED ALMONDS AND STRAWBERRY POWDER TO ANOTHER BOWL.

4. THROW THE DATES INTO THE NOW-EMPTY FOOD PROCESSOR BOWL, AND PULSE A FEW TIMES TO ROUGHLY CHOP UP THE PIECES. THEN, PULVERIZE THE DATES UNTIL THEY FORM A STICKY BALL THAT THWACKS AGAINST THE SIDE OF THE WORK BOWL.

5. ADD THE STRAWBERRY POWDER, ALMONDS, AND A PINCH OF SALT TO THE STICKY DATE PASTE IN THE FOOD PROCESSOR BOWL.

6. PULSE A FEW TIMES UNTIL COMBINED. THE RESULT SHOULD BE A DENSE MASS THAT COMES TOGETHER AS A NUTTY DOUGH.

7. PINCH OFF ABOUT A TABLESPOON OF THE DOUGH AND ROLL IT IN YOUR PALMS TO FORM A SMOOTH BALL. REPEAT 'TIL YOU'RE OUT OF DOUGH.

8. PUT THE TOASTED SHREDDED COCONUT IN A SHALLOW PLATE. TOSS EACH OF THE BALLS INTO THE COCONUT, MAKING SURE TO COAT THE ENTIRE SURFACE.

9. YOU CAN REFRIGERATE YOUR BALLS IN A COVERED CONTAINER FOR UP TO 1 WEEK, OR FREEZE 'EM FOR UP TO A MONTH.

BEYOND
READY!

BLUEPRINTS
FOR EVERYDAY
COOKING

HOW CAN I POSSIBLY GET
BEYOND READY?

So you've stocked up your kitchen with essentials, loaded your icebox with prep-ahead meals, figured out how to make over your leftovers, and know how to whip up emergency rations. If you've made it this far, you're more than ready to take your cooking to another level. But what's next?

The answer is really up to you, because in my book (literally!), going "beyond ready" can actually mean two very different things:

> **1** It can mean becoming so supremely organized that you always have a week (or more) of meals scheduled and prepped in advance;
>
> or
>
> **2** It can mean transforming yourself into a kitchen ninja who cooks on the fly using whatever's on hand, producing meals by taste and feel—all without relying on detailed recipes.

Some people are consummate planners. You know who you are: You diligently mark up your cookbooks and copy down shopping lists before heading to the grocery store. You own at least two kitchen timers, you know what *mise-en-place* means, and you never fail to clean as you go. You're a cooking machine.

Others of you prefer to improvise. You live in the moment, and like to run with scissors around blind corners. (That's just a metaphor, kids. Never run with scissors.) You love tossing ingredients into a pot even if you have no idea what the finished dish will look or taste like. Still, you're no kitchen dummy, so you know the results will be delicious.

I don't care if you're a meticulous planner or a play-it-by-ear kind of cook. I've got you covered either way.

First, for you planners out there, I'm offering up day-by-day dinner plans that'll take you through four delicious weeks of meals. Each week is accompanied by a detailed shopping list, as well as instructions for what to make and when to make it.

Then, for you kitchen improv artists, I'll run down a few of my favorite "no-recipe" recipes. In other words, I'll share with you the main gist of how to cook up a bunch of tasty grub—but I won't hem you in with specific ingredients or measurements. After all, I certainly don't want to be responsible for suffocating your culinary creativity!

BUT WHAT IF I WANT TO BE BOTH A METICULOUS PLANNER *AND* A FLY-BY-THE-SEAT-OF-MY-PANTS COOK?

THAT'S BEEN THE ULTIMATE GOAL ALL ALONG!

Remember: The whole point of this book is to get you excited to roll up your sleeves and create beautifully prepared, deliciously nourishing food—no matter the circumstances. That could mean following detailed meal plans to cook up a week's worth of meals, or it might mean throwing open the refrigerator doors and letting inspiration (or a falling head of cabbage) hit you in the face. But ultimately, it's about doing both—sticking closely to a set of blueprints when you're craving structure in your life, but keeping the door open to culinary improvisation and creativity when you feel like loosening up.

As you build up confidence in your own culinary awesomeness, you'll start whipping up tasty meals by sense memory, using the stuff you've already stockpiled in your kitchen. You'll develop new umami-packed flavor combinations, and invent fantastically butt-kicking recipes. You'll come up with your own meal plans and kitchen shortcuts, and you'll make yourself and your loved ones healthier and happier to boot. In short, you'll be beyond ready.

And that's when I'll come knocking on your door, demanding to be fed.

FOR THOSE OF YOU WHO LIKE TO STAY ORGANIZED, I'VE CREATED FOUR WEEKLY DINNER PLANS THAT'LL GET YOU THROUGH SIX NIGHTS OF DINNERS EACH WEEK, ALL WITHOUT HAVING TO DO A TON OF COOKING DURING THE WEEK!
ALL OF THE RECIPES IN THESE PLANS ARE WHOLE30-FRIENDLY, TOO!
YOU HEARD ME, NOMSTERS! I'VE PUT TOGETHER...
4 WEEKS OF DINNER PLANS!
THESE PLANS WERE DESIGNED FOR A FAMILY OF FOUR, SO IF YOU HAVE A BIGGER HOUSEHOLD, DOUBLE THE RECIPES. AND IF YOU HAVE FEWER MOUTHS TO FEED, MAKE LESS, OR SAVE THE EXTRAS FOR BREAKFAST OR LUNCH.
HERE'S THE GAME PLAN: USE THE WEEKLY SHOPPING LISTS TO GATHER EVERYTHING YOU'LL NEED. THE INGREDIENTS ARE GROUPED TOGETHER BY LOCATION IN THE GROCERY STORE.
ON PREP DAY, GET A HEAD START ON THE WEEK BY PREPARING A FEW MAKE-AHEAD RECIPES FROM THE "GET SET" AND "READY" SECTIONS OF THIS BOOK.
PLAN ON EATING ONE OF THEM, TOO!
WOLF
THEN, DURING THE WEEK, YOU CAN REHEAT AND SERVE THESE READY-MADE DINNERS...

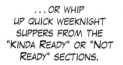

...OR WHIP UP QUICK WEEKNIGHT SUPPERS FROM THE "KINDA READY" OR "NOT READY" SECTIONS.

NOT SURE WHAT TO SERVE AS A SIDE DISH? MAKE A GIANT GREEN SALAD OR ROAST A PAN OF VEGETABLES. IT'S FAST AND EASY!

THE GOAL IS TO HAVE DINNER READY IN LESS TIME THAN IT TAKES TO WATCH AN EPISODE OF A CHEESY REALITY SHOW.

AND IF YOU DON'T WANT TO STICK TO MY PLANS, NO PROBLEM. YOU CAN ALWAYS MAKE YOUR OWN!

JUST REMEMBER TO STOCK UP ON MAKE-AHEAD MEALS FROM THE "READY" SECTION ON YOUR PREP DAY, AND USE RECIPES FROM THE OTHER SECTIONS WHEN YOU'RE SHORT ON TIME OR PATIENCE.

AND DON'T FLAME OUT! TAKE A DAY OFF FROM COOKING EACH WEEK TO REST AND RECHARGE.

I REST AND RECHARGE SEVEN DAYS A WEEK!

319

WEEK 1 DINNER PLAN:

PREP DAY / DAY 1

MAKE A JAR OF ALL-PURPOSE STIR-FRY SAUCE (PAGE 67), A POT OF SUNDAY GRAVY (PAGE 152), AND SOUVLAKI (PAGE 136). FOR DINNER, SERVE HALF THE SOUVLAKI WITH A BIG GREEN SALAD.

DAY 2

USE HALF THE SUNDAY GRAVY TO MAKE SUNDAY ZOODLES (PAGE 155) IN A FLASH! (DON'T WORRY IF TODAY'S NOT SUNDAY.)

DAY 3

QUICKLY REHEAT THE REMAINING SOUVLAKI IN A GRILL PAN OR IN A 300°F OVEN. WHIP UP SOME CUMIN CILANTRO LIME RICE (PAGE 81) TO SERVE AS A SIDE DISH.

DAY 4

TURN THE REMAINING SUNDAY GRAVY INTO HANGRY SOUP (PAGE 178), AND SERVE IT WITH A BIG GREEN SALAD DRESSED WITH EXTRA-VIRGIN OLIVE OIL AND BALSAMIC VINEGAR (OR YOUR FAVORITE DRESSING).

DAY 5

MAKE SOME PAPER-WRAPPED CHICKEN (PAGE 204), AND SERVE EACH PACKET ON A BED OF ZOODLES. NO NEED TO COOK OR SALT THE SPIRALIZED VEGGIES; THE JUICES FROM EACH PACKET WILL SOFTEN AND FLAVOR THEM.

DAY 6

USE THE ALL-PURPOSE STIR-FRY SAUCE TO MAKE ASPARAGUS BEEF (PAGE 230), AND SERVE IT WITH LEFTOVER CUMIN CILANTRO LIME RICE OR A FRESHLY-MADE BATCH OF CAULI RICE (PAGE 80).

DAY 7

TAKE A BREAK FROM KITCHEN DUTY. HEAT UP LEFTOVERS, OR GO OUT FOR A NICE MEAL. BETTER YET, HAVE SOMEONE ELSE MAKE YOU DINNER FOR A CHANGE!

WEEK 1 SHOPPING LIST

PRODUCE

1	pound thin asparagus stalks
1	pound bok choy
2	medium cauliflower (or 40 ounces fresh or frozen riced cauliflower)
1	small cabbage head, 1 bunch of Swiss chard, or 1 bunch of kale
5	medium carrots
2	celery stalks
8	medium zucchini
½	pound shiitake mushrooms
1	small bunch scallions
1	big bunch fresh basil
1	bunch fresh cilantro
1	big bunch fresh Italian parsley
2	(10-ounce) clamshells salad greens
6	lemons
2	limes
½	pound Yukon Gold potatoes
2	large garlic bulbs
2	small yellow onions
1	medium red onion
3	large shallots

MEAT / SEAFOOD

3	pounds boneless pork loin or shoulder roast, leg of lamb, or skinless chicken thighs (for Souvlaki)
4	(6-ounce) boneless, skinless chicken breasts or thighs (for Paper-Wrapped Chicken)
2	pounds boneless pork country-style ribs from the shoulder (for Sunday Gravy)
3	pounds flank steak (for Sunday Gravy and Asparagus Beef)
1	pound sweet and/or hot Italian sausage (for Sunday Gravy)

REFRIGERATED GOODS

½	cup orange juice (or 2 large oranges)

SPICES

- Dried bay leaves
- Cumin
- Garlic powder
- Ginger powder
- Dried oregano or dried marjoram
- Red pepper flakes
- Kosher salt
- Freshly ground black pepper

DRY GOODS

- Arrowroot powder

VINEGARS + OILS

- Balsamic vinegar
- Sherry vinegar (optional)
- Extra-virgin olive oil or avocado oil
- Ghee

CANNED / JARRED FOODS

7	cups chicken stock (if you don't have Bone Broth [page 76] at home)
3	(28-ounce) cans whole San Marzano tomatoes
	Tomato paste

ETHNIC / SPECIALTY FOODS

- Coconut aminos
- Fish sauce
- Rice vinegar
- Sesame oil

IF NO ONE'S COMING TO THE STORE WITH ME, NO ONE'S ALLOWED TO COMPLAIN ABOUT WHAT I BUY!

WEEK 2 DINNER PLAN:

PREP DAY / DAY 1

MAKE ROAST-AHEAD CHICKEN BREASTS (PAGE 84), GINGER SESAME SAUCE (PAGE 66), PRESSURE COOKER OR SLOW COOKER KALUA PIG (PAGE 128), AND GREEN BEAST DRESSING (PAGE 48). EAT HALF THE KALUA PIG, AND SERVE WITH GRILLED ROMAINE AND BROCCOLINI SALAD (PAGE 186). REFRIGERATE EVERYTHING ELSE.

DAY 2

USE THE GINGER SESAME SAUCE AND HALF THE ROAST-AHEAD CHICKEN BREASTS TO MAKE CHILLED ASIAN ZOODLE SALAD WITH CHICKEN + AVOCADO (PAGE 183).

DAY 3

CRISP UP SOME OF THE LEFTOVER KALUA PIG AND SERVE IT WITH A BIG GREEN SALAD TOSSED WITH GREEN BEAST DRESSING.

DAY 4

THAT'S RIGHT: IT'S TACO NIGHT! GRAB SOME OF NATURE'S TORTILLAS (PAGE 79) AND MAKE LEFTACOS (PAGE 212) WITH THE REMAINING ROAST-AHEAD CHICKEN BREASTS OR CRISPED KALUA PIG. IF DESIRED, TOP WITH GUACAMOLE, SALSA, DICED WHITE ONION, AND CILANTRO.

DAY 5

MAKE POT STICKER STIR-FRY (PAGE 304) AND SERVE IT WITH ROASTED CARROTS WITH GINGER-SESAME SAUCE (PAGE 180).

DAY 6

COOK A POT OF CHICKEN CURRY IN A HURRY (PAGE 286) AND SERVE IT OVER CAULI RICE (PAGE 80) AND ROASTED GINGER SESAME BROCCOLI (PAGE 66).

DAY 7

IT'S BEEN A LONG WEEK, AND YOU DESERVE A BREAK FROM COOKING. EAT LEFTOVERS, DINE OUT, OR MAKE SOMEONE ELSE COOK.

WEEK 2 SHOPPING LIST

PRODUCE

2 medium avocados (plus 3 more ito make your own guacamole for Leftacos)

2½ pounds broccoli

1 pound broccolini

1 small green cabbage

1 small Napa cabbage

1 medium cauliflower

4 medium carrots

1 pound young carrots

1 large butter lettuce

2 heads romaine lettuce (about 1 pound)

1 (10-ounce) clamshell salad greens

1 medium fresh ginger root

1 medium red bell pepper

¼ pound shiitake mushrooms

4 medium zucchini

2 bunches fresh basil

3 bunches fresh chives

1 bunch fresh cilantro

1 bunch fresh mint

1 bunch fresh Italian parsley

3 bunches scallions

2 garlic bulbs

1 medium red onion

1 small yellow onion

1 small white onion

2 shallots

2 mandarin oranges

2 lemons

1 lime

MEAT / SEAFOOD

1½ pounds boneless, skinless chicken thighs (for Chicken Curry in a Hurry)

2 whole bone-in, skin-on chicken breasts (about 1½ pounds each) (for Roast-Ahead Chicken Breasts)

2 pounds ground pork (for Pot Sticker Stir-Fry)

5 pounds bone-in pork shoulder roast (for Kalua Pig)

3 slices thick-cut bacon

REFRIGERATED GOODS

¼ cup orange juice (or juice from a large orange)

½ pint guacamole (or make your own with 3 ripe avocados)

SPICES

Coarse Alaea red Hawaiian sea salt or fine Alaea red Hawaiian sea salt

Kosher salt

Sesame seeds

Freshly ground black pepper

VINEGARS + OILS

Avocado oil or extra-virgin olive oil

Ghee or coconut oil

CANNED / JARRED FOODS

1 small bottle apple juice

2 (14-ounce) cans full-fat coconut milk

Roasted tomato salsa (or Salsa Ahumada [page 72])

ETHNIC / SPECIALTY FOODS

Coconut aminos

Fish sauce

Rice vinegar

Sesame oil

Tahini

Thai curry paste (red, yellow, or green)

WEEK 3 DINNER PLAN:

PREP DAY / DAY 1

Make Duxelles (page 75), a Tex Mex Beef + Rice Casserole (page 146), and Braised Pork in Coconut Water (page 126) in the slow cooker or pressure cooker. Shred and refrigerate the Brussels sprouts in preparation for Day 2. Use the Duxelles to make Duxelles Chicken (page 201) and serve with stir-fried kale.

DAY 2

Reheat half of the Braised Pork in Coconut Water, and make a batch of Asian Citrus Brussels Sprouts Slaw (page 258). Serve the pork with half of the slaw and refrigerate the rest.

DAY 3

In a 300°F oven, heat up the Tex Mex Beef + Rice Casserole. Want more veggies? Make a green salad.

DAY 4

Use the rest of the Duxelles to make Weeknight Meatballs (page 222). Refrigerate half of the meatballs, and serve the rest with the remaining Asian Citrus Brussels Sprouts Slaw.

DAY 5

Use the rest of the previous night's meatballs to make Meatball Soup (page 223). When the soup is nearly done cooking, add a handful of baby spinach to the simmering pot and stir until wilted. Serve immediately.

DAY 6

Shred the remaining Braised Pork, and combine it with some chopped veggies to make Choose-Your-Own-Adventure Egg Muffins (page 200). Serve with my go-to easy veggie side: a green salad.

DAY 7

Time to take a breather. Finish off those leftovers or ask a special someone to dinner and a movie!

WEEK 3 SHOPPING LIST

PRODUCE

2¼	pounds Brussels sprouts
1	medium cauliflower (or 1 pound fresh or frozen riced cauliflower)
1	pound baby kale
1	pound baby spinach
3	medium carrots
6	cherry tomatoes
2	pounds cremini mushrooms
¼	pound shiitake mushrooms
1	red bell pepper
4	jalapeño or serrano peppers
1	fresh medium ginger root
1	bunch fresh thyme sprigs
1	bunch fresh chives
1	bunch fresh cilantro
1	bunch fresh Italian parsley
2	bunches scallions
2	(10-ounce) clamshells salad greens
4	large shallots
2	small yellow onions
2	large garlic bulbs

MEAT / SEAFOOD

2	pounds ground beef (for Tex-Mex Beef + Rice Casserole and Weeknight Meatballs)
1	pound ground pork (for Weeknight Meatballs)
2	pounds boneless pork shoulder (for Braised Pork in Coconut Water)
8	bone-in, skin-on chicken thighs (for Duxelles Chicken)

REFRIGERATED GOODS

18	large eggs

¼	cup orange juice (or 1 large orange)

SPICES

Kosher salt

Freshly ground black pepper

Dried oregano

Chili powder

Sesame seeds

DRY GOODS

Coconut flour

Powdered gelatin

VINEGARS + OILS

Coconut oil or ghee

Sherry vinegar

CANNED / JARRED FOODS

6	cups chicken stock (if you don't have Bone Broth [page 76] at home)
16	ounces coconut water
1½	cups roasted tomato salsa (or Salsa Ahumada [page 72])

ETHNIC / SPECIALTY FOODS

Coconut aminos

Fish sauce

Rice vinegar

Sesame oil

WEEK 4 DINNER PLAN:

PREP DAY / DAY 1

Make slow cooker or pressure cooker Kabocha + Ginger Pork (page 120), Thai Citrus Dressing (page 47), Smoky Chestnut Apple Soup (page 92), and a pair of Roasted Dijon Tarragon Chickens (page 106). Serve one of the chickens with Smoky Apple Chestnut Soup and a green salad with Thai Citrus Dressing.

DAY 2

Take the Kabocha Ginger Pork out of the fridge and reheat it. Serve with Thai Mushroom Stir-Fry (page 256).

DAY 3

Using the rest of the Thai Citrus Dressing, make Thai Green Apple Slaw (page 191). Heat up the remaining Roasted Dijon Tarragon Chicken and serve.

DAY 4

Make a pot of Hobo Stew (page 250).

DAY 5

Roast up and scarf down a Sheet Pan Sausage Supper (page 298).

DAY 6

Make lettuce-wrapped Nomster Burgers (page 300) and serve them with your favorite fixin's (like crispy fried eggs, sriracha, etc.).

DAY 7

And on the seventh day, the busy cook rested. Go take a hike, munch on something tasty, and chillax!

WEEK 4 SHOPPING LIST

PRODUCE

1	head butter lettuce
1	small cabbage
7	medium carrots
1	medium fennel bulb
½	pound green beans
2	tomatoes
1	large red bell pepper
1	Thai chili pepper or serrano pepper
2	pounds mixed mushrooms
¼	pound shiitake mushrooms
1	large leek
1	bunch scallions
1	bunch fresh basil
1	bunch fresh cilantro
1	bunch fresh Italian parsley
1	bunch fresh mint
1	bunch fresh tarragon leaves
1	bunch fresh thyme
1	fresh medium ginger root
1	(10-ounce) clamshell salad greens
5	ounces fresh baby kale or frozen kale
2	medium yellow onions
2	small red onions
3	shallots (1 small, 2 large)
3	large garlic bulbs
1	pound potatoes
1	small kabocha squash
3	medium Braeburn, Cortland, Empire, Fuji or McIntosh apples
2	Granny Smith apples
3	limes

MEAT / SEAFOOD

4	slices thick-cut bacon
3	pounds ground beef (for Hobo Stew and Nomster Burgers)
2	(4-pound) whole chickens (for Dijon Tarragon Chicken)
3	pounds boneless pork shoulder (for Kabocha Ginger Pork)
4	Italian sausages (for Sheet Pan Sausage Supper)

REFRIGERATED GOODS

4	large eggs
1	cup orange juice

SPICES

Crushed red pepper flakes

Kosher salt

Freshly ground black pepper

DRY GOODS

¼	cup dry-roasted cashews

VINEGARS + OILS

Aged balsamic vinegar

Avocado oil or extra-virgin olive oil

Ghee or coconut oil

Sherry vinegar

CANNED / JARRED FOODS

8	cups chicken stock (if you don't have Bone Broth [page 76] at home)
1	(12-ounce) jar Dijon mustard
10	ounces roasted and peeled chestnuts
	Tomato paste
	Honey (optional)

ETHNIC / SPECIALTY FOODS

Coconut aminos

Fish sauce

Rice vinegar

Sriracha (optional)

> **LAST BUT NOT LEAST, LET'S MASTER THE ART OF NO-RECIPE COOKING!**

To truly be an anytime cook, you can't always rely on recipes. But if you know just a few basics—how to oven-roast vegetables or whip up a quick stir-fry, for example—you can change up the ingredients and use different spices and sauces to make your meals pop with flavor. At first, cooking without a recipe can feel like jumping out of a plane without a parachute, but with just a little bit of practice, you'll soon see how much more creative your cooking can be.

Start with these "no-recipe" recipes. These blueprints contain only basic instructions and ingredients with just a few quantities listed. Instead of prescribing exactly how much garlic, salt, or pepper to toss into your dishes, I want you to taste while you cook; that way, you can adjust the seasonings to match your own palate. Once you master how to throw together these dishes, you'll be able to seamlessly weave them into your weeknight rotations.

GARBAGE SOUP

Henry hates the name, but it reminds me that if I didn't make this soup, many of the vegetables in my refrigerator would go to waste. Start by heating some ghee or your fat of choice in a pot; then, add sliced onions, mushrooms, carrots, and/or whatever vegetables are left in your crisper. Cook until the onions are softened. Stir in a bit of tomato paste if you want. Then, pour in about 1½ cups of Bone Broth (page 76) or store-bought stock per person. (Four eaters? That would be 6 cups. Math!) Bring to a boil, and then lower the heat to maintain a simmer. Toss in about 2 cups of greens per person, and cook until tender. Add roughly 1 cup of cooked leftover meat per person at the end, and stir to heat thoroughly. Taste and adjust for seasoning, and serve.

> **I LIKE TO ADD DRIED SHIITAKE MUSHROOMS, NAPA CABBAGE, AND LEFTOVER KALUA PIG (PAGE 128) TO MY GARBAGE SOUP!**

CAN I PRESSURE COOK IT?

Want to make some Garbage Soup in an electric pressure cooker? Follow the same instructions, but rather than simmering it on the stove, cook the soup under high pressure for 3 to 5 minutes or until the veggies are tender. It won't save you much time, but with an electric pressure cooker, you won't have to babysit the soup!

KITCHEN SINK SALAD

Fill up a big salad bowl with about 2 cups of lettuce per eater, and toss with sliced carrots, cucumbers, cooked beets (there's no shame in purchasing pre-cooked beets, people), bell peppers, avocado, or anything else left in your refrigerator. Got some leftover roasted vegetables? Throw 'em in. Add your protein of choice—whether it's hard-boiled eggs, roast chicken, sliced steak, kalua pig, or canned fish. Top with toasted nuts or seeds if you have them. Season with salt and pepper, and add your favorite dressing before tossing. No dressing at the ready? Just drizzle on some extra-virgin olive oil and your favorite vinegar.

FAST FISH FILLETS

Blot the fish fillets dry, and sprinkle both sides with salt. Heat a good amount of your fat of choice in a pan over medium-high heat, and then sear the fillets for 1 to 2 minutes on each side or until cooked through. Plate the fish, and sprinkle your favorite seasoning blend on top. If cherry tomatoes are in season, toss them in the empty (but still hot) pan until warmed through, and serve with the fish. Squeeze fresh lemon juice over it all, and top with fresh herbs.

WEEKNIGHT CHICKEN

In a large bowl, combine 3 pounds of bone-in, skin-on chicken pieces (breasts, thighs, and/or drumsticks) with a 14-ounce can of full-fat coconut milk, some herb seasoning, salt, and a splash of acid (like lime juice). Be generous with the salt. Marinate for up to 24 hours, shake off any excess marinade, and then arrange the pieces on a wire rack placed atop a rimmed baking sheet. Roast the chicken in a preheated 425°F oven (or 400°F on convection mode for crispier skin!) for 35 to 45 minutes, flipping the pieces halfway through. They're done when the breasts register 150°F and the thighs and drumsticks register 165°F on an instant-read meat thermometer.

EMERGENCY STIR-FRY

Heat a tablespoon of your fat of choice in a pan over medium-high heat. Add some thinly sliced onion and a pinch of salt. (I like to throw in diced carrots, too.) Once it's softened, toss in about ¼ pound of ground or sliced meat per eater. Cook until no longer pink, and then add about 2 cups of chopped leafy greens per person and some All-Purpose Stir-Fry Sauce (page 67). (No All-Purpose Stir-Fry Sauce on hand? Just add fish sauce, coconut aminos, and a bit of acid like citrus juice or vinegar.) Cover until the greens are thoroughly cooked. Garnish with fresh herbs like chopped cilantro, mint, or green onions.

Feeling adventurous? Mix in a heaping spoonful of Spicy Kimchi or Wimpchi (page 62) at the end, and stir to warm it through before adding the herbs.

ROASTED VEGETABLES

Cut vegetables into uniform pieces and toss with salt, pepper, and olive oil on a rimmed baking sheet. Don't be stingy with the oil, and make sure the vegetables aren't overcrowded. If desired, season with your favorite herb or spice blend. Pop the tray in a 425°F oven (even better: 400°F on convection mode) for 20 to 45 minutes, depending on the type and size of the veggies.

(This isn't a complete guide, but zucchini and bell peppers take about 15 minutes, carrots, broccoli, and cauliflower take about 25 minutes, and heartier root vegetables like butternut squash, potatoes, and onion wedges take about 40 minutes.)

Flip the vegetables halfway through the cooking time. When the vegetables are browned on the outside and tender on the inside, take the tray out, and add a drizzle of aged balsamic vinegar or a squirt of citrus.

SOUPER-CIZE IT!

Got extra roasted vegetables? Transform them into a comforting soup! Combine some broth and roasted vegetables in a pot and bring to a simmer. Blitz everything until smooth with an immersion blender. You can make this a complete meal by stirring in leftover shredded meat and a handful of baby spinach.

SAUTÉED GREENS

Heat a tablespoon of your fat of choice in a pan over medium-high heat. Then, add thinly sliced shallots or garlic (or both), and stir until fragrant. Toss in your favorite greens (like spinach, bok choy, Napa cabbage, or baby kale) and a sprinkle of salt. Cook, stirring, until the greens are wilted. Add fish sauce, coconut aminos, and a bit of acid (like lime juice or rice vinegar) to taste. Or better yet, add a splash of All-Purpose Stir-Fry Sauce (page 67) if you've got it.

CONVERSIONS!

OVEN TEMPERATURES

200°F	95°C
225°F	110°C
250°F	120°C
275°F	135°C
300°F	150°C
325°F	165°C
350°F	175°C
375°F	190°C
400°F	200°C
425°F	220°C
450°F	230°C
475°F	245°C
500°F	260°C
525°F	275°C

WEIGHT

¼ oz	7 g
½ oz	14 g
¾ oz	21 g
1 oz	28 g
1¼ oz	35 g
1½ oz	42 g
1¾ oz	50 g
2 oz	57 g
3 oz	85 g
4 oz	113 g
5 oz	142 g
6 oz	170 g
7 oz	198 g
8 oz	227 g
16 oz	454 g

LENGTH

¼ in	6 mm
½ in	1¼ cm
1 in	2½ cm
2 in	5 cm
2½ in	6 cm
4 in	10 cm
5 in	13 cm
6 in	15¼ cm
12 in	30 cm

VOLUME

¼ tsp	1 ml	
½ tsp	2.5 ml	
¾ tsp	4 ml	
1 tsp	5 ml	
1¼ tsp	6 ml	
1½ tsp	7.5 ml	
1¾ tsp	8.5 ml	
2 tsp	10 ml	
1 T	15 ml	½ fl oz
2 T	30 ml	1 fl oz
¼ C	60 ml	2 fl oz
½ C	120 ml	4 fl oz
¾ C	180 ml	6 fl oz
1 C	240 ml	8 fl oz

BYE!

Information compiled from a variety of sources, including *Recipes into Type* by Joan Whitman and Dolores Simon (Newton, MA: Biscuit Books, 2000); *The New Food Lover's Companion* by Sharon Tyler Herbst (Hauppauge, NY: Barron's, 1995); and *Rosemary Brown's Big Kitchen Instruction Book* (Kansas City, MO: Andrews McMeel, 1998).

THANKS!

I'm sure there's a proper way to write a recipe book, but whatever it is, we ignored it.

Instead, like last time, we kind of winged it. After coming up with a general concept and jotting down a simple outline, we just started cooking and writing. In fact, we completely wrote, shot, and laid out each recipe before moving on to the next one.

Of course, this doesn't mean we didn't work our butts off. I poured myself into each recipe, testing and re-testing steps, tweaking instructions, and refining flavors. When I was (at last!) satisfied, I'd create the dish once more, with Henry hovering next to me with his camera, snapping away as I demonstrated each step. And then we'd sit down and eat what I'd made.

The rest was up to Henry. Whenever he wasn't busy at his day job, he edited photos, re-worked my prose, plotted out comic-book-style layouts for each recipe, and drew cartoons to spice up the pages. Every inch of every page was painstakingly hand-designed by my bleary-eyed, detail-obsessed husband over the course of two years. So first and foremost, I need to thank my co-author and partner in all things.

But Henry and I weren't the only cooks in this kitchen.

We started writing cookbooks back in 2012 because our friends **Melissa Joulwan** and **Dave Humphreys** encouraged us to chart our own (crazy) path. And for this book, we drew inspiration from countless meals with family and friends. My big sister **Fiona Kennedy** was my sounding board, and our parents, **Rebecca** and **Gene Tam** and **Wendy** and **Kenny Fong**, were our cheerleaders. **Sidney Majalya** and **Jory Steele** (and meat-loving **Matthew Majalya!**) served as our human guinea pigs. **Gregory Gourdet** and **Justin Boreta** generously shared their recipes. And my fellow Salon members—**Emma Christensen**, **Sheri Codiana**, **Coco Morante**, **Cheryl Sternman Rule**, and **Danielle Tsi**—were a constant source of advice and support. I especially want to thank **Sheri**

for serving as our official recipe tester; without her amazingly detailed notes, my recipes wouldn't be the same. (Meaning they'd be rife with errors and incomprehensible instructions.) Others helped me stay sane by distracting me with juicy gossip and cracking me up on a daily basis. I'm looking at you, **Shiraaz Bhabha**, **Susan Papp**, and **Maria Zajac**. And especially you, **Diana Rodgers**.

I couldn't do what I do without the help of **Loren Wade Rednour**, whose work behind the scenes at Nom Nom Paleo makes it possible for me to focus on the stuff that matters to me—namely, food.

Special thanks go to friends who opened the door to new food experiences these past few years, especially **Mark Ritchie**, who made us fall head-over-heels in love with Northern Thailand, **Cuong Pham**, who let us see Vietnam through his eyes, and **Anya Fernald**, who gave me a close-up look at sustainable farming and hands-on experience with butchery (and let us crash at her farm every time we made the drive between Portland and the San Francisco Bay Area).

We're forever indebted to our editor, **Jean Lucas**, our publisher, **Kirsty Melville**, and the entire Andrews McMeel family. Without their guidance and support, this book wouldn't have made it into the world.

Henry just reminded me that if we don't mention our children, we'll never hear the end of it. So thanks, **Owen** and **Ollie**, for being our all-time favorite kids, and for eating everything I make—even when it's gross. Our hearts are bursting with love for you, and we hope you're not too embarrassed by this book.

Lastly, Henry and I want to thank all of you, our loyal Nomsters, for cooking with us, sticking with us, and inspiring us. You make it all worthwhile.

GET SET!

		WHOLE30-FRIENDLY	NUT-FREE (NOT INCLUDING COCONUT)	EGG-FREE	NIGHTSHADE-FREE	FREEZER-FRIENDLY	PAGE
SALAD ESSENTIALS	Smoky Lime Pepitas	★	★	★			46
	Thai Citrus Dressing	★*	★	★			47
	Green Beast Dressing	★	★	★	★		48
	Creamy Onion Dressing	★	★	★	★	★	49
	Paleo Mayo	★	★		★		50
	Tonnato Sauce	★	★		★		51
	Roasted Garlic Mayonnaise	★	★		★		52
	Garlicky Devils	★	★				52
	Nutty Dijon Vinaigrette	★		★	★		53
ASIAN FLAIR	XO Sauce	★	★	★			54
	Nom Nom Sriracha	★	★	★		★	56
	Sriracha Ranch Dressing	★	★				57
	Spicy Thai No-Nut Sauce	★	★	★			58
	Chicken Satay Skewers	★	★	★			58
	Sunbutter Hoisin Sauce	★	★	★			59
	Fauxchujang		★	★		★	61
	Spicy Kimchi	★	★	★			62
	Wimpchi	★	★	★			62
	Kimchi Applesauce	★	★	★			64
	Romesco Sauce	★		★		★	65
SAUCY BASICS	Ginger Sesame Sauce	★	★	★	★		66
	Roasted Ginger Sesame Broccoli	★	★	★	★		66
	All-Purpose Stir-Fry Sauce	★	★	★	★		67
	Cran-Cherry Sauce	★*	★	★	★	★	68
	Umami Gravy	★	★	★		★	69
	Fruit + Avocado Salsa	★	★	★			70
	Fried Green Plantains with Nectarine Salsa	★	★	★			71
	Salsa Ahumada	★	★	★		★	72
	Pesto Pomodori Secchi (Sun-Dried Tomato Pesto)	★		★		★	73
FOUNDATIONAL FOODS	Fridge-Pickled Cucumbers	★	★	★			74
	Duxelles	★	★	★	★	★	75
	Bone Broth	★	★	★	★	★	76
	Grain-Free Tortillas		★	★	★	★	78
	Nature's Tortillas	★	★	★	★		79
	Cauli Rice	★	★	★	★	★	80
	Cumin Cilantro Lime Rice	★	★	★	★	★	81
	Pressure Cooker Hard "Boiled" Eggs	★	★		★		83
	Roast-Ahead Chicken Breasts	★	★	★	★	★	84

* if honey is omitted

READY!

		WHOLE30-FRIENDLY	NUT-FREE (NOT INCLUDING COCONUT)	EGG-FREE	NIGHTSHADE-FREE	FREEZER-FRIENDLY	PAGE
SOUPS, SALADS, AND SIDES	Smoky Chestnut Apple Soup	★		★	★	★	92
	Honeydew Lime Gazpacho	★	★	★			94
	Roasted Onion Soup	★	★	★	★	★	96
	Fried Green Plantains	★	★	★	★	★	98
	Buffalo Cauliflower Things	★	★				100
	Buffalo Wings	★	★				102
	Mok Mok Wings		★	★			104
POULTRY	Roasted Dijon Tarragon Chicken	★	★	★	★	★	106
	Orange Dijon Chicken	★	★	★	★	★	106
	Chicken Breasts with Ginger Scallion Pesto	★	★	★	★	★	108
	Bacon-Wrapped Chicken + Lemon-Date Sauce	★	★	★	★	★	110
	Chinese Chicken in a Pot	★	★	★	★	★	112
	Chinese Chicken in a Slow Cooker	★	★	★	★	★	113
	Chinese Chicken in a Pressure Cooker	★	★	★	★	★	114
	Easy Chicken Tinga	★	★	★		★	116
	Duck Confaux	★	★	★	★	★	118
MEAT	Slow Cooker / Pressure Cooker Kabocha + Ginger Pork	★	★	★	★	★	120
	Bacon Apple Smothered Pork Chops	★	★	★	★		122
	Salt + Pepper Fried Pork Chops	★	★				124
	Braised / Slow Cooker / Pressure Cooker Pork in Coconut Water	★	★	★	★	★	126
	Pressure Cooker / Slow Cooker Kalua Pig	★	★	★	★	★	128
	Pressure Cooker Bo Ssäm		★	★		★	132
	Slow Cooker Bo Ssäm		★	★		★	134
	Souvlaki	★	★	★	★	★	136
	Bangin' Baby Back Ribs	★	★	★		★	138
	Pressure Cooker Pork Ribs	★	★	★		★	142
	Pressure Cooker / Slow Cooker Carne Mechada	★	★	★		★	144
	Tex-Mex Beef and Rice Casserole	★	★			★	146
	Primetime Rib Roast	★	★	★	★	★	148
	Sunday Gravy	★	★	★		★	152
	Pressure Cooker / Slow Cooker Sunday Gravy	★	★	★		★	153
	Sunday Zoodles	★	★	★			155
TREATS	Vanilla Almond Milk			★	★		160
	Piña Colada Tapioca Pudding		★	★	★		162
	Tangerine Dream Tart				★		164
	Orange Cream Tart				★		164
	Rustic Chocolate Cake				★		166
	Cherry Chocolate Chip Ice Cream			★	★	★	168
	Strawberry Almond Semifreddo + Berry Balsamic Sauce				★	★	170

KINDA READY!

	WHOLE30-FRIENDLY	NUT-FREE (NOT INCLUDING COCONUT)	EGG-FREE	NIGHTSHADE-FREE	FREEZER-FRIENDLY	PAGE
SOUPS, SALADS, AND SIDES						
Hangry Soup	★	★	★		★	178
Roasted Carrots with Ginger Sesame Sauce	★	★	★	★		180
Bacon Brussels Sprouts with Kimchi Applesauce	★	★	★			181
Chilled Asian Zoodle Salad with Chicken + Avocado	★	★	★	★		183
Sriracha Sunbutter Zoodles + Chicken	★	★	★			184
Red Pesto Coodles	★		★			185
Grilled Romaine + Broccolini Salad	★	★	★	★		186
Mexican Watermelon + Cucumber Salad	★	★	★			189
Winter Date Night Salad	★		★	★		190
Thai Green Apple Slaw	★		★			191
Flank Steak Super Salad	★	★	★			192
Asian Flank Steak Salad	★	★				193
Whole Roasted Cauliflower with Nutty Dijon Vinaigrette	★		★	★		194
Roasted Cauliflower with Whatever You Want	★					194
SEAFOOD						
Roasted Catalan Shrimp	★		★			196
Macadamia-Crusted Sriracha Ranch Salmon	★					198
Naked Salmon on a Hot Pan	★	★	★	★		198
POULTRY						
Choose-Your-Own-Adventure Egg Muffins	★	★			★	200
Duxelles Chicken	★	★	★	★	★	201
Orange Sriracha Chicken		★	★		★	202
Paper-Wrapped Chicken	★	★	★	★		204
EAT WITH YOUR HANDS						
Thanksgiving Bites	★	★		★	★	206
Jíbaritos (Fried Plantain Sandwiches)		★				210
Leftacos		★				212
Pork Chicharrón Nachos		★	★			214
MEAT						
Sunday Stuffed Peppers	★	★	★		★	217
Monday Frittata	★	★				218
XO Pork with Blistered Green Beans	★	★	★			220
Spicy Pork with Green Beans	★	★	★			221
Weeknight Meatballs	★	★	★	★	★	222
Meatball Soup	★	★		★		223
Meatballs 'n' Gravy	★	★	★	★		223
Prime Rib Hash	★	★	★			227
Hoisin-Glazed Burgers	★	★	★			229
Asparagus Beef	★	★	★	★		230
SNACKS						
Spicy Bacon Honey Nuts						232
Hurricane Pig Nuts						232
Chia Muesli Parfait			★	★		234

INDEX!

Ready or Not! copyright © 2017 Michelle Tam & Henry Fong

All rights reserved. Printed in China. No part of this book may be used or reproduced in any manner whatsoever without prior written permission except in the case of reprints in the context of reviews.

This book is intended for general informational purposes only, and not as personal medical advice, medical opinion, diagnosis, or treatment. The author and publisher expressly disclaim responsibility for any adverse effects that may result from the use or application of the recipes and information contained in this book.

Andrews McMeel Publishing
a division of Andrews McMeel Universal
1130 Walnut Street, Kansas City, Missouri 64106
andrewsmcmeel.com

17 18 19 20 21 TEN 10 9 8 7 6 5 4 3

ISBN: 978-1-4494-7829-2

Library of Congress Control Number: 2017930875

Recipes by Michelle Tam
Book design, illustrations, and photographs (except for those listed below) by Henry Fong
Photographs on pages 8 and 332 by Oliver Fong
Photograph on page 33 by Danielle Tsi
Photograph on page 176 by Michelle Tam

ATTENTION: SCHOOLS AND BUSINESSES: Andrews McMeel books are available at quantity discounts with bulk purchase for educational, business, or sales promotional use. For information, please e-mail the Andrews McMeel Special Sales Department: specialsales@amuniversal.com

For more recipes and information, visit **nomnompaleo.com**